JEWISH FAMILY

THE MODERN JEWISH EXPERIENCE

Deborah Dash Moore and Marsha L. Rozenblit, *editors*

Paula Hyman, *founding coeditor*

JEWISH FAMILY

IDENTITY AND SELF-FORMATION AT HOME

ALEX POMSON AND
RANDAL F. SCHNOOR

Indiana University Press

This book is a publication of

Indiana University Press
Office of Scholarly Publishing
Herman B Wells Library 350
1320 East 10th Street
Bloomington, Indiana 47405 USA

iupress.indiana.edu

Manufactured in the United States of America

Library of Congress Cataloging-in-Publication Data

Names: Pomson, Alex, author. | Schnoor, Randal F., author.
Title: Jewish family : identity and self-formation at home / Alex Pomson and Randal F. Schnoor.
Description: Bloomington, Indiana : Indiana University Press, [2018] | Series: The modern Jewish experience | Includes bibliographical references and index.
Identifiers: LCCN 2017055812 (print) | LCCN 2017056533 (ebook) | ISBN 9780253033109 (ebook) | ISBN 9780253033086 (hardcover) | ISBN 9780253033093 (pbk.)
Subjects: LCSH: Jewish families—Ontario—Toronto—Longitudinal studies. | Jews—Ontario—Toronto—Identity. | Toronto (Ont.)—Ethnic relations.
Classification: LCC HQ525.J4 (ebook) | LCC HQ525.J4 P66 2018 (print) | DDC 306.85/089924—dc23
LC record available at https://lccn.loc.gov/2017055812

1 2 3 4 5   23 22 21 20 19 18

For Mum—kin-keeper extraordinaire

Alex

CONTENTS

ACKNOWLEDGMENTS

Working together on a project in which we submitted the final manuscript more than fifteen years after we originally launched our work, we have benefitted from the support of a great many institutions and people over an extended period. We want to recognize those who made a decisive contribution to the completion of this project.

First and foremost, we are fortunate to have received two significant grants from the Social Sciences and Humanities Research Council of the Government of Canada (SSHRC). A first SSHRC grant in 2003 supported the three-year study that laid the foundations for our research. This grant resulted in our first book, *Back to School*, published in 2008. A second grant, in 2009, made it possible to return to the families who had participated in the first study, something we had not originally expected to do.

The professional and lay leadership of the Paul Penna Downtown Jewish Day School gave us access to a wonderfully diverse group of families. While the children in those families had all moved on from the school by the time we completed the study, we would not have been able to get started on any aspect of this project without the school's initial support.

Over many years, faculty and leadership at the Koschitzky Centre for Jewish Studies at York University have generously supported our efforts. Year after year, they provided a comfortable space for us to meet where we could cover a long table with transcripts and piece together an emerging narrative over the course of multiday meetings. Over the years, the menus that fueled these intense sessions changed—we transitioned from deli-sandwiches to healthier fare—but the hospitality provided by the Centre was unchanging. We especially thank the Centre directors who provided a home for our work: Michael Brown, Marty Lockshin, Sara Horowitz, and Carl Ehrlich.

We're grateful to have had the opportunity to test the ideas that emerged during our research with students at York University and at the Hebrew University, specifically at the Melton Center for Jewish Education. Mirroring the evolution of our work, the courses we taught started out with a focus on schools, they then placed a spotlight on schools and families, and in later years, they have specifically explored the life course of families. On numerous occasions, almost annually, conference sessions at the Association for Jewish Studies and the Network for Research in Jewish Education also helped move forward our thinking.

When one of us transitioned away from a full-time position at the university, that move could have been fatal to the kind of emergent inquiry in which we were engaged. The support of colleagues at Rosov Consulting, Alex Pomson's professional home for the last five years of this project, has been critical to the completion of this endeavor. We thank Wendy Rosov, in particular, for her generosity, guidance, and friendship. But for her vision, we would never have brought our efforts to a successful conclusion.

Dee Mortensen and the team at Indiana University Press deserve a special shout-out for their interest in our work. Their encouragement inspired us to think bold and work hard. We are honored that Deborah Dash Moore and Marsha L. Rozenblit have welcomed this volume into The Modern Jewish Experience series. We appreciate their leadership. And we are especially grateful for the input provided by two anonymous reviewers at the press for offering suggestions that significantly helped improve our work.

Concluding a longitudinal study of families' lives, we have experienced significant family life course changes of our own over the same period. We ourselves and our own children have reached important milestones: some of our children now have families of their own; a few have even developed an interest in our work. Alex Pomson would like to thank his wife, Tanya, especially, for her commitment to and encouragement of his work, and for many other things besides. Her support has been a remarkable constant over a great many years. She has maintained and sustained the family system that made this book possible. Randal Schnoor would like to thank his wife, Marsha, for her constant support in everything he does. Randal's family has traversed through the life course with his two children entering Jewish day school at the early stages of our research and culminating in the recent very joyous and personalized Bat Mitzvah celebration of his daughter upon the submission of the manuscript for this book.

Beyond the dinner selections, it is fair to say that over a decade and a half, the authors' relationship evolved as well, from a productive professional collaboration to a close friendship. Randal has even acquired an interested in British football! We look forward to future work together.

Last, but not least, we are immeasurably grateful to the sixteen Toronto families that stuck with us over the course of our research. Their willingness to open their homes and their lives to us is a gift we will treasure.

JEWISH FAMILY

"Growing into Our Skin as a Jewish Family": Proposing a New Approach to the Study of Jewish Self-Formation

In the fall of 2003, Sandy Kleinman and Carla Lowe started Jewish day school for the first time: Sandy in kindergarten and Carla in first grade. The school they joined, the Paul Penna Downtown Jewish Day School (DJDS), had been founded five years earlier with just ten students and a staff of three. When the girls started school, there were seventy children in five grades.

The girls' parents had spent some of their own school years in Jewish day schools, but they were deeply ambivalent about the choice they had made for their children. That wasn't because of the quality of the education provided; both couples had visited a number of other schools before opting for DJDS and were pleasantly surprised by the school's progressive approach to education, its warmth, and the inclusive Jewish environment. The parents were ambivalent because they had never thought of themselves as Jewish day school parents. Carla's mother, Karen Lowe, had wanted to stay clear of what she called the "ghetto." As she elaborated, "I didn't want Carla's world to be too narrow. I didn't want her only to be friends with Jewish kids." The ambivalence of Sandy's father derived from a different source. Joe Kleinman feared that in choosing a Jewish day school he was selling out on his commitment to public education. "For me, I think the ideological and political aspects of the decision to send a child to private school weigh down on me more.... We really support the public system!"

In the last months of 2003, we first interviewed these two sets of parents, along with twenty-six other families who had children in kindergarten, first grade, and fifth grade at DJDS. We were starting a research project to explore the relationship between parents and their children's schools. At the time, these two sets of parents and others in our sample talked with palpable emotion about the first few months since their children started school.

Joe Kleinman—a secular Jew, exploring Suki Gakai Buddhism and expressing doubts about God and about what he called "the Israel question"—remarked that "because Sandy started learning about [Judaism] and I see how that is for her, it reinforces that I want to be part of that as well." His wife, Michelle, someone who thought of herself as a cultural Jew, was enjoying becoming closer with other Jewish families. She reported being almost moved to tears when she heard the children sing the *Hatikvah* (Israel's national anthem) at the start of the school day. Joe revealed that the school "seems to be helping us along a path that really goes where we need to go."

The story at the Lowes' home was different. Despite her ambivalence about Jewish schools, Karen had agreed to join the school's board. The couple seemed pleased with their school choice. They saw how their daughter could really be herself—100 percent Carla, as they put it—within the warmth of the school environment and how she now had no inhibition about singing the *Hatikvah* while out in the local supermarket. But they didn't see why that should change anything in their own lives. Karen explained, "I just think if you are going to a school that is going to immerse you in that, why do you have to be immersed everywhere else in your life?" Describing herself and her husband as loners, Karen claimed, "I'm not really a member of any community. We are not really those kind of people. . . . I wouldn't use the school for something like that."

Two years after these first interviews, we returned to the homes of the two families to see what, if anything, had changed in their lives over the intervening period. We discovered that both families had in fact withdrawn their child from the school within fourteen months of starting. The Lowes had transferred their daughter after a month in second grade into a non-Jewish private school. They had been deeply disappointed with the new teacher hired to teach the second--grade class and the school's refusal to replace her. Karen clarified, "There is a nice and homey feel to the school, but they're still sort of wild . . . and we are academic, we believe in homework." Recognizing that Carla was now missing a Jewish dimension to her education, they resolved to send her to Jewish summer camp. Karen continued: "That was our thing: if she goes to a Jewish school she can go to secular camps. If she goes to secular school, she has to go to Jewish camps. I actually got more of a sense of being Jewish from Camp Shalom than I did from my day school." Repeating something that they had said at the first interview—that they didn't need the school to provide their social circle—she conveyed that switching schools was clearly more of a struggle for their daughter than it was for them.

Joe Kleinman—whose wife Michelle was not available at the time of the second interview—reported that they switched Sandy at the end of kindergarten into a progressive, alternative public school. The tipping point for them was being prevented from observing the first-grade class into which their daughter was due to continue, and about which they had some concerns. They also had concerns about "some very specific [patriarchal] notions of God" that their daughter was acquiring at school, and the sense of socio-economic privilege that they felt in the school community. Having withdrawn Sandy from a Jewish school, Joe made clear that it was now their "responsibility to introduce her to Judaism and to expose her to it, as opposed to the school's.... I feel like I have to take the initiative. I just can't leave it to the teachers." Joe acknowledged that this was a special challenge because the private Hebrew teacher they had hired at the start of first grade had moved to Australia a few months later. Part of the problem, he reported, was that there really wasn't any obvious community, let alone synagogue where they felt comfortable as cultural Jews. Leaving the school had somewhat cut them off from an immediate community of Jews.

At the end of our research in 2005, these two families seemed like outliers. Almost all the other families whose children had started alongside theirs had remained in the school, certainly for more than one year. Many celebrated the ways in which their Jewish lives had been touched and even changed by the school choice they had made, much as the Kleinmans had done in their first interview. Most other families were closely connected to the school community. The book we wrote about the experience of these families, *Back to School: Jewish Day School in the Lives of Adult Jews*, explored how adult identity—specifically adult Jewish identity—can be shifted through the interaction with one's child's school, particularly at the point of transition into elementary school (Pomson and Schnoor 2008).

Over the following few years, we wondered how "our" families were doing, but in the interim we both moved on to other projects, such is the flow of university life. In 2010, we were awarded a second grant by Canada's Social Sciences and Humanities Research Council (SSHRC). We had proposed a follow-up to our study of the transition to elementary school, this time following Jewish families through the transition from elementary school to high school. Developing the proposal, we had not intended to return to the DJDS families: their children were already in high school. Some of the children of those we had interviewed were already moving on to university.

And yet, our curiosity got the better of us. A year after the start of this new project, we decided to devote a small part of our research funds to tracking down and interviewing some of those we had interviewed ten years previously; after all, we rationalized, they too had transitioned into high school at one point. We started tentatively, resolving to interview only three or four of the families we had previously studied. When we reviewed what we found, we realized that we should not stop with just four families. We began to wonder if what we were learning from this small sample of interviewees might prove more significant than what we were learning from the almost thirty families in the high school–transition study. Over the ten years since we had first met them, the Jewish lives of those we had previously interviewed had moved on in remarkably diverse and often unexpected directions. Those changes called for exploration and explanation. We recognized that we were launching an inquiry that was no longer just about Jewish schooling but about Jewish family life and its complex dynamics.

Ten years after we had first met with them, the Lowe family was not hard to find. Although not in the same house, they were living in the same comfortable Toronto neighborhood. Carla, now sixteen years old, was still attending the same private school to which she had transferred from DJDS. Her younger sister, born since the last interview, was there too. Carla had attended Camp Shalom for the previous nine summers: "It's where I get my entire Jewish identity from," she said, sounding a lot like her mother. Like her mother, it was also where she made her closest friends, some of whom were the children of her parents' friends. She was very comfortable in the more religiously observant environment of camp. Carla expressed an interest in the family being, what she called, "more Jewishy." But, it seemed as if her parents had long ago found a point of Jewish equilibrium at home that was unlikely to change now.

Almost repeating verbatim something she said ten years earlier about her aversion to settling in an overtly Jewish neighborhood, Karen stated: "I don't understand ... why you would choose to be in a ghetto? That's my thing." Karen's husband, Adam, had become interested in exploring theological questions but preferred to do so by listening to podcasts in his car. He pulled back from attending seminars at the synagogue about such things because, as he put it, "I don't want to get co-opted." Their resistance to committing too far was likely why they had not encouraged Carla to consider switching to a Jewish high school with her friends from camp. In Karen's words, they were reacting to the way they had been raised: "I grew up with, you go to Jewish day school, you go to Jewish camp, you go to Jewish this, you go to Jewish that, all your friends are Jewish, you only go out with Jewish boys."

In the years since we had previously interviewed them, their Jewish lives had changed little. Three times a year they attended synagogue alongside Adam's parents; it was the synagogue where Carla had marked her Bat Mitzvah. They did not tend to celebrate Shabbat; Adam was invariably working on Friday night. They were always with their parents for Seder, although—in what they saw as a major departure—their parents now came to their house rather than them going to their parents. They expressed a sense of being comfortable with who they were as Jews and how their children were turning out.

When we tracked down Joe Kleinman, we found that he had moved to a lower-income area of Toronto—more than twenty miles from where he had first been interviewed. We might not have been able to find him had he changed his email address. He was no longer married to Michelle.

Ten years later, Joe had a new partner, Liesha, a non-Jewish woman. Joe had continued his exploration of Buddhism, more seriously than before. He found it completely compatible with his being Jewish. As he continued, "After being with Liesha I feel more Jewish than I ever have." Sandy, his daughter, did not however feel very Jewish at all. She elaborated: "I don't know much about the religion, and so [asking if] it means something to me, I don't really know all of what it means because I don't know what exactly being Jewish means." She had not celebrated a Bat Mitzvah, and had received little Jewish education since kindergarten. She explained that there had not seemed to be much point going to Jewish after-school programs "because I wasn't sure why I was [there]. I wasn't interested in it so much. . . . There is a focus on God in some places, and that part . . . I'm interested in it, but it's not something that I believe in, so it's hard for me to sit in the room, and talk about God."

Joe expressed disappointment that this is how things had turned out. He told us that he would love to celebrate Shabbat, but without an extended family nearby, he and Sandy found it hard. They had tried to devise their own secular Seder ritual for a couple of years, and had even created their own *Haggadah*, but that had fizzled. He said that he would love to recover the Hebrew from his childhood that he seemed to have completely forgotten, but "it was a question of time, you know." He'd also love to go to Israel, but "it's a lot of money." He knew that he had committed to taking more responsibility for educating his daughter Jewishly but, he reflected, "You have to choose your battles, you know, and that was not a high enough priority. There were other things that had to be attended to, like splitting up, and divorcing . . . and the pressure of [advancing in my career]."

Sociological Paradigms for Studying Jews

The contrast between the Kleinmans and the Lowes is dramatic. Their lives had overlapped for one year, and for a short period seemed to be headed in similar directions. When we first met them, they had both traveled what we called in our last book a "long and winding road" to choosing a Jewish day school for their children (Pomson and Schnoor 2008, 37). Ten years later, although the parents in these two families continued to identify as Jews, what being Jewish meant to them had substantially diverged. What being Jewish meant in terms of their expectations for their children had diverged further still.

This book explores the sociological reasons why families' Jewish lives develop in such diverse ways. This exploration straddles two traditions of research: the sociology of Jewry and the study of the family life course. In this conjunction lies the point of departure for our work from most recent studies of contemporary Jewry.

Toward the end of the last century, the sociology of Jewry took an inward turn, as did the broader field of the sociology of religion. For the first decades after World War II, sociologists of North American Jewry, using primarily quantitative survey methods, studied what Jews did and how they behaved. This was a paradigm that produced classic works such as Gans's (1958) "The origin and growth of a Jewish community in the suburbs" and Sklare and Greenbaum's (1967) *Jews on the Suburban Frontier.*

At end of the century, there was a move away from studying how people *acted as* Jews toward studying how people, individuals, *thought of themselves* as Jews. The shift was prominently expressed by Cohen and Eisen's succinctly entitled volume, *The Jew Within* (2000). But, as the book's authors acknowledge, their inquiry followed a path that Bellah and his colleagues, and that others too, had started to navigate two decades earlier. Interviewing Americans about their religious and spiritual lives, Bellah's group had found that for "most Americans ... the meaning of one's life ... is to become one's own person, almost to give birth to oneself" (1985, 82). As Baumeister subsequently elaborated, this implied that "realizing oneself meant *breaking away from family, home, and community* as well as from the views and teaching imposed by the larger society" (1991, 108, emphasis added).

The act of "breaking away from family and home" was at the axis of what Roof and McKinney (1987) coined the "new voluntarism," wherein individuals felt less and less constrained to maintain previous generations' patterns of religiosity (Davidman 2007). In a sense, they were free to create themselves or, in Arnett and Jensen's terms, they felt empowered to build "a congregation of one" (2002). For sociologists, in this context, to understand people's religious lives called for studying the choices people made as individuals and how they achieved religious identities rather than how they assumed ascribed identities. This work privileged the investigation of people's inner lives, uncovering how people made meaning and how they constructed and reconstructed their sense of who they were. This is what Warner called a "new paradigm for the sociological study of religion" (1993). Thus, when Wuthnow (1998) influentially explored the shift in American religion from what he called a spirituality of dwelling to one of searching, his study was constructed around interviews in which people described their journeys, or what he called their exploration of their inner selves. His inquiry was not, however, that of a psychologist. As a sociologist, he was interested in the social and cultural significance of the multiple individual odysseys he charted.

Against this intellectual backdrop, the sociology of contemporary Jewry for the last twenty years has been as much concerned with studying the inner landscape of Jewish lives, the self-formation of Jews, as it has been with studying the landscape of Jewish communal life. During this time, the regnant modality for studying Jews, especially when employing qualitative research, has been the exploration of how Jews define and understand themselves. Scholars have been concerned with the stories Jews tell themselves about who they are (Charme 2009), how they negotiate between different aspects of their identities (Barack Fishman 1995; Horowitz 2000; Hartman 2007), and how they use language to authentically express themselves as Jews (Benor 2012; Fader 2009). In these instances, the drama of contemporary Jewish life is presumed to play out on a biographical stage, within the life story of the individuals who, as Thompson put it, are "Jewish on their own terms" (2013).

Research into conversion and into the lives of *ba'alei teshuva* ("returnees" to Orthodox Judaism) is paradigmatic of the focus on the inner life of the individual. From this perspective, few life choices are a stronger expression of individuals' capacity to reinvent themselves whether in taking on a different faith or in returning to a different version of themselves (Aviad 1983; Davidman 1991). It is no wonder that Christians conceive of such transformation as being "born again" (Johnston 2012). As Bellah implied, it is a paradigmatic American act of self-invention. In a similar vein, to be a Jew by choice is paradigmatic of the Jewish condition today. As one influential Jewish foundation expressed it, the current era is one where all Jews are Jews by choice (Charles and Lynn Schusterman Philanthropic Network 2014). Converting to Judaism, or returning to Judaism, gives full expression to individuals' capacity to construct an achieved identity for themselves. In these terms, they recover or uncover their authentic selves.

One can readily see how Joe Kleinman's spiritual journey can be viewed from within this individualistic paradigm. Joe's spiritual odyssey, and the waxing and waning of his interest in Jewish life reflects the meandering course typically taken by one of Wuthnow's seekers. And yet—as was shown in the brief narration of his story—this is a journey that Joe does not undertake by himself. It is pursued in the company of significant others (what we later call "fellow travelers") and through interplay with them. How Joe thinks of himself is strongly colored by how he thinks of himself as a son (he connects his own restlessness to his mother's readiness as an identifying Jew to find spiritual peace by spending time in churches), as a partner (inspired first by his culturally Jewish wife and then by his non-Jewish partner), and finally as a father (creating new rituals together with, and for the sake of, his daughter). Of course, he conceives of himself in relation to other significant coordinates too: his gender (to which we will return later), his profession as a human-rights lawyer, his left-wing politics, and his social class. There are numerous different stories that he—and we—might tell about him, and not just that of a family man. But, as we reflect on the story he told us, we notice how much would be missed if our unit of analysis was Joe himself, and excluded the family, or if our analysis relegated the family to the background.

The family context is also critical to making sense of the Jewish lives of Karen and Adam Lowe. These two people are strongly self-aware of their discomfort with groups and with being ascribed roles by others. The two of them are very much religious dwellers in Wuthnow's use of the term, and it is their home that anchors their settled sense of who they are. They expressed limited desire to change or to reconstruct the Jewish lives that together they long ago chose for themselves. Their children may experiment with new and intensive Jewish experiences, at camp especially, but whatever new ideas they bring back with them are smothered by the fixity of the Jewish culture at home. The family is the arbiter and shaper of their Jewishness in powerful ways.

Bringing the Family into Focus

Returning to Warner's (1993) identification of paradigmatic shifts in the sociology of religion, between what he calls the tribal, on the one hand—the larger social groups to which people belong—and the individual, on the other, it seems that sociologists these past thirty years have overlooked the potential in the family as a unit of analysis, located somewhere in between the two horizons of the tribe (or to use more contemporary language, the community) and the "sovereign self." Perhaps as the family has fractured as a stable social institution in later modernity, and as it has weakened as a medium for intergenerational religious transmission, it has seemed misplaced to approach the study of identity through the lens of those groups of individuals bound to one another through genealogy or marriage (to employ the language that Boyarin [2013] proposes to define family kinship). To do so has seemed too much aligned with a conservative political orientation (Cherlin 2010). Attributing primacy to the family has been out of sync with the prevailing sociological ethos of privileging the individual and with an emerging sociological reality—in which, as Putnam and Campbell state, "it is misleading to think of religious identity in America as an inherited and stable characteristic" (2010, 137).

Yet, while the sociologists of religion, and of contemporary Jewry in particular, have narrowed their attention to the sovereign self, a robust field has matured over the last sixty years that seeks to make sense of human functioning and meaning-making within the context of the family as a system (Jensen and Jensen 1999). During this time, the field of family studies has often been driven forward by the work of therapists and social workers. Having noticed that psychotherapeutic changes in one member brought on new problems for other family members, therapists concluded that it was more efficient to work to change the entire family system than to try to change each constituent member of that system (Broderick and Schrader 1981; Fingerman and Bermann 2000). These therapeutic assumptions were buttressed by the emerging field of general systems' theory whose central premise, ultimately traceable to Aristotle's notion that the sum is greater than the total of its parts, was that the entirety of a system is more than and different from the arithmetic addition of its individual parts considered in isolation (Bertalanffy 1968; Buckley 1967). Out of this intersection of therapeutic practice and sociological theory, scholars have found it productive to view the family as a goal-delivering system (Broderick 1993); a subsystem for value socialization (Bronfenbrenner 1979); and a context for life course development (Uhlenberg and Mueller 2004), to name some of the most influential family-system conceptions to have emerged. A common thread across these conceptual frameworks is that it is not possible to understand the development of human agency independent of the family, given the family's foundational role, across cultures, in shaping and providing individuals with their biological and psychological DNA (Coontz 2006).

Of course, sociologists of religion have not ignored the family. They explored the role of family as a contributing variable in the development of individual commitments, values, and beliefs (Edgell 2006). There have been extensive studies of the relationships between adolescent religious commitments, on the one hand, and any number of family characteristics, on the other, including: parenting style, family structure, parental beliefs, and divorce or marital conflict (Heaven, Ciarrochi, and Leeson 2010; Bader and Desmond 2006; Ellison et al. 2011; Petts 2015). In studies of contemporary Jewry, there have also been important contributions to the understanding of Jewish well-being and identity in terms of the family context (Barack Fishman 2004; Cohen and Eisen 2000; Hyman 1989). But, the focus of these studies has ultimately been on individuals, and on how they are shaped by their family circumstances and context. In these terms, family, like community or school, is one among a set of important contextual variables that socialize, model, or instruct individuals at formative stages of development with lasting impact over the course of their lives.

In an important piece, Prell came close to moving beyond the person-focused paradigm we previously sketched to one that identified the family as a site for study of the construction of American Jewish identity (Prell 2000). Prompted by her study of families in two Conservative synagogues, Prell called for a new social scientific orientation that is more faithful to the contemporary experience of being Jewish than were prevailing methods. Prell proposed an approach that captured Jewishness as a changing and developmental process best facilitated by attention to biography and life course. She characterized the study of identity that she had in mind as the study of self-construction, something she conceived as a cultural matter rather than a psychological one.

All of this of course was fully aligned with the inward turn her colleagues were taking at the time; ultimately, she explained, she was interested in the work of self-construction. Yet, the data she cited and the conclusions she reached conveyed how the sites within which individuals constructed their identities lay first and foremost within the family. Self-construction took place most often at those moments when the boundaries between individual and family were blurred.

Reflecting on what she learned about her interviewees, Prell wrote, "Perhaps more importantly, as American Jews, they have transformed Judaism's focus on communal and personal obligation to creating a unique identity for a family. Judaism's significance for them rests in transmitting those meanings to another generation, to avoid assimilation, and to shape the family as unique because its members are Jews.... The family, in contrast to synagogue, community, and organizations for these late twentieth-century Conservative Jews is the most important setting for creating identity and meaning, the best venue for being a Jew" (50).

The notion of family as "the best venue for being a Jew" provides the starting point for this book. But, this book goes further. We argue that family not only provides a venue, or context, for being a Jew. More importantly, family provides the essential content of being a Jew as well. We argue that it is first and foremost as family members that those we interviewed think of themselves as Jews. Or, to put it differently, when they think of themselves as Jews, our interviewees conceive of themselves as mothers, sons, daughters, and fathers. These are the personal forms within which their understandings of what it means to be Jewish are most fully expressed.

Saying as much in this introductory chapter, we are getting far ahead of ourselves. Initially, when we began our research, we were not drawn to a family systems paradigm. For the last twenty years, our own scholarly work has been carried out within prevailing individualistic norms for studying Jewish identity. Those norms shaped the first book we wrote about these same families and the ways their children's school prompted their own various adult Jewish journeys. It was not disappointment with these norms that prompted a move in a different direction. It was our experiences in the field, over subsequent cycles of interviews with families, such as the Lowes and the Kleinmans, that led us to search out additional theoretical frameworks that helped make sense of what we were finding. We turned to family systems theory, and to a family life course perspective in particular, to help comprehend what at first had struck us as odd or unexpected until we kept encountering it again and again across our interview sample.

In our work, even when we were not looking for it, family inserted itself into our interviews. At some point during each interview, in our study of high school transition as well as in our return to the DJDS families, we asked interviewees to characterize their Jewish lives or how they thought of themselves as Jews. Frequently, they answered the questions by describing moments of being together with family, invariably their children, especially on Friday nights or Seder night. These specific occasions were referenced more often than any other (a phenomenon to which we will return in chapter 5). It was rare that interviewees cited an experience that they undertook by themselves or with members of the community beyond their immediate families. These consistencies across the sample were striking but not altogether surprising given that our adult interviewees were at stages in their lives when they still had dependent children living at home. What was more surprising was that interviewees rarely talked about themselves (how they thought of themselves as Jews and not just what they did as Jews) without talking about their families. Occasionally, for some interviewees, it was difficult to know where they as individuals ended and where their families started. We might say that in these instances it was the family not the self that was sovereign.

There was no more dramatic instance of this than when Ian Maybaum, someone who talking about his son's Bar Mitzvah, explained that "it's been a while since I felt very proud to be who I am and where I came from." Ian described the night before his son's Bar Mitzvah when reading the draft of his son's Bar Mitzvah speech. He conveyed the sensation of how "the light shone for me." In words spoken haltingly, he elaborated with astonishing lucidity on what he meant.

> But it's not about me. To me it's not about. . . . It's about my kids. And whatever light is shining, it's because of them, not because I am going through an epiphany. Or it's not because I am you know in a moment of rapture, it's not that, it's that they do things that just make me, make me smile. They just do things that . . . I am in disbelief that, despite all the shortcomings of who I am as Jew, or the things I haven't done or the things I haven't participated in, that they've got it. . . . They may not always have it; they may turn into me.

Ian conveys how he came to see the fullest meaning in his life ("the light shone") through the performance of his children as Jews. He came to see that whatever he conceived as his own inadequacies as a Jew, he had managed to pass something substantive about what Judaism meant to his own children ("they've got it"). As he says, it is about them; but as he also powerfully indicates, and despite his protestations, it is also about him. He is fully realized through his children. It is in seeing what his children have become that he has gained the clearest sense of himself as a Jew and in seeing some larger purpose in his life.

Of course, in many families, the lives of different family members are less implicated in one another. These families might function as aggregates of individuals whose lives frequently or periodically intersect, or their lives might be completely fractured, connected almost coincidentally to one another because of previous interrelationships. We saw something of that fractured trajectory in Joe Kleinman's story, for example. Family systems theory allows us to see that the members of such families might be disconnected from one another, but they are still components of the same system, albeit one with low levels of cohesion; the adults in this loosely coupled system connect to one another through their children.

Most dramatically, a family systems' perspective can change the meaning of religious conversion, an act we previously suggested was paradigmatic of a conception of identity and of identity-research that is focused on the individual's inner landscape. Although conversion seems to constitute the ultimate expression of individuals' capacity to reinvent themselves as autonomous persons, we have learned through our research how integral family can be to the process of reinvention. Family gave purpose and meaning to this act.

Take the case of Joanna Fine. Joanna was not born Jewish but had spent part of her childhood in the home of older Jewish relatives, a couple she referred to— using the Yiddish terms—as her *bubbe* and *zeide*. Reporting that she always dated Jews, and that she had "felt Jewish" for a long time, Joanna characterized herself as "practicing Judaism in the way I wanted to" even without having undertaken formal conversion. There was much in the details of her story that was reminiscent of Bellah's well-known case of Sheila, a woman who for his team exemplified the personalization of religion through the creation of what in effect was her own version of Christianity, what they called "Sheilaism" (1985, 221). Yet, unlike Sheila, Joanna did begin the process of formally converting to a normative faith. The prompt, she reported with great emotion, pausing many times to wipe away tears, was coming to realize that she "was standing in her [daughter's] way." She reported that her daughter, Lisa, "considers herself Jewish and someone told her she wasn't because Jewish is mother-born and her mom is not Jewish." She elaborated further:

> [*Speaks the following while crying*]: She was really, really hurt that all the people in the world would not consider her Jewish, and then I felt like I was standing in her way and if I just did this formality then it wouldn't matter because then as [the medieval rabbinic authority] Maimonides said . . . when the person converts you can't refer anymore [to their past in another religion], and so whoever said to her, oh yeah but you are not really Jewish because your mom

converted, they would not be behaving in a Jewish way. And I kind of thought that would help her and make things a little more clear-cut or whatever.

A family system perspective does not discount the force of individual choices, and the inner journeys that individuals undertake, as highlighted by a long tradition of sociological research, but it does widen the frame through which those journeys are viewed. Joanna's relationship to Judaism waxed and waned over the course of our research in highly individual and frankly idiosyncratic ways. In fact, after a number of years of preparation, we learned that she never did formally convert to Judaism. Her journey becomes a lot more comprehensible when seen in relation to shifting family relationships with her adopted parents, with the Jewish father of her children from whom she had separated before our first interview, and above all with her two children who because of their physiological and emotional development became first more and then less dependent on their mother. As her daughters' dependence on her waned, so did their mother's commitment to conversion.

Real-Time Rather Than Retrospective

We have elaborated at length on the ways in which this study departs in conceptual terms from earlier studies of identity. We believe that our work also involves a second, methodological departure that is no less important: while almost all qualitative studies of Jewish lives and identities employ a retrospective research design, our research entails the close qualitative study of the Jewish lives of a cohort of individuals over a ten-year period, in real time.

Employed most commonly in medicinal research, the study of cohorts of individuals sharing some common characteristic (e.g., birth year) or experience (e.g., exposure to pollutants) has been going on for much of the last one hundred years (Pearson 2016). In recent years, "cohort studies" has become an established subdiscipline of sociology and social psychology (see e.g., Bynner et al. 2000). As Payne (2006) explains, social scientists have come to conceive such studies as a special form of longitudinal design that promises a more rigorous investigation of change over time than is possible through comparing individuals of different ages within the same sample. One of the longest running, and best-known social science studies of this sort, combining the Berkeley Guidance and Oakland Growth studies, has been gathering data about a group of men and women born in Northern California since the 1920s (Dillon and Wink 2007).

In the social scientific study of Jewry, the best-known instance of a longitudinal study with a cohort design is the ongoing investigation, launched in the year 2000, of Taglit-Birthright alumni: the tens of thousands of eighteen- to twenty-six-year-old participants in a free ten-day trip to Israel. The Birthright research draws on survey data provided by program participants and a control group of nonparticipants (Saxe et al. 2009). On a smaller scale, for almost twenty years, Kosmin and Keysar (2000, 2004) have been studying a cohort of teens in Conservative high schools. More typically, especially when utilizing qualitative methodologies, studies of Jewish identity and Jewish lives employ a retrospective design: they ask subjects to report and reflect on their lives or experiences over a length of time running from anything from one year to a lifetime (Cohen and Eisen 2000; McGinity 2009; Schuster 2003). These studies have established that Jewish commitments wax and wane over the life course. Yet, most of what is known about such changes has been learned through retrospective interviews that ask people to reflect on changes in their lives up to the time of the study.

A retrospective approach to researching human lives is more financially feasible to undertake and promises findings without having to wait long lengths of time. But, retrospective approaches are also fraught with difficulties that are often overlooked due to the lack of available alternatives. First, people don't remember well what they learned in an earlier time; with the passage of time, memory straightens out the twists and turns that life takes (Kohler Reissman 1993). There is also a tendency among interviewees when participating in retrospective interviews to assume a teleological perspective, that is, to see everything as leading to a point in time in the present (the moment of the interview) when everything finally comes together or makes sense, at least until the time of the next interview, if there is one (Measor and Sikes 1992; Pomson 2004).

During our research, we became aware of some of the pitfalls of retrospective inquiry. Returning to interviewees between six and ten years after we previously met them, we asked at different points in the interview whether certain things had changed—for example, whether or not they were in the same line of work, or (more challengingly) whether or not there had been changes in their Jewish lives since their children had withdrawn or graduated from the Jewish school system. While some interviewees discerned shifts in their own and in their children's lives (something we came to notice as an indicator of a cohesive family system), a great many commented how they had not been aware of such things until we asked, or they claimed that little had changed, contrary to what we then learned during the remainder of the interview.

Of course, there is great deal that does not change in people's lives over a ten-year period. For example, we previously commented on the anchored quality of the Lowes' Jewish family life, and noted how Karen Lowe used more or less the same linguistic-imagery in interviews conducted ten years apart. Karen was not the only person to express such fixity. It seems that a person's view of the world, and how they talk about it, once established in early adulthood, changes little over time. Yet, at the same time, and this became increasingly clear to us, there is much that people don't notice either because it shifts imperceptibly as they and their families age, or, at the opposite extreme, because they are living through periods of significant historical change that they only notice after the event.

During the early years of our work, we noted that little changed in the Weinstein family's Jewish life as a result of their children starting Jewish elementary school. During that phase of our research, returning to the family three years after our first interview with them, we attributed this stability to the high levels of social and religious capital in the family: Carolyn was the daughter of a rabbi; Zev, her husband, was highly educated and quite self-sufficient in Jewish terms. Whatever their child brought home from his Jewish day school added little to the already-rich Jewish culture in the home. When we revisited the family some six years later for a third interview, Carolyn cautioned us that "things don't change." It was a theme she returned to later in the interview when reflecting on the stability of the family's Jewish practices. She speculated: "Your sense of the cycle of Jewish time would be unchanged, because it comes from the home, you know." In the early years of our study, as observers of this family, we too reached a similar conclusion about the role of the home in diminishing the adults' receptiveness to new Jewish stimuli from school. The richer the culture at home, the less impacted it is by cultural artifacts brought home by the child.

Yet, because in the later years of our research we came to our interviews keenly aware of what had been told to us in earlier interviews (before revisiting a family, we always reread previous transcripts), we often noticed changes that the family members had not themselves noticed. In that first interview, Carolyn used martial language to describe how Yoni—then age five—was her "comrade in arms" in persuading her somewhat cynical husband to sing zemirot (Hebrew songs) on Shabbat. Yoni, she reported, assisted her in further intensifying the Jewish culture of the house. Eight years later, however, it seemed that Yoni had switched sides. Still using martial imagery, Carolyn reported that as a consequence of Yoni's resistance, "I have given up the battle on meat with a glass of milk. We don't cook milk and meat together but the glass of milk is on the side for the kids. I have given in." Revealingly, although her comment opened a window on a shift in family dynamics and a consequent change in the family's religious culture, a few minutes later Carolyn returned to her theme of the lack of change at home. She reassured us and perhaps herself too: "I think probably I have gotten worn down in terms of fighting, completely no support for certain ritual elements, so that maybe has evolved but not, not core things. I mean we, other than that, I think that's the only thing that's different."

Our point is not that repeat interviews conducted over an extended length of time enabled us to detect inconsistencies in what people said or to challenge people if they contradicted something they had said or done many years earlier. We underline, rather, that in investigating people's lives in real time, we have been able to observe changes that they may not have noticed themselves, or that a researcher engaged in retrospective inquiry would not have uncovered. By interviewing the same people a number of times over a period of years, we don't just have to rely on what they tell us about the past on the latest occasion we interview them. Rather, we benefit from a continuous narrative of their family lives over time.

It is not coincidental that retrospective narrative inquiry attributes great importance to "critical incidents," those peak moments that interviewees identify as having constituted a fork in their lives' journeys (Clandinin and Connelly 2000). Those are the moments in life that people remember. Life course theorists refer to these occasions as moments of generational change— a change in school, a marriage, a death. As those theorists indicate, change can also occur at a different pace and with less visibility: that's what they refer to as ontogenetic change; change associated with physiological development or aging (Bengston and Allen 1993). In the case of Carolyn Weinstein, those less dramatic kinds of changes might have gone undetected or might have seemed of no great significance, but they help explain why there has been a shift in the Jewish balance of power at home, and why in addition Carolyn was more involved now at her synagogue, a causal connection she made herself: "Now that the kids are older I am back on the ritual committee." This was not a landmark change, nor a fork in the road, but an outcome associated with the aging of her children.

Ed Manning, the non-Jewish father in a family we interviewed three times over ten years, reflected on these same processes in our final interview with him when talking about his son's Bar Mitzvah. He provided us ultimately with language that brings into focus what we were observing in many homes.

> Again, I'm not Jewish but I help represent a Jewish household with my wife and my children and, you know, part of Max's *dvar torah* was about all of a sudden going from a Jewish school to being the only Jewish kid in his class, and all of a sudden he has this realization that not everybody is Jewish, and he realizes he is a representation of his cultural group and has to do it appropriately. The family, as well, we're carrying ourselves as, we would like to believe, a good representation of our Jewish faith. But are we doing anything exceptional or extraordinary? No. We're just living our lives. Like I said,

I think *we've been growing into our skin as a Jewish family*. We're more comfortable than when we first met you. [Emphasis added]

Prompted by Ed's insight, we have come to appreciate that our research has been akin to watching skin grow, observing change that lacks drama or uniqueness, so much so that it is barely noticeable. The interviewees themselves might only be aware of these changes at moments of generational change, at a Bar Mitzvah or at the time that one of the children changes school, for example. (We earlier quoted Ian Maybaum, another interviewee, making a similar point about how that life cycle moment revealed some deeper meaning in his own Jewish life.) But, as Ed indicates, what we are able to see over time is the unexceptional but highly significant matter of family lives developing over part of the life course. Over time, in real time to be precise, we have been able to observe the intersecting influences of ontogenetic, generational, and historical changes on families' Jewish lives. In Ed's case, his comfort as a non-Jewish parent "representing" a Jewish family is surely an expression of changes in historical norms that have seen the non-Jewish members of Jewish families assume public roles in their families' Jewish lives. Ed references, too, the processes of ontogenetic change and of generational change as they have played out at home. And, to return to our earlier theme, he indicates also how adults' identities are so much absorbed in their roles as family members.

The short interview extract with Ed offers an extraordinarily vivid instance of what is revealed at the intersection of the conceptual and methodological paradigms that frame this study. Viewing adult Jews as members of family systems through the aperture of a life course research design, we are able to see why, over time, some individuals lead more intense Jewish lives and others become increasingly disengaged from other Jews and from Jewish culture.

In recent years, Jewish communal policy debates about diminishing Jewish engagement have been strongly inflected with concern about the consequences of high-rates of intermarriage. As we will see in the following chapters, intermarriage is undoubtedly a factor informing how some of these families' Jewish lives develop. At the same time, we will also see that our research design enables us to propose explanatory factors that rarely get a viewing when debate about intermarriage is on the stage and "hogging the limelight."

Dramatis Personae: The Participants in the Study

Examined in this way, at the intersection of these two research paradigms, we think there are insights to be found in the study of these sixteen families that have significance for the broader Jewish community and for those who study contemporary Jewry. We make no claim that these families were identified for study because they were somehow representative of the broader mass of Jewry in North America. The families constituted an opportunity sample. They are connected to one another almost by coincidence. It so happens that at one time their children all attended the same school in downtown Toronto, Ontario, the DJDS. Their families' lives then moved in profoundly different ways from that point of overlap. As we have already indicated, some remained at the school for just one year. Two or three stayed at the school for the following eight years and played prominent roles as volunteers.

When we first sought out these families, we were interested in studying the interacting influences between schools and the families whose children spent their days within their walls. Over time, and as the lives of these families moved further and further apart from one another, their shared origins at DJDS became less and less important to our inquiry. Therefore, readers will find that the story of DJDS fades somewhat from the pages of our analysis. We are still curious about schools, but this book is not primarily about schools. In this introduction, we discussed why this has become a book about families and about how the family is a critical (perhaps *the* critical) space in which Jewish life is experienced.

In effect, the fortuitous circumstances of our connection with this group of families left us with a diverse research sample whose lives we had the opportunity to study over an extended period of time. Moreover, these circumstances have provided us with access to a group of families many of whom are today marginally engaged in Jewish life. The circumstances of our first point of connection with them do not seem to have determined what came next other than providing us with access to a diverse set of Jewish families at a period of the family life course when some of their children were becoming adolescents and some were even leaving home for college. We got lucky!

Originally, in the fall of 2003 and winter of 2004, we interviewed fourteen sets of DJDS parents whose children at the time were in kindergarten or first grade, as well as a further fourteen sets whose children were in fifth grade. Two or three years later, we succeeded in returning to nine sets of the parents whose children had previously been in the younger two grades. Six to eight years after that, that is eight to ten years after the first interviews, we were able to track down sixteen sets of the original families, whatever grade their children had originally been in. Eight of these sixteen families had been in the sample of those we had interviewed for a second time in 2005. In the next chapter, we will introduce these families more fully. (There are also short descriptions of all sixteen families in the appendix.) We will describe at greater length the Jewish culture of their homes when we first met them at the start of the project. We contend that the

Jewish social and cultural capital (the Jewish networks and cultural resources) to which parents had access when beginning to build their family lives was a significant factor in shaping the subsequent Jewish trajectory of their families.

To clarify how we came to learn their stories: At first, when the children were younger, we visited their family homes to interview the parents. Often, the conversations took place in the evening, and we were introduced to the children as they made their preparations for bed or for school the next day. At that time, because we were very much interested in the school their children attended, we also conducted participant observations at school events and within the daily life of the school. These proved useful opportunities for learning more about the families (e.g., when sitting alongside people at school board meetings or at special festive occasions over the course of the year). At that time, a member of our research team also conducted brief interviews during the school day with some of the children and with their teachers.

Ten years later, we no longer conducted observations. All of our data came from visits to family homes where we made every effort to interview children alongside their parents, and, as far as possible, if the parents were not estranged from one another, we interviewed both adults together too. In these later interviews, the conversations were generally structured so that we began talking with the whole family together, and then often the children left us to talk with the parents alone. As mentioned above, before returning to a family, we made a point to be fully familiar with earlier interview transcripts. This enabled us to make sure that we followed the threads of families' stories over an extended period of time, although as we discuss below this resulted in some methodological challenges.

Methodological Cautions

As we have argued, we believe that this research design has enabled us to learn about the development of Jewish life and identity in unusually insightful ways. At the same time, we recognize that our approach may have skewed some of the data we collected. By interviewing people in their own homes, where it was quite usual for family members to come in and out of the interview space, we may have prompted people to talk about their lives in terms of their homes and their families. It is possible that if we had met interviewees at their places of work or in some neutral space, such as a café or library, they might have highlighted other themes where family was less central. We are confident that this was probably not the case, based on our experience interviewing a few separated or divorced individuals in settings away from their family home. The foci of these particular interviews did not seem especially different.

Another methodological matter to which we have had to be alert is that, in some respects, we have come to know people better than they know themselves. In the course of our first round of analysis, when we were working on our first book about these families, we spent hours poring over their words. By contrast, our interviewees had long forgotten what they had said to us on previous occasions and often what they themselves had done in the past. They sometimes expressed surprise that we "remembered" some incident they had described on a previous occasion. At these moments, we had to remind them that we had reviewed the transcripts from earlier conversations. In a sense, returning to interview the same individuals after the passage of a number of years was a bit like reconnecting with an old family friend who remembers a lot less than you do about the past times you spent together. This awkward dynamic had potential to lead to a problematic power imbalance in the interview relationship. Often, it meant that we had to play down what we knew about the interviewee, so as to foster as natural a conversation as possible.

A last challenge, less easily resolved, was that in the last phase of our work we were returning to people who might not only be unsettled by how much we "remembered" about them, they were also often aware that we had written and published about them. (In one case, we arrived at an interview to find a copy of our previous book on the coffee table.) There was a great danger that, under these circumstances, people would talk in ways they presumed to be socially desirable. We found, therefore, that it took time, over a necessarily long interview, to get to a point where interviewees might let go enough of the self-consciousness created by these circumstances.[1] The reader will have to judge whether or not we overcame these challenges.

Structure of the Book

In the coming chapters, employing a series of sociological frameworks, we view the lives of sixteen Jewish families as they have played out over a period of up to ten years. As already mentioned, first—in chapter 2—we provide an orientation to the families while employing the constructs of social and cultural capital. In this way, we make explicit the diversity evident in our sample, and we lay down a baseline in relation to which to observe future changes in its members' Jewish lives.

In chapter 3 we introduce the three central analytical lenses of life course theory. Viewing families' Jewish stories through these lenses, we see how change can be driven most visibly by generational change (the life cycle movements and role transitions of family members) and less obviously by ontogenetic change (the physiological development of family members from embryo to adult) or as a consequence of historical change (macro-social shifts through which families live). We show how the interplay between these life course processes can result in profound changes in families' Jewish lives.

In the following chapter—chapter 4—we tackle the question of why some families' Jewish lives change more than others. Drawing on Olsen's circumplex model, a powerful application of family systems theory, we demonstrate how the interplay between the dimensions of family *flexibility* and *cohesion*, on the one hand, and features of the family structure, on the other (such as whether families members share the same religious faith, whether parents are single, married, or divorced, as well as gendered family patterns) accounts for the extent to which life course processes result in change in Jewish lives over time (or what sociologists call the balance of morphostasis and homeostasis in their lives).

In chapter 5, we apply elements of the analysis from the previous chapters, specifically a life course perspective and family systems theory, to the interpretation of the stories that families tell about home-based family rituals. We show how recurring family rituals, such as Friday-night practices or Seder nights, and rituals associated with the High Holidays and Chanukah, serve both performative and formative functions for families. These rituals, we propose, also act as indicators of what does and does not change in families' lives over time, what accounts for those changes, and most unexpectedly the contribution of children as "kin-keepers" in the observance and development of family ritual.

In chapter 6, we take the opportunity to look closely at the children in this study, all of whom were teenagers at the time of their final interview. We highlight the insights gained from talking with teens at home when other family members are around in contrast to most recent studies of teens where every effort has been made to interview teens away from their families' shadows. This analysis reveals a profound difference between how these young people talk positively about themselves as Jews and how they think about intermarriage when compared with their parents.

In our final chapter—chapter 7—we argue that, together, the theories we have deployed contribute to a new paradigm for analyzing Jewish lives. This paradigm is especially timely at a moment when scholars and practitioners are wrestling with the significance of profound changes in the Jewish family, and in how the Jewish family is conceived. We elaborate on the potential contribution of our analysis to disciplines that study contemporary Jewry and to the decisions of policy-makers and practitioners who work with Jewish families and Jewish teens.

Notes

1. The documentary filmmaker Michael Apted describes wrestling with a similar challenge when making his long-running series "7-Up," "14-Up," and so forth. He argues that it is hard for an interviewee to maintain a performance for the interviewer over the course of a long interview. Eventually, the interviewee's self-consciousness in front of the camera fades away (Maxwell-Stewart 2012).

TWO

Dreidels on the Christmas Tree: Jewish Capital in the Family

The cast of individuals about whom we develop an account of Jewish growth and change is made up of a sample of sixteen families who at one time enrolled their children at the Paul Penna Downtown Jewish Day School (DJDS). To review, all the families were interviewed at least twice, and some of them three times, over a ten-year period (2003–2013). The families were made up of two groups: nine families whose children were in kindergarten or first grade when we first met them, and who were starting high school when we met them for the final time; and seven families whose children were in fifth grade when we first met them and had just started university when we met them for a final time.

Downtown Jews

Differing from one another in their family composition, in their Jewish backgrounds, and in their socioeconomic profiles, this group of sixteen families with whom we enjoyed a professional relationship over a decade of their lives share some important sociocultural features. First, they have all made their homes in Toronto, Canada's largest city, with a population of more than three million. Toronto has never quite shaken the well-known quip that depicts it as "New York run by the Swiss" even while it has become one of North America's most diverse cities in which approximately two hundred languages are spoken. It is a thriving metropolis where the rough edges of capitalism are softened by Canadian, collectivist civic culture.

The Jewish community of approximately two hundred thousand has grown in three waves since World War II; with the arrival of Holocaust survivors in the 1950s (in one of the largest influxes outside Israel), migrants from Montreal in the 1980s (during the most intense period of separatist turmoil in Quebec), and Russian-speakers and Israelis since the demise of the Soviet Union in the 1990s. The first two groups have shaped a strong community ethos reflected in the high per capita contribution to the Jewish Community Federation. They have also sustained a strong commitment to Jewish day school education, with more than a third of Jewish children attending all-day Jewish schools, until recently, that is. While the community has grown, it has in large part remained concentrated, extending ever further north into the distant suburbs along Bathurst Street, a single thirty-mile artery. This geographic feature is perhaps the most visible point of departure for the families in this study.

These families are part of a trend of Jews who choose to live in the less Jewish-concentrated, more multicultural urban core of large North American cities (Hoffman 2011; Weiss 2009). Most of their own parents had moved to the suburbs when they achieved a certain level of economic well-being (Diamond 2000; Sklare and Greenblum 1967). By contrast, these families—our sample— have to a certain extent become disaffected with conventional denominational suburban Jewish life. They prefer to return downtown, many relying on public transportation rather than cars to get around. They are more interested in living in close proximity to the creative core of the city where they have ready access to educational and cultural institutions rather than to suburban shopping malls. A few members of the sample were employed at a major downtown North American university. They tend to have liberal political and religious values, reflecting their social-geographical positioning as self-proclaimed "downtown" Jews, rather than more traditional and conventional "uptown" Jews found in the northern or suburban reaches of the city. They are unusual as private school parents who at least for a period of time chose to pay about $10,000 a year for their children's schooling. As one observer explained to us, "For these parents what is important is more the kinds of kids they have, than the things their kids have."

In socioeconomic terms, however, this is a far-from-homogeneous collection of families. While the group includes doctors and lawyers, there are many more that work in the creative arts (acting, film, or music), intellectual professions (journalism, psychiatry, or academics), and welfare services (nursing and social work). Members of these families, consisting of a pastry chef, a costume designer, and a national newspaper editor, formed a core group on the board of directors of their child's Jewish school during its early years.

More than a quarter of the families are intermarried, and there is a sizeable number of single parents, "older" parents, and same-sex couples. This contrasts with the majority of families in Jewish day schools in North America, where families conform to certain normative structures, where both parents are Jewish, heterosexual, and typically start families before they turn thirty (Bechhofer 2011; Pomson 2011). Conventionally, social scientists view synagogue membership as a key indicator of Jewish communal connection. Yet, while approximately 90 percent of day school families in North America hold synagogue membership, only about half of these families do, and a quarter of them are members of what Wertheimer (2005, 53) calls a "progressive niche synagogue," a local fellowship where Jews band together periodically for prayer and other activities. Those parents who do hold memberships at full-service synagogues tend to prefer the style at a downtown traditional egalitarian service rather than in one of the denominationally based congregations in the city's midtown or suburban neighborhoods. This particular traditional egalitarian congregation became a strong connector for families once their children graduated or were withdrawn from the school.

The previously mentioned trends of religious individualism and of religious seeking play an important role in understanding the Jewish orientation of these families (Bellah et al. 1985; Wuthnow 1998). They feel comfortable leading privatized Jewish lives, beyond the institutions once assumed to mark out the terrain of an engaged religious life. Through their own personal enactment of lived religion, they construct Jewish meaning in often spontaneous, frequently innovative, and entirely personal fashion (Hall 1997; Davidman 2003). One of the most vivid instances of such religious personalization (and one we have often cited to our students when we teach about the shifting nature of contemporary Jewish identities) is the phenomenon we call "Apple Orchard Jews" as expressed by the Richards family when we first met them in 2003. Jean Richards explains:

> We still feel connected to our Judaism but not necessarily in the traditional way; a little more secular. Neither of us like synagogue, we haven't really found a place that we like to go as a family and our kids completely hate it and we don't want to make them go.... So, we sometimes do go to Shaarei Chesed [a conservative synagogue] sometimes to be with John's father in respect to him.... Otherwise on Rosh Hashanah we like to apple orchard [in the original interview recording this term appears as a verb], and to have our own family ceremonies as well. We sit in the orchard and talk about what our new year's resolutions are and we will go around and say what we want to do.... Or on Yom Kippur we go to a ravine and we ask for forgiveness from one another. We do things that are personally meaningful.... Generally, it is the six of us doing it together.... Our neighbor wanted to come with us this year; she is like a surrogate aunt. She is not Jewish but she is a surrogate aunt; so, she came with us.

It is these increasingly common types of individualized and customized Jewish family practices (what Davie [1994] describes as instances of "believing without belonging") that call for close examination if we are to gain a better understanding of the contemporary lives of Jewish families, and particularly those in our research sample.

As we have explained, the families whose stories we are recounting were not deliberately chosen in an attempt to find a representative sample of North American Jewry; as we have indicated, they were an opportunity sample. The parents happened to send their children to the same school at the same time, during the year we launched our research. Indeed, some children only attended the school for just that one year. In some ways then this is an unusual group of Jewish families. They might best be characterized as hybrid Jews. On the one hand, they construct highly personalized Jewish lives, display liberal values, demonstrate relatively low levels of traditional Jewish engagement and, in large part, as public school graduates themselves, are advocates of the public-school system. In these ways, they are reasonably representative of North American Jews in general. Their profiles align quite closely with the secularizing trends highlighted in the 2013 Pew study of American Jews (Cooperman, Smith, Hackett and Kuriakose 2013). On the other hand, for some period of their lives (longer for some, shorter for others), they chose to enroll their children in a private Jewish day school. This behavior places them somewhat outside of mainstream Jewish trends: in both Canada and the United States, approximately one third of Jewish children attend Jewish day school for at least one year. Perhaps this hybridity is related to the Canadian context. A similar profile of families in the less traditionally Jewish United States would be less likely to make the ideological and financial commitment to an exclusively Jewish educational setting. Perhaps, because in Ontario there is a long tradition of public funding for Catholic schools, and because generally there is a cross-cultural consensus that values a cultural mosaic over a social melting pot, politically liberal families are less wedded to the virtues of public education for all (Schnoor 2011; Weinfeld 2001). As the interviewees told us themselves, Toronto families that in Jewish terms are moderately engaged and in political terms are liberally inclined can still feel comfortable sending their child to a Jewish day school, especially when it is pluralistic, progressive, and downtown.

Overall, whatever the peculiarities and even idiosyncrasies of the members of this sample with respect to their Jewish affiliations and expressions, we feel that many Jewish families in North America—day school families and non–day school families alike—will see reflections of themselves in the lives we describe over the following pages. We will demonstrate that the insights we glean are significant for the broader Jewish community and for those who study contemporary Jewry.

Jewish Social and Cultural Capital

Two conceptual constructs we have found helpful in illuminating the primary Jewish features of our sample are those of social and cultural capital, derived from the work of Pierre Bourdieu (1986) and Robert Putnam (2000). Putnam describes social capital as the "social networks among individuals . . . and the norms of reciprocity and trustworthiness that arise from them" (2000, 19).

We can thus think of *Jewish* social capital as the extent to which an individual has an array of Jewish family connections, friendship networks, and professional associations with other Jews. Individuals with high levels of Jewish social capital tend to live in geographic areas with high levels of Jewish residential concentration and spend the majority of their personal and professional lives within Jewish orbits.

Cultural capital, as defined by Bourdieu, refers to forms of knowledge, skill, education, and any cultural advantages people may have that afford them a higher status in society. By Jewish cultural capital, we thus refer to the extent to which an individual has knowledge of or competence in aspects of Jewish secular culture or religious practice. Examples of this could include individuals with a long history of regular synagogue attendance, extensive formal Jewish education in Jewish day schools, high levels of Jewish cultural socialization through Jewish summer camps, or fluency in Hebraic culture due to spending extensive time in Israel.

By classifying our families in relation to these two constructs we, first, lay down a baseline in relation to which we can chart subsequent changes in the families' Jewish lives. In this way, we are able to observe the extent to which families accumulate or deepen their Jewish social and cultural assets—that is, how much they extend their Jewish connections and their Jewish cultural advantages. At the same time, classifying these families in terms of their Jewish social and cultural capital at the time when we first met them, we can establish expectations about the kinds of resources on which they might draw over the subsequent years. In this sense, we view capital not just as an asset that is banked, an indicator of Jewish wealth, but also as a fluid, or fungible, resource that enables individuals to realize certain life choices. As Lareau has vividly shown, cultural capital can be conceived as the set of cards a family is dealt at the start of the "game of life" (Lareau 2000, 296). Different families make better or worse use of these cards; how they fare in the game is not prescribed, but, undoubtedly, the cards one is dealt make a difference to one's chances of success regardless of one's skills as a cardplayer. If we map the Jewish social and cultural assets that families held when we first met them, we can develop some reasonable expectations about how their lives might subsequently develop.

Low Jewish Social and Cultural Capital

As we argued in our first book, more than half of our sample could be characterized as having limited Jewish social or cultural capital. When we first met these families, a number of them lacked extensive Jewish family and social networks and many, by their own admission, experienced a partial or unsatisfactory Jewish education in their formative years. The Ruben-Fine family gives us a sense of what such a family can look like when it lacks both Jewish social and cultural capital. Michael Ruben, a screenwriter, did not attend any Jewish day schools growing up. His private elementary school had very few Jewish students. Because of the academic pressure of this school, he released his energy by consistently misbehaving in his temple's Sunday school. He does not remember this as a meaningful Jewish experience. He did attend some summer camps over a few years that had significant numbers of Jewish campers and did spend one summer in Israel as a young adult. When we first interviewed him, he reported that he attended synagogue only on High Holidays. He referred to himself as an atheist who is also "shaky on his Zionism." He had never placed a high priority on his two children attending Jewish schools, or even attending schools that have high proportions of Jews. In fact, he himself admitted that he is "not one hundred percent comfortable in a Jewish environment." Although he had some Jewish friends, he explained that for a long time he had spent most of his time with "gentiles."

Michael's partner, Joanna, who we met in the previous chapter, was not born Jewish. For part of her childhood she was raised by Jewish relatives who had passed away by the time we first interviewed her. After she met Michael, she began a conversion process to Judaism, in large part because of the prejudice she perceived her daughter to experience as the Jewish child of a parent who was not Jewish. The conversion process became stalled when the couple did not agree to send their children to the religious day school recommended by the rabbi facilitating the conversion. Joanna lamented that she still had not learned very much Hebrew. She would like to improve on this. From the outset, Michael was lukewarm about Joanna's conversion. He felt that her sponsoring rabbi "takes the religion far too seriously." He strongly resented the suggestion that he become more ritually observant to support his wife on her journey. Joanna tried to make Shabbat for the family, but when work or school got in the way, Shabbat did not happen.

Although their younger daughter was at DJDS at the time of our first encounter, their older daughter never attended day school. Jewishness was present in their home to some extent, but in a low-key way. The family did not live in a part of downtown Toronto where many other Jews lived, and so the children did not have much exposure to Jewish life in their social circles around the neighborhood. It was almost entirely lacking in their extended family circles. While there were certainly elements of Jewish pride and identity in the mix in this family (intermingled with Jewish ambivalence), and this affirmative sense of Jewishness did account for their enrolling in a Jewish day school for a short period of time, overall the Ruben-Fine family possessed relatively low levels of social and cultural capital from which to draw. As we will later see, these resources were further fragmented by subsequent life choices made by various members of the family.

High Jewish Social and Cultural Capital

The Reinhart family provides a profile of a different type. Here we see parents who did not attend Jewish day school but acquired substantial Jewish social and cultural capital in other ways as they grew in to adulthood. Donald Reinhart attended public school and went to Hebrew school on Sunday at his local Reform temple. He found his Hebrew school more enjoyable than did most of his friends, immersing himself in "worthwhile" Jewish projects and benefitting from some "inspiring" teachers. While his family attended temple services only sporadically during Donald's childhood, he became involved in his temple's youth group. In addition to these experiences, Donald explained that there was "another branch" of his Jewish upbringing, which provided him with a strong religious foundation. On his frequent visits to his grandparents' home in a small town, Donald would attend his grandfather's Orthodox synagogue, where he was drawn into "the mystery of the religion."

Donald's wife, Sandra, also found certain Jewish outlets in her upbringing that stimulated her passion for Judaism. While she attended a nominally Christian private school and grew up in a family with low levels of Jewish observance, there was a feeling that everyone needed to stay home for Friday night dinner. There was little synagogue attendance, but the family enjoyed a trip to Israel to celebrate Sandra's brother's Bar Mitzvah. Sandra reluctantly stayed in religious school in her Reform temple so she could have a Bat Mitzvah. It was here that she began to get interested in her Jewish studies and decided to stay until tenth grade. She became immersed in Jewish literature, particularly Holocaust novels, and while she reported being "turned off" by formal religion, she found herself drawn to many synagogues and Jewish memorials on her travels as a young adult through Europe.

It was in Israel that Donald and Sandra met and became close. Through this year of religious study, Donald developed an interest in a fusion between Orthodoxy and Jewish Renewal. He relished a free-spirited nondenominational Judaism, which connected with Sandra's interest in "whole natural world energy." She began to incorporate more Jewish values into her understanding of the world. The two spent time together in chanting circles in Tzfat, a city in Israel with a long-established spiritual subculture, and then with an Orthodox community in Australia. Donald explained that he had exposure to many shades of Judaism—Reform, Reconstructionist, Jewish Renewal, Orthodox, Conservative, Jew-Bu—and he "adores them all." Donald and Sandra gradually began to take on a more observant Jewish lifestyle together. And whether as a cause, effect, or totally coincidence, around the same time, Donald's father became a *ba'al teshuva* (newly Orthodox), further intensifying the Jewish culture and engagement in the extended family.

Although they grew up in already dense Jewish social networks, we see here the gradual accumulation of more and more Jewish social and cultural capital as the couple progressed through their life course. As Donald and Sandra raised their family, they instilled their love of Judaism and Jewish rituals in their children. In a later chapter, we will describe how they regularly attended Shabbat services with their children at a small, local Orthodox synagogue. In time, they transitioned to a Shabbat service in their own home with a neighboring family, combined with a chanting group. They hosted many guests in their home for Shabbat dinners, conducting all of the traditional prayers. The youngest child in the family, Herschel, age five, had been particularly inspired by his experiences in Jewish day school and wanted to sing the Shabbat *brakhot* at home at every opportunity. In comparison to most families in our sample, Donald jokingly referred to his own family as "religious fanatics." On our first encounter with them in 2003, the Reinharts were a strong example of a family—parents and three children—who collectively shared high Jewish social and cultural capital.

A Capital Map

These two families, at least at the time when we first met them, mark out poles in the Jewish sociocultural worlds of those we studied. In the extent of the Jewish social and cultural capital they evidenced, the Reinharts resemble the plurality of families whose children historically have attended Jewish day schools in North America, even while the family's journey to this point is somewhat idiosyncratic. The Ruben-Fines, by comparison, were a decidedly atypical day school family in their limited Jewish social and cultural capital, and in their deeply ambivalent relationship with Jewish life. If it wasn't for Joanna's emotional response to what she perceived as antisemitism in her daughter's public school, at a time when she was engaged in her own exploration of Judaism, they would not have been interested in enrolling any of their children in a Jewish day school.

In figure 2.1, we depict in impressionistic fashion how we classify all of the families in our sample at the time of their first interviews in 2003, in relation to the extent of their Jewish social and cultural capital.[1] To make clear, our classification is not based on a set of quantitative measures. This figure depicts graphically (schematically) what we learned through repeated lengthy interviews about the complex compound of Jewish social and cultural assets that these families possess. The specific location of each of these families in relation

High Cultural Capital

Reinhart
Wagner   Weinstein
                                                                Funk

                                          Elbaz
                                          Lowe
                        Stern   Goldman

                                Richards

Low Social Capital ── High Social Capital

                Wallace
                        Manning   Lombard

                    Silver   Maybaum

        Kleinman
        Ruben-Fine

Low Cultural Capital

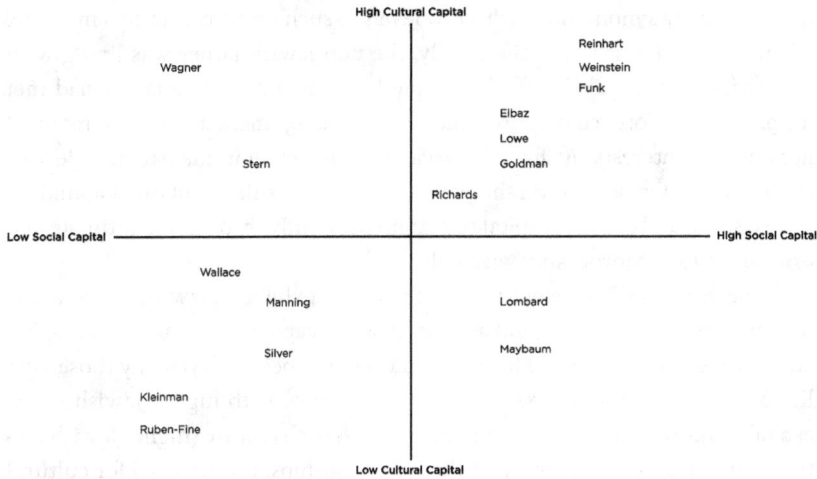

Figure 2.1. The Jewish social and cultural capital of the research sample

to the X and Y axes represents a reconciliation of the independent but largely overlapping assessment of the two authors following repeated reviews of the interview transcripts collected from these families. We are confident about having assigned families to the appropriate quadrant, even while the precise location of some families within each of the quadrants is more tentative.

The most significant aspect of this figure is that although our sample was originally built from a population whose children attended day school, fewer than half of these families (seven in total) exhibit both high Jewish social and cultural capital—a combination one would expect to find among those who at some point chose to pay more than $10,000 a year to send their child to an all-day private Jewish school. Thus, although these sixteen families shared a connection to day school education, they include a sizable number of individuals who would not typically be found in such social communities.

Least typical of those whose children are enrolled in private Jewish day school are adults located in the low social and cultural capital quadrant. Although we did not purposely assign them to the same quadrant, it turns out that all of the five parents in this quadrant are or have been involved in interfaith relationships. These families possess limited Jewish social networks of friends and families, and the Jewish parent in the relationship (three men, two women) has retained little interest in Jewish culture even if he or she might once have possessed more extensive Jewish cultural assets.

One interfaith family in the sample (the Elbaz family) is not located in this quadrant, but rather in the upper right-hand quadrant with both high Jewish social and cultural capital, thus demonstrating that an interfaith relationship is not necessarily synonymous with low levels of such resources. In this instance, when we first interviewed the family, the non-Jewish father was living with his Jewish partner, although the couple later separated. The father had met his partner in Morocco on a freelance writing assignment and shared many of her cultural interests. At first, he became quite active in his partner's Jewish social circles. On separation, however, the mother still maintained abundant Jewish social and cultural capital to sustain the family through her intimate and extensive ties to Moroccan Jewish culture.

The families who are outliers are those that exhibit, in Jewish terms, a mix of either higher cultural capital and lower social capital, or higher social capital and lower cultural capital. This is an unusual mix because typically those who live among strong networks of fellow Jews (those with higher Jewish social capital) acquire a substantial familiarity with Jewish culture (higher Jewish cultural capital) as a consequence of these relationships. It is unusual for cultural and social capital to be uncoupled in this way. Isolated toward the corner of the top left-hand quadrant is a family that can truly be classified as an outlier: the Wagners, a conversionary family where the father converted to Judaism after they married. The parents, in this instance, have little extended Jewish family (Jewish family members were barely referenced over the course of three long interviews), but the parents are highly educated about Jewish culture and Jewish practice, largely as a result of their own independent efforts and interests. This family unit (both parents and children) was one of the most religiously observant in the whole sample.

As an indicator of the role of capital as a resource and not just as an asset that is banked, the families in the bottom right-hand quadrant—those with higher Jewish social capital and lower cultural capital—were among the interviewees whose Jewish lives intensified the most over the course of the study. It seems that, over time, social capital can be translated into increased cultural capital. By contrast, cultural capital is not readily translated into social capital. Indeed, as seen in the next example, without sufficient levels of social capital, it seems that cultural capital can actually erode.

Eroded Jewish Social and Cultural Capital

In contrast to what is indicated by the cases of the Ruben-Fines and the Reinharts, described above, there is evidence that Jewish capital is not always something that an individual or a family consistently accumulates or that remains inert over an extended period of time. In some cases, we observed how capital may have been higher in the distant past, but had declined by the time of our first contact with the family. Capital, it seems, is not resistant to decay. We thus introduce the previously overlooked construct of what we call "eroded capital," the wearing-away of cultural knowledge and social networks, a phenomenon not previously considered in Bourdieu's or Putnam's formulations.

The Wallace family is located in the bottom left-hand quadrant of figure 2.1. Dave Wallace grew up in a very traditional Jewish environment. His home was strictly kosher and all Jewish holidays were observed. Through his nine years of Jewish day school education and his tight-knit family experience, immersion in Jewish culture was unavoidable. In his own words, Dave explains:

> My mother was very observant ... my grandfather was there, my aunt was there, my brother was there, my brother and I both went to the same [Jewish] school. The environment included all kinds of things that would connect me in a stronger way.... A large part of attitude is behavior and habit. You get used to doing something. You're going to have an attitude that reflects that. A positive attitude. And I was immersed in going to shul, from ... a pretty young age: six or seven. And I went every Saturday and we went to all the holidays together.

Dave further recounts that he lay tefillin every day until age twenty-one and served as a counselor at a Jewish camp where he achieved high proficiency in Hebrew.

Dave's wife, Adele, is not Jewish. She was raised an atheist but as a teenager became interested in exploring spiritual questions. This exploration took her on a journey through many traditions: native spirituality, Bahai, and Buddhism, among others. Adele expresses a profound attraction to Jewish people, tradition, and culture. When we first met her, she explained that she was happy to raise her son Sam as a Jew since she sees Jewish culture as rich with historical and moral content. As an educator, she took the leading role in deciding to send her son to Jewish day school. She explained, "I felt he had a right to that cultural heritage and I really wanted him to have that, and I know I couldn't do it."

With this combination of backgrounds, one might reasonably expect Sam to have grown up in a home environment with reasonably high Jewish cultural and social capital. We were surprised to observe that this was not the case. While Adele has put what effort she could into bringing Jewish capital into the household, Dave has not done the same. On his departure from his home-town in early adulthood, he became turned off by his synagogue experiences and broke his close ties to organized Jewish life. Geographically separated from his family, particularly his mother, his Jewish support structure was significantly reduced. There was little evidence to suggest that he and Adele had found sufficient Jewish social ties to replace it. Dave's knowledge of Jewish ritual and tradition seemed to be there in the recesses of his childhood memories, but he did not bring it out, express it and share this cultural heritage with his wife and son. It seemed to have worn away over time.

As we pick up the story of the Wallace family later in the book, this erosion of Dave's Jewish social and cultural capital will become more visible. We will have a chance to hear some of Dave's regrets of not maintaining the capital he once possessed. His regrets echo those of Franz Kafka in his famous letter to his father in which he bemoaned his father's failure to pass on what he called "the few flimsy gestures he performed in the name of Judaism"; these customs and practices simply seemed to "dribble away" in Kafka's evocative phrase (cited in Mendes-Flohr and Reinharz 1995, 254–255). Dave Wallace had the potential to engage his son more in Judaism and infuse more of a Jewish spirit into the home. He did not do so. As mentioned, Adele was always interested in raising her son as a Jew, but she required an active partner working alongside her. When we met with the Wallace family in their home in late December 2012, more than eight years after our first encounter, Sam did not demonstrate much passion for Judaism. In the living room stood a Christmas tree decorated with dreidels. The high levels of Jewish capital that were once there had gone through a gradual process of erosion. As we will see later, the decorations on the tree provide a powerful symbol of the hybrid culture produced by the family system in this home.

As we argued in our previous book, *Back to School: Jewish Day School in the Lives of Adult Jews*, the families we met at DJDS provide strong evidence of how schools can impart Jewish meaning to families (Pomson and Schnoor 2008). Our sample was composed of a significant number of families with relatively lower levels of Jewish social or cultural capital, and it is these Jewish families who were most influenced by their interactions with their children's school. They were more inclined to develop Jewish social networks together with the parents of their children's classmates and to engage with the Jewish content of what their children brought home from school. If this sounds like a tautological claim—that those who gained the most from encounters with day schools were those who had the most to gain from them—it is worth noting how much this claim departs from previous assumptions about the relationship between non-Orthodox families and Jewish day schools. Research in the 1970s and 1980s had shown that less traditional families enrolled their children in day schools *despite* the Jewish education being offered (Kapel 1972; Kelman 1979; Zeldin 1988). Many of the parents in those earlier studies were prepared to tolerate the Jewish studies, as long as it was not too intensive, as the price to pay for access to high-quality schools for their children. Our own earlier work reached a different conclusion, that low levels of prior Jewish engagement and interest do not necessarily inhibit parents' interest in the school's Jewish content or their responsiveness to their children's Jewish learning.

Our first book helped us understand the ways that Jewish social and cultural capital within the family play an important role in informing the shape and content of Jewish family lives. At the same time, we ended our work with more questions than answers. If it is true that Jewish elementary schools can serve as a locus of Jewish identification for a sample of moderately engaged Jewish parents, what will happen to these families once the children graduate or leave the day school system? What role will the families' Jewish social and cultural capital play in this ongoing process? Why might some families deepen their Jewish engagements beyond the day school walls, while others see their Jewish connections and commitments dissipate? Beyond the Jewish capital with which these families start, what are the drivers of Jewish change over the life course? What role does family cohesion play? What role does family structure play? These are some of the questions we will tackle in our next chapters.

Notes

1. Inspiration for this graphic representation comes from James Coleman's (1994) schematic depiction of the decline of social capital in families relative to the rise of financial capital.

THREE

"Reversing Some Screwed-Up Thing": Changes in Families' Jewish Lives over the Life Course

> You know, I think when I was in high school and a young adult
> I was not comfortable with being Jewish. I didn't feel connected to it in
> anyway.... Where I am at now, I feel good that I am connected to it....
> I feel much more comfortable with who I am, in my own skin.
> —Joyce Silver

For Joyce Silver, the path toward feeling at ease with who she is today was neither straight nor smooth. Her life story, as she tells it, is closely interwoven with the lives of family members across four generations, from her grandparents to her only child, Ruby. In this chapter, we view such journeys from a "life course perspective," through a collection of analytical lenses that makes visible the drivers of change in individual and family lives (Elder, Johnson, and Crosnoe 2003). This theoretical perspective is a powerful aide in making sense of the extraordinarily varied directions taken by different families' Jewish lives over the same period of time and in more or less the same geographic place.

Joyce's sense of herself is deeply imprinted by her childhood relationship with her grandparents, by their active role in the Jewish community, and by their traditional Jewish lifestyle, down to the food at their *sukkah* table. When we first interviewed Joyce, she recalled how her ease with this traditional culture was interrupted by her parents' divorce just as she was turning thirteen. "My upbringing, the whole part of the tradition ... didn't feel like it included me anymore," she explained. In her words, she became "the freak girl whose parents were the first in the whole school to be divorced."

Joyce described how she reacted to this turn of events.

> When my parents split up, when I was thirteen, it was a very different time all of a sudden in my life ... everything kind of fell apart; everything fell apart. So, although I have this traditional background and loved it, I was living with my mother who was

kind of on the other side of the fence. She is not that religious, and so I had a lot of conflict in my religion. . . . I became extremely rebellious against Judaism and against anyone who is Jewish. Although I continued to participate in all the family traditional holidays because I love them—I loved them all the way through—I didn't spend any time with anyone who was Jewish. I had no friends that were Jewish. . . . Every single possible way you could rebel, I just did. . . . I was exploring drugs and I was promiscuous and I was adventurous . . . I started working at thirteen-years-old so I could pay for whatever I wanted, and I just grew up really quickly. So, I was buying the clothes I wanted to wear and going out to night clubs. . . . I had a job and looked a lot older than I was. . . . I was very much rebelling, did all sorts of things that I wasn't supposed to do— skipping school, not participating in the things that I should have been doing at thirteen and fourteen years old.

Although Joyce remained in touch with her parents and grandparents, she charted her own course in life. She left home at sixteen, as soon as she could. She put herself through college, and launched her own business, one that in time became very successful.

Today, Joyce's Jewish rebellion has long since dissipated. She hosts a Seder in her own home, she and her daughter build their own *sukkah*, she recently spent a couple of years on the board of her daughter's Jewish elementary school, she's dating Jewish men, and, as we saw, she now "feels comfortable with being Jewish. . . . I feel good that I am connected to it in ways around food and traditions, and just the way it makes me feel."

When asked what prompted so much change in her life, she put it like this: "You know, I think I felt a little bit lost. You know, I think that, I think that maybe when I became single and had a baby. I didn't make a conscious thought, 'okay, I want to turn to my Judaism,' but I think that I found some kind of comfort in going back into that past." Undoubtedly, when we view the trajectory of Joyce's life, the birth of her daughter, Ruby, the child of a non-Jewish man whom Joyce never married, proved a decisive moment. Ruby's birth did not constitute a sudden turning point. It was not a life-changing event (what narratologists like Clandinin and Connelly [2000] call a "critical moment"), but because Ruby's life is interwoven so closely with Joyce's, Ruby's development and experiences have over time set Joyce's life in a different direction. Ruby's maturation from infant to adolescent and then emergent-adult, and the transitions in her life to Jewish elementary school, public high school, and university as a Jewish studies major, have established the pace and even direction for her mother's own life journey.

The search for an elementary school for Ruby led Joyce to the Downtown Jewish Day School (DJDS), a place that, in our first interview, Joyce memorably described as feeling perfect for her: "it was the school for freaks, the Jewish Downtown freak parents." Explaining her choice of school, Joyce's reasons seemed to have less to do with Ruby's needs than with her own: "I liked the idea of the way it would get me back to participate in some of the holidays with Ruby.... This way, I thought, you know, I thought, it would be a good way to enrich that part of my life that was in the past, and bring it into the present." The school provided Joyce, for the first time in many years, with a Jewish community that she felt comfortable with. And despite academic challenges, Ruby remained at the school. It seems that membership in this community meant so much to both daughter and mother that they were reluctant to leave even once Ruby had reached eighth grade, the final grade.

Ruby's personal development, and not just her transitions through different institutions, brought about a steady thickening of the family's Jewish culture. When we first interviewed Joyce, when Ruby was in fifth grade, Joyce talked about how moving it was to hear Ruby make *Kiddush* on Friday night. "I mean I can hum along with it, but I never really learned it, and it gives me great joy that Ruby knows the blessings." Nearly ten years later, Joyce relished how Ruby (her Jewish cultural skills deepening with the passing years) had been leading the family Seder, and how for the last couple of years Ruby has "honored" a non-Jewish friend with an invitation to come join them.

Over the years, there has been a change in the conversation at home that reflects Ruby's maturation as a person. When we first met, when Ruby was still at DJDS, Joyce reflected how, inspired by "God-talk" time at DJDS, the two of them discussed their relationship to God—Joyce doing so in what she called her own Jewish-Buddhist way. Ten years later, Ruby was at university but living at home and getting ready to major in Jewish studies. During our interview, now with both mother and daughter, they repeatedly referenced conversations about a host of serious matters, some prompted by Ruby's studies, or her transition from DJDS to a non-Jewish high school, and at other times connected to her experiences with Jewish and non-Jewish friends, as well as to her Jewish boyfriend, someone a couple of years older than her who she'd been dating for the last few years.

Wrapping up our interview, Joyce reflected on how her relationship with Ruby, how the events of Ruby's life, and especially her experience of Jewish education, provided an opportunity to repair some of the trauma of her own childhood. Joyce suggested that because her siblings never had any children of their own, they never had the chance to reevaluate the principles they had previously rejected or to change the trajectory of their lives as she had. Close to the end of the interview, Joyce tied together a number of these thoughts, reflecting on the counterpoints in her life over the course of many years:

> My Bat Mitzvah did not mean a thing to me because my parents had just divorced and it was like, why am I even here, they're fighting. I looked out there and my father is scowling and my mother is scowling and my aunts won't be at the same side as my father. This is not about me at all, right? So, my growing up, I was not connected to a good feeling about that at all, and I think that Ruby has had such an enriched feeling about Judaism and Jewish education, and still knows that her father is not Jewish. I mean we go celebrate Christmas at Kyle's house and I love that, and it's part of, you know, a really important part of our life. But, but we are Jewish, and it's really incredible to have that experience and to learn from her, through her, it's kind of like reversing, reversing some screwed up thing.

Panning Out from the Particular

We dwell on the Silvers' story because it vividly brings to life the theoretical perspective that has helped us make sense of the diverse changes we observed among all sixteen families we have studied. A life course perspective draws attention to the processes that mold human behavior over time by bringing together both micro- and macrolevels of analysis. To elaborate: in a family context, this perspective makes visible the interplay between processes of ontogenetic change (the movement of individual family members from embryo to adult), generational change (the life cycle movements and role transitions of family members) and historical change (the macrosocial developments through which families live) (Bengston and Allen 1993). In later work, Bengston, Putney, and Harris (2014) summarize these processes as the intertwined forces of biographical time (age), generational time (cohort), and historical time (period).

One of the most useful insights of the life course perspective is that of "linked lives"—the idea that as individuals develop, their development is enmeshed with and within the developing lives of others in their social network, particularly parents and grandparents (or children and grandchildren). This insight derives from a view of the family as a microsocial group within a macrosocial context, a collection of individuals with personal and shared histories who interact within ever-changing social contexts across ever-increasing time and space (Bengston and Allen 1993). In these terms, making sense of changes in individual lives calls always for consideration of the person's biography, her social networks—especially the family network—and the historical context in which her life plays out.

We are not aware of any previous studies of Jewish lives that explicitly draw on these assumptions and theoretical frameworks. In fact, the paradigmatic studies in the life course field are generally of families living through acutely challenging times, through war, or dramatically changed economic circumstances. Other life course studies have explored the multigenerational family histories of victims of sexual abuse (Elder 1974; Hareven 1982; Gilgun and Reiser 1992). If our interest in the Jewish trajectory of families' lives seems benign by comparison, we propose that the adults we have interviewed, the oldest of whom were adolescents in the 1960s, have in fact lived through a good deal of social and cultural turbulence, especially in the sphere of Jewish communal norms. As their individual and family lives have developed, they have been shaped by these larger circumstances.

Re-viewing the Silvers' story through the lens of a life course perspective, we readily see the intersecting forces we have just enumerated: the historical, the generational, and the ontogenetic. We see, in the broadest terms, how the family's story has been able to unfold in certain ways because of historical or macro-social changes. As a child in the 1970s, Joyce was ashamed of her parents' divorce, and her shame—strongly colored by social norms at the time—contributed to her rebellion. Today, Joyce is fully comfortable with being a single, unmarried mother. Her daughter expresses no discomfort—only amusement—over her mother's serial relationships with both non-Jewish and Jewish men. And those relationships have not problematized Ruby's own Jewish growth. In another dramatic historical change, it is noteworthy that liberal Jews like Joyce have become fully comfortable enrolling their children in parochial, all-day Jewish schools. When Joyce was a child, this was not an option that her parents, members of one of Toronto's prominent Reform congregations, would have considered. Progressive Jews viewed such schools as socially separatist and educationally inferior. Joyce's comfort with this choice for her child created opportunities for her own and her daughter's Jewish life to be enriched in dramatic fashion. A last indication of the changed cultural circumstances in which their lives have unfolded is in their comfort with practicing their Judaism among and with non-Jews, something that would have been an anathema to earlier generations of Canadian Jews (Weinfeld 2001). In doing so, they express Jewish identities that are neither exclusive nor threatened, and their comfort with practicing Jewish life in the company of gentiles has resulted in the stimulation of their own Jewish learning and growth. Because of their readiness to explicate and demonstrate their Judaism for others, they have been impelled to become better informed about their own ethnic and religious culture.

While these are some of the historical circumstances in which the family's life has evolved and which have also shaped that life, there have been a number of significant moments of generational change within the family. These are discrete, identifiable, life cycle related forks in the road that have made a differ-ence to the developing lives of family members. We have discussed at length two of the most significant transitions: Joyce's parents' divorce and Ruby's enroll-ment at a Jewish day school. Ruby's graduation from eighth grade at DJDS was, it seems, another no less significant moment of change for mother and daughter. In the weeks prior to Ruby's transition to a large public school for the arts, she became anxious about losing what she called the "anchor" provided by DJDS. She looked closely at the option of transferring to a community Jewish high school instead. Ultimately, she and her mother decided that, in Joyce's words, transfer-ring to such a school "didn't feel like it was a really organic move for our family." Instead, to ease the transition into the public sector—"to create a bridge ... a transitional thing"—they got together with other families to support a monthly after-school program at DJDS for recent alumni. No less significant, Ruby's departure from DJDS also prompted her mother to join the school's board, the first time in her life that she had sat on the board of directors of a Jewish institution. This proved a useful way to soften the impact of this transitional moment, Ruby's departure from full-time Jewish schooling, and helped "make sure that I had something to do with keeping the essence of why that school, why I chose to go to the school." Interestingly, moments of generational change that were significant for other families we studied—such as the death of parents or grandparents, or a child's Bar or Bat Mitzvah—did not loom large in Joyce's and Ruby's story. It seems that the family's Jewish trajectory, whether toward greater or lesser Jewish engagement, was already set in motion by other forces.

In addition to these forces of historical and generational change, one more collection of forces plays out at an entirely different rhythm and with a different degree of visibility at the microsocial level. Within the life course perspective, these microsocial changes are referred to as ontogenetic changes. They occur due to the ceaseless process of human aging from the time that an individual is born until his or her last day. In the Silvers' story, it is possible to discern these forces as well. They continue to drive forward the movement of the family's Jewish life. These are the kinds of changes associated with Ruby's maturation from a dependent (an infant) to someone who now serves as an inspiration and model for her mother. We noted already how Ruby, as she became more adult, brought ever richer Jewish capital into the home, in terms of what she knew about Judaism and in her developing competence to perform Jewish rituals. Ruby's growing independence—another facet of ontogenetic development—has also meant that the family is now *less* likely to mark Shabbat or Jewish festivals at home, simply because she is much less often at home. At the same time, Ruby's intellectual and emotional development as a young adult has also stimulated a change in the quality and focus of Jewish conversation at home. It is also surely no coincidence that, as Ruby has started dating and maintains a stable relationship of her own with a young Jewish man, her mother for the first time in her life is also starting to date Jewish men too. The trajectories of mother and daughter Jewish lives are closely intertwined; they serve as models for one another.

The Silvers' story is unusual because of the readiness one can discern within it, in holistic fashion, the interplay between the three major life course processes identified by the life course perspective.[1] To gain a more nuanced sense how each of the life course processes of ontogenetic, generational, and historical change operate, we turn now to examining each in turn. We describe how they manifest in the lives of a variety of families. In the next chapter, when we look at how family systems function, we ask why, given that all families experience the influence of these powerful life course forces, the Jewish lives of some families change more than do others.

Ontogenetic Change

We noted in an earlier chapter that conventional, retrospective studies of Jewish identity and Jewish life tend to overlook the processes of ontogenetic change, that is, the ways in which individuals develop as a consequence of relentlessly dynamic biological and physiological processes. The challenge for researchers is that interviewees themselves don't notice such changes, certainly not while they are experiencing them, and often not after the event either; they seem so unremarkable or inevitable. As we previously expressed it, observing such change is like watching skin grow. Perhaps the only genre of Jewish socio-logical research that has paid systematic attention to these ontogenetic phenomena is that which looks at the elderly. A number of studies have looked at how a looming awareness of mortality—or how, for retirees, the availability of many more hours in the day for altruistic activity—results in an intensification in religious activity and interest (Dillon and Wink 2007; Schuster 2003; Sered 1992).

Bringing a life course perspective to what we learned over a period of almost a decade during the course of repeated interviews with the same families, we have become aware of the pervasiveness of these ontogenetic processes. They may appear unremarkable, but their significance should not be underestimated. They can result in the gradual intensification of Jewish life at home just as they can result in the steady erosion of Jewish engagement, sometimes in the same family. And they deserve attention among young adults, no less than among the geriatric or terminally ill. We provide some examples below in order to convey a sense of their steady and unremitting influence on both the intensification and weakening of Jewish engagement.

In the Wagner family, Gary, an exceptionally bright boy, was in kindergarten when we first met his parents. The Wagners described themselves as traditional Conservative Jews. They lived the furthest north in the city of all our families, choosing a highly Jewish-concentrated neighborhood in the suburbs. Indeed, they were probably the most religiously observant members of our sample: they kept kosher in and out of the home, did not drive on Shabbat, and Brian, the father, a convert, was exceptionally serious about Jewish learning; he had been taking a weekly Talmud class for a number of years before he converted. The family embraced the diversity and egalitarian ethos of the DJDS community, aware that they differed from most other families in the school.

Over the years, as Gary matured, we noticed how he became an intellectual and social companion for his father, accompanying and enabling his father's Jewish growth. At the time of our second interview, when Gary was finishing first grade, he was making an hour-long walk to synagogue with his father each Shabbat, armed with a supply of bananas. By the time we returned for a third interview, when, having skipped a grade, Gary was already at the Jewish community high school, we learned how he and his father would walk almost three miles to a synagogue that they both particularly enjoyed. Upon arrive at their home for this third interview, we interrupted father and son learning Talmud together. As Brian explained, "[Gary] told me about this long extracurricular conversation he's had with [his Talmud teacher at school] and I said, 'I need to teach you a piece of Gemara; it'll help you with that.'" Over time, Gary had grown from a dependent to a partner of his father's, his deepening interests and abilities immeasurably enriching his father's Jewish life.

At the Goldman family, we observed a similar trajectory of intensified engagement due to ontogenetic processes even while at the same time generational changes (especially the transition from Jewish to public school) diminished the intensity of Jewish life at home. Ruth Goldman is a single mother who, when we first met her, identified herself as a Reconstructionist Jew, and as "a hypocrite, in that I know about more than I practice." At the time, Ruth was attending synagogue less frequently than she wanted. The problem was that after dining most Friday nights at Ruth's parents' house and getting home late, Dara—her five-year-old daughter—was too tired to get up for synagogue: "She is still in her pyjamas at 2 o'clock in the afternoon." At the same time, Ruth commented, "I see that Dara is probably going to be [*laughs hard*] forcing me into a little bit more practice if it's what she learns at school and I don't want to be sending her to a day school and not being absolutely hypocritical about things at home."

When we revisited the Goldmans, Dara was just starting second grade. Ruth reported that Dara still preferred "to do nothing" on a Shabbat morning at home but that when whey they do go to synagogue "she loves the services. She never wants to go to the kids' services; she loves hanging out with me—grown up services. It's getting her out of the door that is the difficulty."

We visited a final time when Dara was in eighth grade at a local public school, and we learned that Ruth and Dara went to synagogue every week now. They had switched from the Reconstructionist synagogue where they had been members since Dara's birth. Now, they had become members of a traditional egalitarian congregation. It was closer to home and a number of Dara's old friends from elementary school also attended. Dara was leading services for younger children and reading Torah quite frequently. Ruth, meanwhile, had joined the board of directors, having made many new friends. Dara's maturation (the steady playing out of ontogenetic change) had set in motion significant changes in Ruth's religious, communal, and social life.

In most other families we studied, ontogenetic processes seemed to have resulted in the decline rather than the intensification of Jewish activity at home. As children became more independent, especially the older members of the teen sample who had left home for university by the time of our last round of interviews, parents reported making less effort to mark Jewish events at home. At the Manning family, for example, when the children were in the younger grades of elementary school, they marked Shabbat most weeks. As Ed explained at the time: "Now that [Max] gets a challah every Friday and brings it home, there's reason to do the Friday night prayers that we didn't normally do at all before ... Most Fridays we say the prayers and incorporate it into our weekly life. It's something I look forward to but it's not like a special event anymore. It's a part of what we do." Six years later, by the time of our third interview, Shabbat dinner on Friday night had become a less frequent event; the change driven again by the children. Just as when they were younger, there seemed good reason to mark the onset of Shabbat, now that they were older, there were fewer reasons to do so. As Ed explained, "Some Fridays are chaotic, and if the kids aren't here, you don't think to do it." Sharon, his wife, elaborated, "And we're a family that has dinner every single night and so Friday night isn't the one night we have dinner together. So, as they got older, they were playing here and there outside, and we didn't insist that they come in and we do it."

We encountered a similar dynamic at the Reinhart family, with regard to synagogue attendance and Shabbat observance. Previously, we noted this family's relatively high levels of Jewish capital. Later in this chapter, we will share more about the idiosyncratic route taken by this family whose members were both more traditional than many others in our sample and more inclined to experiment with its Jewish practices. Here, we note specifically how ontogenetic processes drove changes in the family's Shabbat observance and synagogue attendance.

When we first met them, Donald and Sandra explained how when their children were younger, they lived across the street from a synagogue. It was an aging downtown congregation, but they went every week even though they were often the only family with children. "And then," Sandra summed up, "we kind of stopped going gradually." Her words offer a succinct statement of the slow effect of ontogenetic processes. Donald, her partner, expanded on what happened: "Our kids, when they were little, they were doted on and embraced by the community and they weren't very much in the way. As they got older, they got noisier and they weren't that interested in the ritual.... As time went on they were less interested and there were a few people there who found the noise of kids a bother.... That kind of energy around the kids we were not comfortable with, and so it gradually diminished our involvement there."

Drawing on their own Jewish cultural resources, they continued to craft their own Shabbat morning service with another family at their home, in what they called "Jewish renewal" style. When this other family left the street, they launched a "chanting group" on Sunday mornings. At the time of the interview, they insisted the "one thing we have always been consistent with is that Friday nights we have guests, and we do *Aishet Hayil* (an extract from the book of Proverbs praising women) and a blessing of the children and all the rest of it. And in that respect we are like religious fanatics compared to a lot of people that we have in the school community."

Nearly ten years later, both parents reflected wistfully on how their family observances had further evolved, regretting that "it has sort of shifted away." In part, this change was related to a year they spent in Israel (more about this later in the chapter). At the same time, the changes in their observance, especially once they returned to Canada, were associated with their children aging and with their Friday nights being squeezed by other commitments— hockey games, dance practice, and orchestra—"things," as Sandra explained, "they didn't need to consider when the kids were little" but that were really important to them as part of the broader community in which they lived. Additionally, as part of a parallel process, with their oldest child moving out of the house—and being the one who, in her own words "brings a lot of the Shabbat momentum to the family"—their Friday nights have "lost a bit, you know," Sandra reported. "And it's not to my liking. Let's say, I am not, like, great!"

These examples of declining Jewish activity related to the aging of children were repeated across the research sample. In some instances, as children aged and their routines changed, families got out of the habit of performing certain Jewish practices. Sometimes, they didn't even notice these changes. As one father put it, "I don't remember a conscious decision to stop. It just sort of happened, which is too bad." In other instances, parents were tired of insisting that their children took part in Jewish observance. As children got older, it was harder to get them to do things, such as going to synagogue, against their will. So, parents also stopped. At the same time, as their children became more independent, and less needy of attention, others noted that this opened up more time to tend to their own Jewish interests, and that led some of them back to synagogue. As Carolyn Weinstein reported, "Now that the kids are older, I am back on the ritual committee," something she didn't have time for when they were younger. For Dina Funk, too, it meant being able to embrace the opportunity to serve as a *chazanit*, a cantor (a choice we explore more fully later in this chapter). She explained, "I decided that rather than spend all of this energy on my kid's school, I am spending it on music, you know ... It's connected to the kids getting older, feeling like now I am entitled to it."

Generational Change

The ontogenetic processes we have just described have largely been undetected by scholars of contemporary Jewry, although they have been noted in studies of the ebb and flow of religious activity over the life course, such as in Dillon and Wink's (2007) monumental sixty-year study and in other shorter-term instances (Hayward and Krause 2012; McCullough et al. 2005). Conventionally, studies of Jewish life and Jewish identity do not focus on these slowly evolving processes but rather on critical episodes or turning points in people's lives; these are moments that, in retrospect, adults can identify as having signaled or stimulated an important change. Thus, in Cohen and Eisen's *Jew Within* study, the researchers encouraged their interviewees to look back in time, and asked them: "Would you say that there was any particular point in your life where you became either decidedly more or less Jewishly involved than you were before?" (Cohen and Eisen 2000, 210). In *Connections and Journeys*, Horowitz posed a similar question, revealing in her interview protocol the assumptions that lie behind such questions:

> What have been the major *turning-points* in your life and the important *decisions* you've had to make?
>
> (PROBES: Have there been moments when the things that mattered to you changed? It could have been a conventional rite-of-passage such as travel, graduation, Bat Mitzvah or a more personal milestone—periods/events/decision points/experiences. Or decisions such as where to live, what work to do, what sorts of relationships to pursue, what to support.) [Emphasis in original] (Horowitz's 2000, 204)

Life course analysts conceive of such moments as *one* source of change in people's lives, what they call points of generational change—discrete, identifiable experiences or forks in the road that launch people's lives in different directions. These are what Bengston and Allen call "events or family transitions that alter interactions or selves" (1993, 471). In a family context, these moments involve changes in an individual's role or status: as child, partner, parent, or student (van Gennep 1960). They include life cycle moments, involving marriage or divorce, a child's Bar or Bat Mitzvah, or a death in the family (Brodbar-Nemzer 1986; Lawton and Bures 2001). They might be linked to transitions between one phase of education and another, such as children starting school or graduating school or making the transition from elementary to high school. They might also involve formative, one-off experiences, such as a sabbatical or an extended stay in a foreign country that mark out phases in a person's or family's life. As we have already seen, Joyce Silver's story was paced by such experiences: her parents' divorce, her daughter's entry into a Jewish school, and then her daughter's graduation at the end of eighth grade. As we saw in Joyce's case, these changes are rarely experienced independently of the involvement of other family members. On the contrary, these points of transition assume great meaning precisely because they imply a changed relationship with significant others in one's family.

There was no lack of such moments of generational change in the lives of the families we interviewed. In some instances, these were linked to transitions in the family lifecycle, most commonly to the experiences of Bar and Bat Mitzvah, but also to divorce or death. In a great many cases, these moments were associated with educational transitions, a particular interest of ours when we launched this study.

Bar or Bat Mitzvah

Because the children who provided the occasion for this study all turned twelve or thirteen at some point during the span of our research, the one life cycle event that provided an opportunity for generational change among all members of our sample was that of Bar or Bat Mitzvah. It was something about which we asked whenever we returned to families in the final round of interviews.

The most vivid example of the subtle role played by Bar or Bat Mitzvah as an occasion for generational change is provided by the Mannings, a family where we already observed the impact of the ebb and flow of ontogenetic processes. For this interfaith family, the enrolment of their eldest child in first grade at DJDS had set their Jewish lives on a trajectory of intensifying engagement over the following years, despite the erosions produced by ontogenetic processes that we already noted. At the start of sixth grade, they transferred their eldest son to a local public school where he had few Jewish friends, and a year later, at the end of fourth grade, they made the same change for their daughter. They never did enroll their youngest child in a Jewish school.

Once they withdrew their children from DJDS, there were fewer Jewish stimuli in their family's life, for example, fewer reasons to mark Jewish festivals now that their children stayed in school on most of the festivals and fewer reasons to celebrate Shabbat now that their children were not coming home with Shabbat eve packages and activities. Yet, rather than completely atrophy, their Jewish engagement launched on a new trajectory with their decision to mark their son's Bar Mitzvah at Temple Shalom, a liberal synagogue. Their son's Bar Mitzvah introduced a new intensity into their Jewish lives, at least for a period of two years.

In formal terms, deciding to mark their son's Bar Mitzvah at Temple Shalom meant joining the synagogue's Bar Mitzvah program, along with two former classmates; attending classes each week for the next twelve months; and paying synagogue membership. In practice, it meant that all members of the family spent a good deal of time at the congregation. Sharon explained that when they took their son to synagogue for the Bar or Bat Mitzvah ceremonies of one of his twenty-five synagogue classmates, they didn't simply drop off their son and run errands. As Ed elucidated: "He's invited for the service, so if I'm going to drive him up for the service, I might as well stay." Coming to the synagogue so often during this period, Sharon learned about parent education opportunities and participated in some. Ed, meanwhile, although never inclined to convert, also found that he enjoyed being welcomed in the congregation whenever he came: "The people are very warm, very easy going, accepting of someone not being Jewish like myself, and every week it's like, 'Ed, good to see you! Shabbat shalom!' you know, and everything is good. It's a very warm and welcoming shul."

In many respects, the Bar Mitzvah experience for this family bears all of the hallmarks of a generational transition in the life of the family; creating opportunities to build new social networks and to acquire previously lacking cultural capital. And yet when we met Sharon and Ed for the last time, already six months after their son's Bar Mitzvah—an event that had been intense and emotional, especially for Ed—both parents were feeling burnt-out by the experience. "We're a little overdone with it," they said. In fact, they weren't sure that they'd push either of their younger children to go through the same experience if they didn't wish to. And for the moment, having heavily invested in Jewish activity for almost two years, they had become much less conscientious, for example, about marking Shabbat at home: "We needed a break!" they explained. It seems that the Bar Mitzvah had prolonged their Jewish engagement over an eighteen- to twenty-four-month period after their children were no longer in a Jewish school, but it hadn't moved their lives on a fundamentally different track. It had been an important episode in their lives, but it had not been transformative. This is well demonstrated by Ed's answer to a question about whether they would continue going to synagogue now that their son's Bar Mitzvah was behind them:

> I grew up going to church every Sunday. Going to shul is not much different. The ritual of getting up on the weekend, getting dressed a little bit and going and listening to all the singing, all the prayers; to me, the ritual of the service is very comforting. Even though I haven't got a clue what's going on. It's all being part of the sanctuary, the congregation listening to the sermon. I really enjoy it. Whether we will make it a very regular habit, I don't think so, but it's nice to know that we have a place we can go to.

In the next chapter—when we examine how family systems function—we will look more closely at why in some families new patterns of behavior stick and in others they don't. For the moment, we seek to highlight how families (many families in our sample, in fact) experience Bar Mitzvah as a peak episode in their life course, but how ultimately (without additional stimuli or further supporting structures) they experience it as no more than a passing episode. In our first chapter, we saw how, for Ian Maybaum, his son's Bar Mitzvah was a moment when "the light shone" for him, bringing into sharp focus what it meant to be a parent and a Jew. What we did not emphasize at the time is that this epiphany did not change how Ian conducted and thought of himself as a Jew. In his own telling, his Jewish interests and activity continued to be as sporadic as before. In other families too, these were memorable occasions—especially when they were personally choreographed by parents and children—but despite the count-less hours that many invested in designing the experience (about which we will say more below), these investments neither set in motion lasting Jewish change nor established durable new Jewish patterns.

This may be because these occasions were not necessarily experienced as Jewish events. They were more expressions and celebrations of family. Michael Ruben—a screenwriter—captured this paradox well:

> You know it was a meaningful experience, and it was in its con-struction and intention entirely Jewish.... However, it was so per-sonal in a way that, you know ... I don't even barely look at it as Jewish. Not to say that it wasn't because it just ... I guess the people [involved] transcend the Jewishness for me, I guess. Which isn't to say it wasn't, but, I didn't.... I didn't finish it feeling, yea, it's so great to

be Jewish. I felt more how wonderful to have this daughter and this family and to celebrate that in this way.

Unlike other lifecycle experiences, Bar or Bar Mitzvah did not in most cases create a state of permanence or a new reality, something that is a feature of birth and death, of educational transitions, and occasionally of marriage and divorce. It is no coincidence that one of the few families where a Bar Mitzvah marked a genuine moment of transition was where Adele Wallace, a non-Jewish mother introduced in the previous chapter, made clear that she felt that once her son reached Bar Mitzvah, she had fulfilled her responsibility to raise her child as a Jew. "My feeling was always, take him to the Bar Mitzvah and then he does what he wants with it. I have my own personal religious life. It's not just Jewish." With great intention, therefore, she had enrolled her son at a Jewish school "to give him a chance to be part of a Jewish community, with Jewish educators. . . . I felt that [it was] the most effective way to have him know about his heritage, and then he could do whatever he wants with it." She elaborated on how she understood her role as a parent: "I guess in terms of my objectives, that's part of it too. In those first ten years, you have a chance to open as many doors as you can. You did piano, and you got the Jewish education, and he did his Bar Mitzvah. As a parent, that would be how I met an objective: just open the door for him, and then he steps through or not."

For the Wallaces, Bar Mitzvah was a peak family experience—one they created in a public space provided by the local university chapel—but it was also a transition point to a new series of family interactions where Jewish father and son would now have to take charge of their own Jewish resources. And as we will see in the next chapter, neither of them ultimately chose to take up that challenge. As confirmed by a number of studies, Bar or Bat Mitzvah is as likely to serve as a portal on the way out of Jewish communal life as a point of entry into it (Schoenfeld 1987; Schoem 1989).

Divorce

The potential for life course transitions to be intensely meaningful but ephemeral moments or, alternatively, to be a transition point to a new more permanent reality was something we also found in those families where parents went through a divorce or separation. These different trajectories echo studies of the varying influence of divorce on religious engagement. It seems that traditional institutional religious practices and beliefs among young adults are more vulnerable to the effects of parental divorce and discord than personal spiritual beliefs and practices (Ellison et al. 2011; Stolzenberg et al. 1995), but the outcomes differ depending on the gender of the family member, the salience of religion in their lives prior to divorce, and the particular form of religious expression affected (Denton 2012; Zhai et al. 2007).

Two examples from our sample demonstrate these patterns, the cases of Rachel Elbaz and Joe Kleinman. Rachel Elbaz, a secular Jew who spent many years living in Morocco both as a child and as an adult and who met her non-Jewish husband there, started attending a traditional egalitarian synagogue in the years soon after her daughter began attending DJDS. While the synagogue experience complemented her daughter's schooling, she shared with us that the main impulse for attending so regularly was not her child's education; it was because it helped her navigate the disharmony in her marriage. The synagogue was somewhere she could be with her two children, without her atheist non-Jewish husband. The synagogue was a "sanctuary," as she memorably put it. She explained further:

> Initially for me to be to have somewhere to go to with them and to feel that it was the right place to be, instead of like going to the Eaton Centre [shopping mall] or something (which would not have worked . . . it would have been four of us at the Eaton Centre), so yea he didn't feel comfortable because I had been to a Jewish day school. . . . I know the prayers, I am comfortable. But it wasn't because I felt comfort in the prayer. It was simply a welcoming safe place where the kids could enjoy, where the kids could play.

Attending synagogue regularly didn't change her own well-established, essentially secular outlook. It provided her children with a sense of community, which continued to be important to them once they no longer attended Jewish schools. But for Rachel herself, with the Bar and Bat Mitzvah of her children behind her, and long ago separated from her former partner, the synagogue was not somewhere she spent much of her time. As she said, "Now I no longer need to go, because I no longer live in the same house as their father. I don't need the sanctuary."

For a period, then, the synagogue assumed an important role in Rachel's life, but not a permanently important one. For Rachel, the supports that sustained her secular Jewish identity continued to come from her extended family and local social network, from frequent visits to Morocco where she also maintained an extensive social network from her past, and more recently from her own children's active involvement in a progressive Jewish youth movement. Those ongoing supports were not provided by the congregation that had played such an important role during a particular phase of her life.

The transitory impact on Rachel's Jewish engagement by her separation from her non-Jewish husband contrasts with the process initiated by

Joe Kleinman's divorce, a story we introduced in our first chapter. Neither Joe nor his wife, Michelle, felt very much at ease in Jewish institutions. They defined themselves as cultural or humanist Jews. They felt like outsiders because of their politics and their atheism. In our final interview with Joe, he complained, "The big problem I have is I feel like I can't find a Jewish community in which I fit in." As a couple, Joe and Michelle nevertheless made efforts to stimulate their eldest daughter's engagement with Jewish culture. They hadn't felt comfortable with the social and cultural milieu at DJDS, particularly because of what they perceived to be the middle-class elitism of most other families. They appreciated how the school enabled them and their daughter Sandy to develop a Jewish identity during the year she attended. They also enjoyed some of the spillover effects in their own home. In our first interview with them, Joe reflected, "It's great that she is acquiring a Jewish identity and that she can do with that identity what she wants to in the future. And we are giving her the option to think about that and to identify as a Jew. I think that's the most we can do."

After they withdrew Sandy from DJDS, they continued to experiment with alternative settings where she might continue to be "exposed to Judaism." Without the prompts provided by the school, they recognized (and even embraced) the fact that the onus was on them "to introduce Sandy to Judaism." At the time, as Joe explained in our second interview, they therefore started to sing part of Birkat hamazon (Grace after meals) when they ate at home on Shabbat. Joe explained, "We decided, she's not doing it in school, so we need to do it at home. [We're] taking more initiative."

We learned subsequently that a few months after this interview, he and Michelle divorced. It seems that, following their divorce, they lacked the shared resources to sustain such efforts. In the years following their separation, Sandy never experienced any systematic Jewish education. When we met her at the age of sixteen, her father had been living with a non-Jewish partner for more than five years. We were struck by how little Sandy said she knew about Jewish matters. (She seemed to have forgotten what a siddur or haggadah were, and she confused Rosh Hashanah with Pesach.) There were many factors that shaped this trajectory of disengagement, but it does seem as if her parents' divorce was a significant (even decisive) element in this process. When they were together, Michelle's interest in providing her daughter with a Jewish education that would be at least equivalent to her own in the early grades of day school and the Jewish social network provided through her own extended family counterbalanced her and Joe's alienation from the normative Jewish community. If anything, their joint sense of feeling as outsiders seemed to have sustained their ongoing wrestling with what it meant to be secular Jews. Living now with a partner who was not traveling this particular journey, Joe found that his stamina to live in an outlier state was sapped. If his daughter was not pushing for more Jewish involvement, he had more than enough other battles to fight. His daughter Sandy succinctly summarized her father's stance in this respect.

> SANDY: I think that if I or [my younger sister] showed interest
> in learning more in Jewish culture it would have, you as a
> parent would encourage us to learn what we were interested
> in. And if we showed interest in that I think it would have
> become more of a priority.
> JOE: Yeah.
> SANDY: But we weren't interested.

To our surprise, even though Sandy's mother, Michelle, was now living with a partner who had been religiously observant until quite recently, she too seemed to have abandoned the project of grounding her daughters' Jewish identities in Jewish learning and experiences. Divorce proved a moment of profound transition in the Jewish life of this particular family.

Educational Transitions

While generational changes associated with the family life cycle seem to have unpredictable and at times surprisingly short-lived consequences, the changes associated with educational transitions—children starting school for the first time, proceeding from elementary to high school or from high school to university—seem profound and far-reaching. Moreover, the consequences of these transitions seem to be experienced not only by the child starting at a new educational institution, but by their families too—a phenomenon that sociologists have been exploring over the last two decades (Ecclestone 2007; Evans 2002; Lam and Pollard 2006).

In our previous study of these families and their peers, we probed how the Jewish lives of many families were changed once their children began attending a Jewish elementary school. Parents were changed by what children brought home with them from school: by the questions their children asked about theologically challenging matters, by the Hebrew songs they sang back at home, and by the expectations their children expressed about what it means to live a Jewish life. Families were changed no less profoundly by parents' own experiences inside their children's school: at school events and rituals, as volunteers, as committee members, and in their interactions with educators and with one another. We found that, for parents, children's Jewish elementary schools assumed the formative roles historically associated with synagogues as houses of prayer, study, and meeting. In concluding that earlier study, we wondered how permanent these effects would be. We speculated that "if the connections that have sprung up around the school are to survive, they will need to be nurtured around additional foci. At this time, these connections, while meaningful as adult experiences, are ultimately contingent on the presence and inspiration of children. When children withdraw from the base of these connections, the surviving superstructure may be no more than a fragile web of memories and good intentions" (Pomson and Schnoor 2008, 162–163). Revisiting families, sometimes more than half a dozen years after their children transitioned from a Jewish day school to other educational settings, to other elementary and middle schools, and to high schools, we were deeply curious about what happened to Jewish life at home. In large part, what we found was much as we had speculated.[2]

For many families, perhaps the greatest change once their children moved on from a Jewish day school was that their lives at home were no longer paced by the rhythms of the Jewish calendar. Jewish day schools are closed on all of the major Jewish holidays, and in some cases on the holiday eve too. This meant that even if parents had not previously marked any aspect of the holiday, once their children were enrolled at DJDS they were now at home on these days and needed occupying. Moreover, because of the intense preparation for the holiday during school time—learning special songs, becoming familiar with special practices, and learning about the roots and rationale for the holiday—many parents began to feel the need to support their children's learning, by "bringing it home" in whatever way they took that to mean. In the weeks leading up to the fall holidays of Rosh Hashanah, Yom Kippur, and Succot, and the spring holiday of Pesach, it was hard for parents not to be caught up in the spirit of the season. That's something parents repeatedly told us during our first two cycles of interviews when many of their children were still enrolled in the school.

Just as we were regaled with excited stories about the changed Jewish culture in homes during the years that their children attended the school, when we revisited families once the great majority of their children had moved on, we heard a similar number of reports, invariably tinged with disappointment, about how Jewish practices and habits had fallen away.

Take the case of Ruth Goldman. We saw before how her daughter's ontogenetic development created opportunities for and even stimulated her own Jewish social, cultural, and religious engagement. At the same time, her daughter's transition from DJDS to a public school led to a loss of intensity in their Jewish life at home. Ruth reflected on these changes with sadness. Having previously been infuriated by how many days of school were lost due to Jewish festivals, even to the extent of leading a parent campaign to address this with the school, she now seemed wistful about missing these pauses in the calendar.

RUTH: The school kept us very connected to life cycles, or not
    life cycles but you know annual cycles ... and certainly the
    school closed as much as it did for holidays it forced that ...
    So, that's not with us to the same extent and I regret that.
    Some of it was nice; some of it was over the top you know;
    two weeks for Passover was a little bit much... they don't
    have to close the school for a whole ten days.
INTERVIEWER: And now Dara is at Pine Crest public school so....?
RUTH: I am not bringing her out of school to miss school.... So,
    yes, so those Jewish holidays go by the by.

We found a similar shift, and an even greater sense of nostalgia for what was lost, with the Sterns, a moderately observant family who were active in a liberal downtown congregation during most of the nine years their youngest son was at DJDS. The Sterns' case is interesting because on the surface it did not seem as if their time at the school had changed much at home. As they explained during their first interview, the family's Jewish engagement was influenced more by a five-month period they had spent in Israel before the younger of their two sons started at DJDS than by his attendance at the school. The time in Israel prompted them to develop their own Jewish family style—what they called, "developing their own thing": they took to keeping kosher at home; they observed aspects of Shabbat until mid-afternoon on Saturdays; Phillip became an active volunteer at the Federation; and Rhonda joined the ritual committee of her downtown congregation.

When their youngest child started at DJDS, their practices were not so much changed as energized. Thus, when we interviewed them for the first time in the fall of 2004, during the High Holiday period, Rhonda provided an insight into the dynamic triggered by the school: "Like even today as we were walking home, Jayden said to me, you know, Friday, mom, we are going to make ... you know how we did last year where we made all the decorations for Sukkahs? He said, yeah, remember we made all these paper chains and we did it the day we got out early for Yom Kippur? Okay yeah, I guess we will be doing that again."

The school prompted them to invest more effort and find more joy in practices that they might anyway have observed. Additionally, their connection with the school drew them into a social circle of people with whom they began to observe these practices. For the first time in their adult lives, it introduced them to a group of other Jewish families with whom they felt comfortable: "The nice thing about the DJDS is that it is a really *haimish* [homely] bunch, you know, nice eclectic sort of urban family groups, which I like. We would be sort of I guess typical of that, like liberal leaning, very easy going and stuff about the religion side, not Jappy and stuff like that."

When we visited them for the last time in May 2013, their son Jayden was no longer in a Jewish school (he had graduated from DJDS five years previously). He conveyed a strong sense of apathy and even antagonism toward all things Jewish. Phillip and Rhonda, in turn, looked back fondly on a less complicated time when their children were not as resistant to Jewish practice or even to thinking of themselves as Jews. As Phillip lamented, "There's not a lot of strengthening going on, at least not in our family."

And yet it's worth emphasizing that transitioning away from DJDS did not lead to the abandonment of Jewish practices in the home. It did, however, produce a change in their intensity, partly because of their son's diminishing enthusiasm and also because of the dynamics of generational change.

> RHONDA: Well the school celebrated every holiday, so there was always something coming home like about holidays. If it was a celebration at school, or whether there was some kind of . . . Right so then they'd have the school calendar, and all the Jewish holidays are marked on it. So, everything was Jewish. I guess up until grade 7. . . . You know we would get together occasionally, but regularly for Friday night dinners with some of the families. You know, and there was a Chanukah party, Purim . . . .
>
> PHILLIP: It was a community.
>
> RHONDA: It was . . . Yeah. I liked that.
>
> PHILLIP: It was like our own little *shteibel*. You know our own little community shul.
>
> INTERVIEWER: People at the school?
>
> RHONDA: Yeah. The class. Not the school so much.
>
> PHILLIP: Because we didn't really know anybody outside the class. But, whatever, how many families? Twelve families? We were really pretty tight actually for a while.
>
> RHONDA: So right . . . that was a disappointment that we didn't stay friends.
>
> PHILLIP: Yeah.
>
> RHONDA: Some of the parents we liked.
>
> PHILLIP: Yeah they were nice people. They are nice people.

Uncannily, Phillip's image of the school as *shteibel*, a Yiddish term for a small congregation, echoes his description nine years earlier of the other families as *heimish* (another Yiddish term). While their son was at the school, those other families provided a context in which to live their Jewish lives. Once Jayden left the school, Phillip and Rhonda seem to have been thrown back on their own resources within the immediate context of their home.

Reviewing the Sterns' story, and others we have referenced, it seems as if there is an inevitable dimming in the intensity of Jewish life following the transition of children (and families) from a Jewish to a non-Jewish school. Yet, it's worth contrasting these families' stories with our account at the start of this chapter of the journey taken by the Silver family: Ruby's graduation from DJDS at the end of eighth grade prompted her mother to join the school board for the first time (the first time in her life that she was ready to play a leadership role in a Jewish institution). It also led both mother and daughter to take an active role in organizing once-a-month Jewish programming for graduates of the school. Leaving the school prompted an intensification in their Jewish social engagement. In parallel fashion, for the Maybaum family, the withdrawal of their oldest child, Elijah, from DJDS at the end of fifth grade prompted them to be much more "consistent," as they put it, about marking Shabbat at home. Carrie Maybaum explained: "You leave Jewish day school but being Jewish is still, this is important, whether you are there or not ... we needed Elijah to see it was important to us. . . . So, not at school and not getting it at school, it's important that they see that it's consistent at home, it's not just when we go to their grandparents' house."

The contrast between the stories of the Goldmans and the Sterns, on the one hand, and the Silvers and Maybaums, on the other, again raises questions about why some families seem to change more than others. This is a question we address directly in the next chapter.

Israel Experience

To conclude our account of generational change, we draw attention to one last form of generational transition that has not previously been noted in the family life course literature: spending an extended period abroad as a family. Even within the sociology of contemporary Jewry where a great deal has been written about the transformative impact of immersive experiences in Israel (Cohen and Cohen 2000; Copeland 2011), no attention has been paid to what such experiences might mean when undertaken by families rather than by individual young or emergent adults. Much of the literature concerned with Birthright Israel, a free ten-day Israel experience program, highlights the unique receptiveness of eighteen- to twenty-six-year-olds to this intensive program at a time of their lives when participants are still in the process of constructing their own identities (Saxe and Chazan 2008; Kelner 2010; Saxe et al. 2014). (Arguably, the sociological frame within which studies of Birthright are conducted with its trope of conversionary experiences is quintessentially located within the personalistic paradigm that we previously critiqued.) Among the sixteen families that we followed during full the term of this research project, we encountered two (the Reinharts and Sterns) who together with their young children spent an extended period of time in Israel. In both instances, this experience seemed to have exercised a great lasting impact on the trajectory of the participants' Jewish lives as a family.

Donald and Sandra Reinhart had previously spent a year in Israel when they were single, in fact they had met there while each was occupied with their own Jewish exploration. That experience had been formative of their own highly literate and creative Jewish-Renewal-inspired melding of different Jewish forms. They decided to spend another year there when their three children were, respectively, going into fifth, seventh, and tenth grade. Donald explained, "The whole idea of going there was to first of all deepen our relationships as a family and second of all to deepen our relationship with Israel and Judaism." At the same time, in reflecting on what the experience ultimately meant for the family, Donald recognized that "obviously, a major adventure like that is going to affect different people in different ways and you can't expect a family full of individuals and individuals that have been encouraged to be forthright, you know self-realizing, to agree with each other all the time."

While their year did not formally change their life course statuses, as is the case with other life course transitions from dependent to partner or high school student to graduate, they did return home thinking differently about themselves, as Jews and as family. In Sandra's words, it was a deepening experience because it enabled them to locate themselves on a Jewish map, within, as her daughter Yael elaborated, "a community of progressive, religious-inspired, forward-thinking individuals."

The intensity of the family's experience in Israel had a series of paradoxical consequences. It meant that, returning to Toronto, they felt that the intensity of their own religious observance as a family "devolved" (by which they seem to have meant, declined) absent the all-encompassing rhythm they experienced in Jerusalem. It was as if they no longer needed to sweat the details of Jewish practice once they gained a bigger picture of how they thought of themselves as Jews. They had outgrown their own local community, feeling more at home in an international Jewish context. In addition, it was actually in Israel, while relishing the experience that observing Shabbat was no longer "socially alienating and isolating," in Yael's words, they became much less stringent about traveling on Shabbat. Donald explained, "It was the only day where we could go on a *tiyul* [an excursion] or something, because of six days of school, and so, as the year went, on we started, you know, we started making dates on Shabbat." By the time they returned from Israel, all members of the family had become much more comfortable with who they were as "serious Jews," and less stringent about the particulars of religious observance. Their Jewishness had become a very strong element in how each of them thought about themselves, but its importance did not find expression in specific religious practices.

The Stern family's experience in Israel also moved them on a trajectory that took them to a place that was markedly different from where they had set off when they first arrived in the country. It is not clear what originally inspired the couple to spend five months in Israel when one of their children was ten years old and the other five. Rhonda, raised in Detroit by proud secular Jews, had spent a year in Israel previously as a student. Neither Rhonda nor Phillip identified themselves as a passionate Zionist before the experience or as engaged in some journey of Jewish discovery. They characterized the move as "going on an adventure" that included putting their children in kindergarten and grade school for a semester.

Phillip, in particular—having initially been reluctant to go—identified the experience has having been transformative.

> We took a leave of absence and went to live in Jerusalem and that pretty much changed our orientation around Shabbat, and getting a lot closer to what's important to us in religion, etc. And that I guess was a big instigator for sending Jayden to the Downtown Jewish Day School. We probably wouldn't have done it otherwise, if we hadn't been to Israel. . . . You know living in Jerusalem was just a remarkable experience, and my late dad had a cousin who lived right across the road from us and they were just wonderful people and they brought a huge amount to the trip. They are great people. They are modern Orthodox as well and it was a great time.

Having not previously sent their older child to a Jewish day school, they enrolled their younger child at DJDS on their return. Phillip himself developed a passion for Israel that he translated into activism on behalf of the local Jewish federation in Israel-related causes. As a family, they became much more interested in marking Shabbat. They both explained:

PHILLIP: . . . it was Israel that did that though, living in Jerusalem.
RHONDA: Because Jerusalem is like that.
PHILLIP: Yeah, and everybody, Friday night, everything shuts
    down Friday night and you walk on the roads.
RHONDA: And no stores are open, and nobody phones you. It was
    very nice.

The narratives of these two families provide a helpful contrast in highlighting how a deep but limited-time immersion in Israel, a quintessentially liminal experience, like other moments of generational change, has the potential to advance families' lives in new and unpredictable directions. As with the experiences of Bar Mitzvah, divorce, and school transition, the outcomes produced by such experiences are not foreclosed. They can, however, set in motion profound changes in families' lives.

Historical Change

We have made explicit how within the context of a single interview, research subjects are often able to identify the moments of generational change that constitute turning points in their lives and in the lives of their families. We have also tried to demonstrate how multiple interviews with the same subject can allow the researcher to identify ontogenetic processes that have resulted in changes in the life of a family. It is rare, however, that interviewees point to a third group of forces that life course theorists identify as enabling change to occur within the family. These are the forces that play out at the macro or societal level, the historical events and societal changes that people live through and that have impact on the ways in which their lives develop. To make clear, these phenomena do not influence individual actors in some deterministic fashion, causing great numbers of people all to act in the same way; rather, they create circumstances that enable lives to develop in ways that would not otherwise have been possible. Individuals rarely notice such phenomena or their particular effects; it is hard to step outside one's historical moment and observe how it is different from those that came before. Life course theorists argue that these historical changes can, however, have as much impact on people's behaviors, social relationships, and values as those generational and ontogenetic changes that play out on a more intimate stage within the family.

Classically, in life course research these macrosocial phenomena are historical events, such as economic crises or wars, or they are technological or cultural changes, such as the invention and proliferation of the motor car or the widespread employment of mothers outside the home (Elder 1974; Hareven 1982). These sociocultural shifts enable changes in the lives of families over time. In our study, we identified a small number of social and cultural phenomena that had not commonly been experienced or practiced by previous generations of Jews in North America, and that seem to have prompted the lives of some families in this sample to move in new trajectories. To be clear, these expressions or experiences were not embraced or enacted by all or even most of our interviewees, but their frequent existence and perceived normality provided new and different opportunities for the development of Jewish family life, or for finding meaning within it.

The Personalization of Rites of Passage

During the three decades after the end of World War II, coinciding with the large-scale move of Jewish families to the suburbs of North American cities, the Bar Mitzvah and (about a decade later) the Bat Mitzvah became a rite of passage that not only marked the maturation of young Jews but also cemented the membership of Jewish families within the organized Jewish community in the synagogues that had become the locus of Jewish communal life in the suburbs (Schoenfeld 1987; Stein 2001). Regardless of widespread handwringing about the miseducative character of Bar and Bat Mitzvah preparation (Aron 2010; Schachter 2010) and the satire of the ritual itself by generations of writers and popular commentators (Roth 1993), one assumption that underlay such occasions was never challenged: important moments of the Jewish life cycle were marked within the embrace of the community. It was most unusual for those who chose to mark these rites of passage to do so anywhere other than in a communal context and anyhow other than in a carefully scripted procedure. Marriages and deaths were observed in similar ways—within the community and according to familiar ritual scripts.

Our interviews with this sample of families indicate that there has been a sea change in communal norms for marking the Bar or Bat Mitzvah as a rite of passage. This is in fact the one historical change that the subjects noticed themselves, with the mothers—in particular—marveling at how different it was to be Bat Mitzvah today compared with when they were younger. In numerical terms, fifteen of the sixteen families in the research sample publicly marked the Bar or Bat Mitzvah of the child who was the original focus of this study. Of these fifteen families, five dramatically personalized how they celebrated this occasion. They took charge of the design of the event, in terms of its timing, location, and content. In all of these cases, the family—working with a specially recruited educator or rabbi—designed its own personalized ceremonial ritual in a location outside a synagogue or conventional Jewish prayer space, relocating to a theatre or church hall, and holding the event at a time of the week other than on Shabbat morning, the conventional time for more traditional iterations of this event. In and of itself, this phenomenon is a fascinating indicator of the personalizing trend in Jewish religious life to which we drew attention in this book's introductory chapter. The personalization of the Bar and Bat Mitzvah calls for further scholarly examination having been noted until now mainly in nonscholarly literature and explored in a limited way by the organized Jewish community (Hollander 2014; Meiser 2013; Oppenheimer 2005; Pickus 2015; Munro 2016). Employing a life course perspective, we are interested in an additional dimension. We see this development as expressing a historical change in Jewish cultural practices that has enabled Jewish families to develop and find meaning in ways that were not previously imaginable.

Elijah Maybaum's Bar Mitzvah provides a window on the implications of this phenomenon for the family life course. Elijah marked his Bar Mitzvah on a Saturday evening at the theatre of the local Jewish Community Centre. The ceremony was planned around a *Mincha/Maariv/Havdalah* service for which the family designed its own *siddur*. As part of the event, Elijah chanted some of his Bar Mitzvah Torah portion and delivered a *d'var torah*. It was a deeply serious event designed with intentionality and with Jewish literacy. Doing it this way, so that the service ran directly into a Saturday evening party, meant that guests—and especially Elijah's friends—couldn't just turn up for the party. They had to come to the service too. As Elijah's mother, Carrie, explained: "I know kids who have Bar Mitzvahs and only invite the kids to the party when they're at public school, and I would never have done that. It was important for me to have the kids there for the service. We did an all in one. We did the *Havdalah* service and then right into the party, but it was really important that anybody who was going to be there had to be there for the service."

When Carrie reflected on why the event was so meaningful, she provided an intimation of the potential significance for families of this historical change in sociocultural norms, a shift especially reflected in the fact that her own grand-parents had been founders of one of the largest Conservative synagogues in Toronto, an institution from which this event was essentially in flight. As Carrie herself emphasized, "It didn't need a rabbi, it didn't need anything." And taking control in this way had consequences for the family:

> I think you have to make a lot of choices, right? I don't think there is a formula for how you do it and I think by going our own way we had to make a lot of choices along the way and we had to talk about what was important to us, and that idea of the intimate service, of making it understood, explaining things as they were going on. We invited people to do English readings and things. That's where we went through the process of articulating what is important to us. And so, for that reason, I think when you do the formula [participate in a conventional service], when you see it done a certain way, and you think that's the way it has to be done, maybe you don't go through those [choices] as much.

Carrie's explanation highlights some important features of this phenomenon: the desire to create something intimate for one's family and friends, and above all to create an experience that is both profound and deeply personal. Through making decisions about how they would mark this occasion, the family felt they gained greater ownership and understanding.

We heard remarkably similar sentiments from the Reinharts when they described their daughter's Bat Mitzvah—an "adventure" to which all members of the family contributed. Yael, eighteen years old at the time of the interview, explained in great detail the personal touches that she and her parents brought to this event, not the least of which was delaying it for more than a year, until she was in eighth grade, "in case I was in a new school and wanted to establish myself socially and have people who are important to me there that I didn't know yet were important to me."

The features that Yael highlighted closely echo those described by Carrie Maybaum, her former classmate's mother:

> We had it in a hall near my house. . . . It's right nearby. It used to be a synagogue and a Jewish community centre that is oriented eastward but it hasn't had Jewish programming as of, say, 30 or 40 years. . . . So, we didn't have a Rabbi. We didn't have a congregation that already met or a shul that met. We made everything up ourselves. I, along with this person who really did it, made the siddur and I led the service along with my dad for the most part.

Describing at length the prayers and tunes that they chose to include in the service, Yael concluded:"They did the ones that I liked and other things, basic things that I liked, because you know I wasn't confined at all by a shul, like already having a way of doing things. So, I got to pick and choose how I wanted to be there."

The impetus for doing things in this way was the opportunity to personalize the experience. We suspect that, in an earlier age, a family like the Reinharts, one so comfortable with and literate in the varieties of Jewish expression, would have surrendered their personal preferences to the will of the community, or at least to communal norms. Increasingly, it seems, families are not willing to do so. Instead, uncoupling themselves from the broader community, they create their own rites of passage in the company of a more intimate group of friends and family. This is a trend much like that seen in more intensive fashion in the 1970s among Havura members who broke away from traditional congregations to form their own microcommunities and to create their own worship services (Prell 1989).

From a life course perspective, this phenomenon represents both an opening up and a closing down of opportunities for family development. Through designing such experiences, families uncover, articulate, and commit to those things that are most important to them. At the same time, by taking such complete ownership of these events they cut off a route to joining a larger Jewish collective beyond their immediate social circle. They seal themselves within a more intimate social grouping.

We suspect that, in these respects, Bar Mitzvah is the thin end of the wedge. We already saw intimations of other rituals evolving in the same way. Michael Ruben claimed that he was inspired to design his daughter's Bat Mitzvah without a rabbi by his experience designing a theatrical performance in memory of a recently deceased colleague. He explained that the memorial show had been about the eighty-six things his close colleague had left behind, and climaxed with the deceased person's partner presenting her ashes before an audience of 450 people jammed in to a Toronto theatre space. Michael reflected: "It was one of the most moving evenings of my life.... And it ... was one of the reasons that I considered putting together an evening [for my daughter's Bat Mitzvah] as perhaps the most meaningful and intimate way to do it. So I think the absence of, literally, a rabbi, a figure that was mediating, and sort of between the congregation and the principle participants, and the absence just brought it closer. It made things more visible, more intimate." Michael's description of this memorial event and what made it so powerful echo those elements in the personalized Bar and Bat Mitzvah rituals that our interviewees highlight.

The Normalization of Interfaith Family Relationships

If the personalization of rites of passage has attracted limited comment and analysis, another historical change, the surge in interfaith marriages and relationships between Jews and non-Jews, has drawn more commentary than perhaps any other social issue within the North American Jewish community. Long before the Pew Research Center's 2013 *Portrait of Jewish Americans* reported that 71 percent of non-Orthodox Jews were marrying non-Jews, and even more so since Pew's publication, there has been extensive debate about the meaning and implications of intermarriage for the Jewish community (Barack Fishman 2004; McGinity 2009; McGinity 2014; Saxe 2014; Thompson 2013; Wertheimer and Cohen 2014).

In the sample of sixteen families that we followed over a decade, there were six families where one of the adult partners in the family was not Jewish. Among the twenty-five adult interviewees in the sample who had been born Jewish, only one reported that he or she had a parent who was not Jewish. This suggests a sea change in behaviors and norms, whose potential implications are being hotly debated. Although our sample might be considered unrepresentative of the broader phenomenon in that all of these interfaith families had enrolled a child in an all-day Jewish school for at least one year, this case does strongly suggest that intermarriage is no longer an expression of disengagement from the Jewish community (Thompson 2013). Looking closely at these families, it is possible to observe the various implications for Jewish family life of these societal changes in ways that support different positions in the debate about intermarriage. We found: (1) families where a non-Jewish partner supported or even drove forward the Jewish engagement and education of children, (2) families where the absence of an extended Jewish family meant that parents and children lacked the stimulus and support for Jewish experiences, and (3) families where a Jewish parent possessed sufficient social and cultural capital to sustain the intensity of Jewish life at home with limited assistance from a disinterested non-Jewish partner.

We have already had a couple of occasions to note the supportive role played by Ed Manning, someone with no intention of becoming Jewish himself, in supporting his family's Jewish practices inside the home and beyond, in embracing the benefits of Jewish schooling for his children, and in generally articulating an appreciation of his family's Jewish identity. We have seen also how Adele Wallace, a non-Jewish woman with a deep commitment to her own spiritual search, sought out a Jewish school for her son and initiated much of the Jewish activity in her family's home, recognizing her husband's lethargy about such matters. As we previously mentioned, she had told her husband that she was "not prepared to do extracurricular Judaism; after-school Judaism like an add-on," so she propelled the decision to enrol their son in a Jewish school. We have also seen how she made clear that once her son reached the age of thirteen, she would no longer play such an activist role in shaping his Jewish identity.

Earlier in this chapter, we observed a different trajectory set in motion by interfaith relationships. We saw how once Joe Kleinman separated from his Jewish partner, he did not have the social or cultural resources to sustain his daughters' Jewish education or their Jewish experiences at home, even though his subsequent non-Jewish partner was someone who described herself as a spiritual person. Much as did Michael Ruben, another Jewish father in an interfaith relationship, Joe found that the lack of an extensive Jewish social network, or an extended Jewish family, reduced opportunities for connecting with other Jews and for participating in Jewish experiences, and that this contributed to the gradual erosion in the intensity of Jewish life in the home for him and his daughters. Both Joe Kleinman and Michael Ruben expressed ambivalent feelings about their own Jewish identity; in the terms of the Pew report, they are "Jews not by religion," and as the only Jewish adults in their home, they expressed limited interest in deepening their daughters' Jewish engagement if their daughters were not themselves especially interested in being engaged. There was a thinness to the Jewish social resources on which they could draw, if they had wanted to, in contrast to those families where both partners were Jewish, even if ambivalent about their Jewishness. (As we discuss in the next chapter, it is significant that in the case of Joe and Michael, the Jewish parent in these interfaith families is male.)

In a different fashion, we came across one instance where a parent who had married a non-Jewish partner with limited interest in their children's Jewish education was nevertheless able to socialize her daughter and son into a strong Jewish identity. Dependent on her own resources, Rachel Elbaz was connected to an extended and communally active Jewish family. She had great familiarity with traditional Moroccan Jewish culture, stretching back to her own childhood. She continued to feel a close affinity to the country, and traveled there with her children at least once year. Although not religious herself, she became connected to a downtown synagogue so as to access communal dimensions of Jewish life that she missed, especially with a non-Jewish spouse. At her encouragement, her children became active members of a progressive Jewish youth movement in Toronto and led active, communally engaged Jewish lives well into their teenage years when we interviewed them for the last time.

A last feature of the normalization of interfaith relationships (although not exclusively a consequence of this phenomenon) is the presence of non-Jewish family members and friends as fellow participants at domestic rituals, such as Shabbat and Seder night meals. In previous generations, these occasions were experienced as intimate enactments of Jewish fellowship, where the inclusion of non-Jewish participants would have been inconceivable. For some of the families in our sample—living at a different historical time—these events have become opportunities for sharing and explaining who they are to others. When those who participate in these events experience them frequently, they can be routine or mundane; the events might rarely possess special meaning. But when performed in the company of non-Jews, especially those unfamiliar with them, they become occasions for explaining to interested others what it means to be Jewish, and in turn for thinking more deeply for oneself about what it means to be Jewish so as to be able to explain oneself more articulately. For example, this is what we noted at the Silvers' on Seder night where an animated non-Jewish guest posed no-end of interesting questions to the Jewish participants in the event.

The Normalization of (Parochial) Jewish Day School Education

A further historical change worth highlighting is evidenced by almost all the families in this sample of liberal Jewish families who chose to enroll their children for at least one year in an all-day Jewish school. When we first researched this sample of families, we noted how their Jewish profiles differed from previous generations of day school families. We previously wrote: "Historically, parents who chose to pay thousands of dollars each year to send their children to all-day Jewish schools were synagogue members and residents of Jewish neighborhoods and had been recipients of a relatively intensive Jewish education themselves. With few exceptions they were Jewish from birth, Orthodox in denominational orientation, and married to other Jews. Paying for all-day Jewish schooling constituted, therefore, the most complete expression of an intensely engaged Jewish identity" (Pomson and Schnoor 2008, 141).

In our earlier study, we found—through a series of six additional school cases—that not only did the families at DJDS depart from this historical profile, so did parents at other Reform, Conservative, Community, and Modern Orthodox day schools, often in significant ways. We found parents in this wider sample, as at DJDS, who did not have extensive Jewish family or social networks and who by their own admission experienced either a partial or unsatisfactory Jewish education during their formative years. This finding—that, in contrast to previous eras, many contemporary day school parents possess limited Jewish social and cultural capital—led us to explore why parents' Jewish lives were so much interrupted once they enrolled their children in an all-day Jewish school. "Having chosen a Jewish school for their child, they seem ready to explore opportunities to learn about Judaism, to experiment with the Jewish practices their children bring home, and to develop meaningful relationships with other adult Jews" (Pomson and Schnoor 2008, 142).

Viewing this sociological phenomenon from a life course perspective, and especially through the prism of the divergent life courses of the sixteen families who remained in our sample over ten years, we see how the turn of liberal families to Jewish day schools has functioned as what life course theorists would conceive of as an instance of historical change. This shift in societal norms, wherein liberal Jewish families have been willing to forgo public school education for their children and instead enroll them in schools that, as previously noted, their own parents would have considered socially separatist, educationally inferior, and prohibitively expensive, has enabled *some* families to develop rich Jewish social networks and deeper Jewish cultural literacy. The key consideration in this situation is that some families' Jewish lives have changed in this altered environment, while others have not. In this sample, made up of families whose children spent at least one year in a Jewish day school, those whose Jewish family lives changed least either withdrew their children from these parochial Jewish settings after very little time (like the Kleinman and Lowe families who switched their children after just one year) or who did not remain long enough to establish stable or lasting Jewish social networks (like the Ruben-Fine family).

Returning to the case of Joyce Silver, with which we began this chapter, we have already noted Joyce's appreciation of the school's transformative role in her own and her daughter's life. Here we underline Ruby Silver's appreciation of the values she gained at school, values she might not have gained elsewhere:

> Looking back ... I am happy that I got that Jewish education espe-
> cially because, like, because it's so egalitarian.... Looking at the
> person I am today and my belief system, I was happy that I was able
> to get educated in a system that was so egalitarian.... I love that.
> And I love that I have kind of, it's not like a huge knowledge base, like
> I don't remember many of the details. I don't speak fluent Hebrew
> anymore, but I do have some core knowledge that I think came from
> them and, I guess, stability in my Jewish knowledge, which is nice.

As we previously saw, six years after Ruby's graduation, Joyce had no difficulty discerning the decisive impact of this experience on Ruby as well as on herself. What she never dwelled on (and perhaps could not have been able to appreciate) was how her decision to embrace what she called "this very special experience" reflected a sociocultural change of historic proportions that was ultimately as decisive in shaping the course of her family's Jewish life as any changes stimulated by her daughter's maturation or the many transitions and changes in status in her own life. Her grandparents had been traditional Jews, and her own parents had been prominent members of established liberal congregations in Toronto, and would probably not have considered sending their own children to parochial Jewish schools. For Joyce, and for others like her who were put off by the bourgeois character of much of the organized Jewish community, it was now possible to feel comfortable in a Jewish day school and not feel as if one had sacrificed one's core values. Her comfort in this parochial school setting represents a profound social change.

Social and Cultural Opportunities for Women

It is axiomatic in twentieth-century life course research that the changing status of women in society has dramatically altered the pathways along which family lives have developed (Rossi 1985; Elder, Johnson, and Crosnoe 2003). With an increasing array of opportunities and obligations beyond the home, women's lives (and to a lesser extent, men's) have incomparably changed over the last fifty years, even while—as contemporary feminist thinkers caution—there is still a great deal more that must change before those opportunities and obligations are truly equitable (Pomerantz, Raby, and Stefanik 2013).

When we brought a family life course perspective to our data, we expected to find that changes in the status of women would be reflected in the different ways in which these families' lives have developed. We expected both to see evidence and hear talk among the mothers about how different their lives are from their own mothers and from their daughters. Yet, the traces of such changes were muted.

In contrast to the other phenomena of historical change we have just reviewed, it seems that major changes in the socioeconomic status of women, in their roles and in their opportunities in society, largely played out while most mothers in our sample were still young, in the late 1960s and early 1970s. These mothers were beneficiaries of such changes in their educational and career opportunities, and in the opportunities they had—for example, to freely choose to start and raise a family without a (male) partner, as in the cases of Joyce Silver and Ruth Goldman. Unlike the phenomenon of intermarriage, the social earth-quake associated with second-wave feminism occurred before the main plot lines of our stories were launched. A new landscape had settled into place by the time these mothers began to raise children (Geffen and Gerstenfeld 2010). In fact, their own daughters seem oblivious to how great a change there had been in the last fifty years, a phenomenon that seems quite widespread among their peers, as noted for example by Barack Fishman (2001).

The one exception to this pattern relates to the roles played by some of the mothers within religious institutions, and especially synagogues, settings that historically have been more resistant to the gender revolution. In Orthodox sectors of the Jewish community, women's roles are still more-or-less unchanged, even while in non-Orthodox communities, Jewish life has been dramatically feminized (Barack Fishman and Parmer 2008). These trends are best exemplified by the case of Dina Funk.

When we first interviewed Dina, she reported how prior to raising a family she had trained as a musician and had worked as a singer in night clubs and piano bars. During the first couple of years of our research, we had witnessed her vocal talents for ourselves as part of an accomplished acapella group of mothers who each year performed at the school's annual Chanukah celebrations. When we interviewed Dina a second time, she shared that she had been invited by another mother to come sing in the High Holidays services at a liberal prayer community in the city's eastside. The congregation was one, Dina clarified, that she and her husband would "never in a million years have been involved with—never!" but the connections she had made through her singing had made this attractive. Her husband would support her whatever his reservations about the congregation.

Six years later, when we interviewed her for a last time, it was evident that Dina had moved further in this new direction. As she explained, "So, you know that I am a musician. You know that I sing. *In my new life*, I'm a Chazanit.... I am the associate cantor at [a Conservative synagogue in the city].... When I'm on the bima, I love it" (emphasis added). Dina's choice of words could not be more poignant when considered against the backdrop of historical changes in opportunities for women within religious institutions. Those changes had allowed her to create what she recognizes (even tongue in cheek) is a new life for herself, one that during her own childhood and given her family circumstances, she would once have considered unimaginable. Having embraced this opportunity, she found it exhilarating.

To be clear, it does not seem that Dina encountered conflict in the institutions where she played this particular communal role. On the contrary, the congregations wooed her. Our point is that others before her likely had to overcome such conflicts. For her, taking on these roles was experienced as an opportunity that would not have come the way of many women in previous generations. Any conflict she did experience was probably at home where there were hints that her husband, more of a religious traditionalist, was somewhat uncomfortable with, although not resistant to, her taking on such a public role as a woman in the synagogue.

Dina's journey to a "new life" is the most dramatic instance we encountered of women, the mothers in our sample, taking on responsibilities in their synagogues. We already noted Carolyn Weinstein's return to the ritual committee in her congregation as her children aged, and we saw also that Ruth Goldman took on a leadership role in the synagogue she joined because her daughter so much enjoyed it there. These developments were not reported as significant episodes, but they were important enough for the interviewees to raise in the course of our interviews. This delicate balance of important but not dramatic conveys well the difference between changes in social and cultural opportunities for women, as a historical phenomenon, compared to the personalization of religious rituals and the normalization of intermarriage. Those latter forces are still playing out with as-yet unknown consequences. In the public domain, at least, the ripples created by changes in opportunities for woman have already reshaped large sectors of the community.

In the next chapter, we will contrast what has occurred in what we call here the "public domain" with what we found inside the home. As we will see, at-home, older, gendered patterns linger. In fact, gender's strong influence on family structure suggests that there still has not been a revolution inside the family system with regards to male and female family roles.

As we have suggested throughout this chapter, the special insight provided by a family life course perspective is that it enables appreciation of the interplay between historical, or macro, changes and other more personal or micro factors.

This perspective brings into view the interplay between the processes that play out within the most intimate and private contexts of the home, within more public spaces where generational changes occur, and on the grandest scale in the context of historical changes that influence social norms and social expectations.

The family life course perspective dramatically alters our appreciation of what might stimulate change in the Jewish lives of families, and of how often change does not occur at a single moment or as a consequence of a single turning point. This perspective offers an opportunity to remove the blinders that have focused the attention of sociologists of contemporary Jewry over the last few decades. Of course, the family life course perspective does not claim to be a "theory of everything." Its great strength is that it draws attention to the interplay between forces invariably studied within different and discrete disciplinary frames. What it does **not** explain is why some families change more than do others when exposed to the very stimuli identified by the perspective: why historical, generational, or ontogenetic shifts stimulate lasting changes in the lives of some families but not in the lives of others. Answering these questions, we propose, is the task of the next chapter.

Notes

1. The shared story of Ruby and Joyce also provides an unusually strong instance of two additional phenomena in the life course literature: first, reverse or reciprocal socialization, whereby, contrary to typical patterns of human development, an earlier generation learns from a later one (Peters 1985; Boyatzis 2003); and second, the phenomenon of what Bengston, Putney, and Harris (2014) call the "religious prodigal," where individuals who start out as religious rebels, rejecting the religious beliefs and practices of their parents at an earlier stage of their lives, come back to embrace those beliefs after a period of time.

2. It turns out that the trajectory of intensifying Jewish engagement we previously described at the Silvers' following Ruby's graduation from DJDS was unusual. Probably, this was because both Joyce and her daughter Ruby—because of their own idiosyncratic story—were so reluctant to let go of the DJDS community and because Ruby had remained in the school for nine years in total, until the end of eighth grade. The children in most other families attended the school for less time; the social relationships that their parents had built during their time in the school were less deeply rooted and the behavior patterns they developed were less deeply grounded. When most other children moved on from school, these relationships and patterns began to dwindle and fray.

FOUR

"It's about the Kids, Right?": Jewish Families as Social Systems

When we met the Lombards and the Wallaces for the first time, both families had a child in fifth grade at DJDS: the Lombards' eldest child, Joshua, and the Wallaces' only child, Sam. Members of these two families were among the most actively involved volunteers in the school. Both Ray and Estelle Lombard were board members at different times, and Adele Wallace had been co-chair of the school's Education Committee and a member of the board as well. Of the four parents, only Dave Wallace had not served as an active volunteer in the school.

In 2004, when we interviewed them for the first time, both families had already been connected to the school for at least half a dozen years. Ray Lombard, a social worker, had sat on the school's founding board and had been involved for a couple of years even before the school formally opened.

At the time of that first interview, both sets of parents highlighted the ways in which the school had enriched their Jewish lives during the previous six to eight years. The Wallaces reported that they would have had "virtually no family Jewish culture except for what we've brought in since Sam has come to this school." Adele Wallace was not Jewish and, though deeply interested in Judaism, was more intent on pursuing her own spiritual search via other means. Her husband, Dave, traditionally observant when much younger, had gradually dropped the practices he had once observed such as keeping kosher and laying tefillin. Over the decades since he left home as a young adult (he was sixty-four at the time of this first interview), he had not attended synagogue at all. In his words, "Why should I pay someone to allow me to pray, when I could do it at home." At the time of our first interview with them, Adele highlighted that "the school was a pivotal decision for us. I kind of said to Dave I'm not prepared to do extracurricular Judaism, after-school Judaism like an add-on. Like I felt if we were going to introduce [Sam] to a Jewish identity, it had to be done authentically and in the context of a community.... I couldn't convey much. I can do a little."

At the time of our first interview—six years after Sam had started at the school—Dave confirmed that this is indeed what had happened: the school provided both context and content for their Jewish lives. "We often will light the candles on Friday night and say *Kiddush*, and because of Sam being at the school I think this leads us to celebrating the holidays in a more, not rigorous, but I guess more routine way because when holidays come up, Sam is involved with school all the time." We learned that since Sam had been in kindergarten, the family had even joined an alternative, monthly, Jewish prayer group that they attended on the High Holidays too.

Over in the Lombards' home, in their first interview, Ray and Estelle high-lighted no less significant changes. Both parents possessed extended Jewish fami-lies, some members of which, like Estelle's mother, were very much involved in community activities. Ray and Estelle led quite secular lives, and setting up a home of their own, they found few opportunities or reasons to enrich them-selves with Jewish culture or practices until a series of serendipitous events led Ray to get involved in planning the launch of DJDS. Once Joshua, their eldest child, started at the school, they then joined a synagogue that became increasingly important for them. Estelle explained, "We thought, well, if our kids are going to a Jewish day school it would also be nice if we belonged to a synagogue.... And we always thought that it would also be a great connec-tion between the school and the synagogue.... There is an overlap of families that belong to both." Some of the parents from the families to which Estelle referred were people they had met and worked alongside at the school, and who became close friends. At the same time, the longer they had been associ-ated with the school, the more that Jewish concepts and ideas became a normal part of family conversation in the house or wherever they might be. They told a memorable story, for example, about a Friday night meal at a local Chinese restaurant where the two children had debated whether sharing their last portion of shrimp might count as a "mitzvah of the week" they could report on Monday morning at school.

When we interviewed the two families nine years later, the Jewish culture of their homes and the Jewish engagement of the two sets of parents and chil-dren had gone in different directions. Sam Wallace had transferred to an elite non-Jewish private school at the end of sixth grade. After his Bar Mitzvah, the Jewish practices that the family marked at home started to peter out. The family still invited friends and extended family to join them at Chanukah or for a Pesach Seder. Adele explained that she was "still very committed to finding meaning in the rituals." But during the rest of the year, outside Chanukah and Pesach, there was little Jewish content, conversation, or activity at home. In our interview, Dave expressed disappointment that Jewish activity in their home had kind of dribbled away without him really noticing. Sam had fewer regrets: "It was just going through the motions. It didn't really mean anything." Adele, from her perspective, had long been comfortable with the situation.

As she put it, "My feeling was always, take him to the Bar Mitzvah and then he does what he wants with it. I have my own personal religious life. It's not just Jewish." The situation in the home was best reflected in an interchange during the interview between Dave and his son Sam. Earlier in the interview, Dave had been pleasantly surprised to learn that Sam had fasted the previous Yom Kippur when he and Adele had been abroad. But after hearing Sam then say that "being Jewish is not an important part of me," he commented: "I am a little disappointed when I hear you talk, son, how Jewish you are. I thought you'd be more.... I thought you'd have picked up, you'd be more influenced by what went on at DJDS." It seemed as if this interview was the first time Dave had confronted the erosion of the family's Jewish culture, a process that had played out over six or seven years.

We heard no such regrets when we visited the Lombards for a last time, just over two years after their youngest child, Lara, had left DJDS at the end of seventh grade, marking the end of eleven years during which the Lombard children had been enrolled at the school. At the time of the interview, Lara's brother, Joshua, who had stayed at DJDS until the end of eighth grade, was at college where he had chosen to minor in Jewish studies and was in the midst of completing an application to participate in Birthright. Lara, who had now been in a public high school for two years was looking for an opportunity to get course credit for studying Hebrew, since it had been her strongest subject in elementary school. The family was continuing to take vacations with families they had met at DJDS and with whom they continued to be close. They told us that they didn't attend synagogue frequently, but we also learned how the children continued to chant their Bar and Bat Mitzvah portions each year, they attended special youth Shabbatot in the congregation, and Ray was taking a course at the synagogue with the rabbi, someone with whom he had developed a close personal connection. They had not become observant religious Jews, but they had easily transitioned from being active members of the school community to being more than occasional participants in the synagogue community. Their relationship was succinctly conveyed by Estelle: "I didn't grow up going to synagogue very much so I wasn't all that comfortable with the actual service but there is something comforting there because we know so many people even though we just go once in a while." At home, meanwhile, there continued to be lively Jewish conversations. We didn't hear any more stories quite as memorable as the shrimp one, but they did report on a recent debate at home in which the children and parents expressed different views on whether love should triumph over religion when it came to marriage (about more of which in a chapter 6).

Contrasting what we found in these two families, we note how, at the Wallaces, Sam's disinterest in Jewish matters compounded his father's similar lack of interest so as to deflate the intensity and extent of Jewish culture and life at home. At the Lombards, by contrast, each family member was taking it in turns to intensify and expand the family's Jewish culture.

When reporting at conferences on the divergent trajectories of these families, we have found it useful to depict their stories in graphic terms, as in figure 4.1. The diagram is impressionistic; we have not developed a quantifiable measure of the intensity of Jewish family life in each home. Nevertheless, the impressions we have gleaned are well conveyed by the different course of the two lines in the diagram, a picture that portrays the trajectories of two complex family stories.

In this chapter, we try to address the central question stimulated by this image: Why do some families' Jewish lives change more than others, even when exposed to similar stimuli? Both the Wallaces and the Lombards experienced the same processes of ontogenetic change; those physiological processes are universal. Both families experienced the same historical changes; those social and cultural processes generally affect all families located in the same places at the same time. And, the two families also experienced many of the same generational changes; those processes are shared by many families. How is it, then, that these stimuli have resulted in such varied outcomes in two families that for a few years seemed so similar?

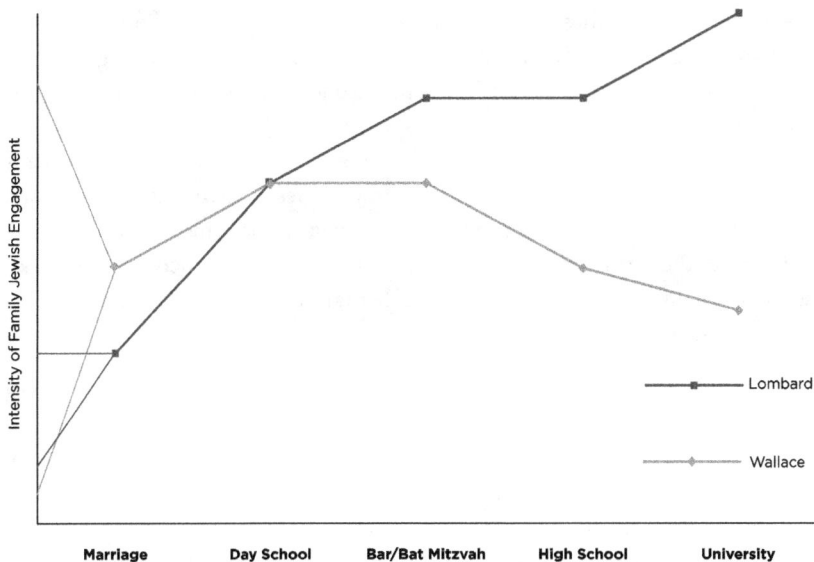

Figure 4.1. The Jewish life course trajectories of the Lombards and the Wallaces

The Lombards and Wallaces as Family Systems

In order to answer these questions, we turn to family systems theory. Family systems theory is built on the assumption that families, as open systems, maintain their internal constancy through a continuous exchange and flow of information with their larger environment. In a crucial insight, it is understood that within the family system, individual members are constrained and shaped in their behavior by their relationships with others in the system (Gerrity and Steinglass 2003).

As we explore the divergent trajectories of the Lombards and the Wallaces, we highlight *structural* and *relational* features in the family systems in these two homes. In conceiving of these families as systems, we follow Steinglass et al. to view them, within a larger context, as "a set of interconnected individuals acting together to produce a unique social unit that changes in a predictable fashion over time" (1987, 13). The structural features of the family-as-system in which we are interested include the composition of the household in terms of the number and status of grandparents, parents, and children (Uhlenberg and Mueller 2004). (*Status*, in this instance, refers to whether the adult members of the family are—for example, unmarried or divorced, of the same or different faiths—and if of different faiths, whether the mother or father is Jewish—and living with or close by other family members.) The relational features of the family-as-system that are relevant to our inquiry include the dynamic quality and character of the relationships between different family members. In particular, we are interested in the extent to which these relationships exhibit features of cohesion and adaptability, aspects of marital and family behavior that Olson and his colleagues identify as foundational dimensions for the multitude of concepts in the family field (Olson et al. 1979).

Over the following pages, we point to the family system features that seem to have made a decisive difference to the trajectories of Jewish life in these two families. We will then further explicate the theories on which we draw when pointing to these features. Finally, we will show how these theories help make sense of the differences between two further families from our sample.

Structure

Wallaces: A Limited Extended Family

At the Wallaces, the almost complete absence of an extended Jewish family is striking. When Dave married Adele, his second wife, he was close to fifty years old. He was fifty-three when Sam, their only child, was born. His own mother, still alive at that time, was the primary source of Jewish capital in the family. When Sam was still young, the family used to travel to Ottawa to spend Passover with her. By the time Sam was six and his grandmother eighty-eight, she could no longer host the family, and they stopped visiting at those times. Sam's grandmother passed away when he was twelve and henceforward the family was entirely dependent on its own Jewish resources. Adele summed up the situation at the time of our first interview, explaining why they had been so dependent on the school for nourishing the family's Jewish culture: "We have very little close family. Dave has two cousins in town so they would celebrate Jewish holidays. And his mom is ninety-one. His father has passed away. His brother lives in Edmonton, and he isn't Jewish at all, so we have virtually no Jewish support structure.... And we do go to Ottawa but it's kind of too late.... She didn't want us there for the holidays, it was just too much to handle."

Wallaces: One Child

The absence of grandparents nearby during most of Sam's childhood was compounded by a further structural factor in the family, the fact that Sam was an only child. This meant that when he concluded his formal Jewish education, there were no other infusions of Jewish cultural capital into the family of the kind that might have been prompted by a younger sibling. Sources of Jewish capital dried up at both ends of the generational chain.

Wallaces: An Interfaith Family (with a Jewish Father)

The less obvious impacts of these features of the family's structure were exacerbated by one further structural feature to which we have already referred: this is an interfaith family. And while Adele was especially energetic in initiating and supporting Sam's formal Jewish education, she was not interested in taking up the slack for her husband's limited effort once Sam had graduated elementary school. Dave's lack of activism in this regard is consistent with gendered analyses of Jewish interfaith families. As McGinity (2009, 2014) has persuasively shown, Jewish fathers in such relationships tend to be much less proactive about raising their children as Jews than are Jewish mothers. Adele Wallace pursued her own personal spiritual journey with unusual intensity but made no demands of the other members of the family, a relational characteristic of the family to which we will return. The members of the family all did their own thing in that regard.

In structural terms, the fact that Adele was not Jewish was a further reason for the limited infusion of Jewish social and cultural capital into the family. As Adele pointed out, when holding a family Seder, it involved inviting second cousins ("not people that we see a lot"); there are no closer Jewish family members in Toronto, and few more further afield. The family's Jewish life was connected to a thin Jewish family and social network. The school had brought more Jewish friends into their orbit, but these relationships were episodic and, again, were driven more by Adele than by either Dave or Sam.

One further consequence of Adele not being Jewish surfaced in the course of our final interview with the family. It became apparent that because Sam was not halachicly Jewish (i.e., because he didn't have a Jewish mother), he was not permitted to mark his Bar Mitzvah at the congregation attended by some of the family's closest friends from school. As we saw earlier in this chapter, this was a congregation that came to play an important role in the Jewish family life of the Lombards. Adele Wallace had wanted Sam to join the congregation's Bar Mitzvah program but her non-Jewish status closed off this potential avenue of growth for the family.

Lombards: A Close-Knit Extended Family

The structural features of the Wallace family contrast dramatically with those at the Lombards. Ray and Estelle presented themselves in their first interview as an unlikely day school family due to their commitment (Ray's especially) to public education and their own limited or nonexistent Jewish education. As Estelle put it: "The last thing on my mind was Jewish day school. It never even entered my realm of thought." Describing her own background, she reported: "I went, I would say, to Sunday school for a couple weeks, and that was about it. My brother and sister and I all refused to go. My brother did not have a Bar Mitzvah and so we were brought up in a very secular household."

At the time of this first interview, Ray and Estelle lightly glossed over the network of family relations in which the couple was intertwined. It was not something to which we paid attention given that, at the time, we lacked a family systems perspective. Instead, we were struck more by how this liberal Jewish family had become so involved at their children's school, and how that involvement led them to develop a thick network of Jewish friends that they seemed previously to lack.

Lombards: Jewish Roots

What we didn't notice at the time was how intertwined Ray and Estelle's lives were with their own parents, their children's grandparents. Estelle's mother might have been a highly untraditional Jew but she was a Jewish community activist. A decade or so earlier she had been a founding member of the only Reform day school in Toronto, and now she became an early member of the DJDS school board, where she sat alongside her son-in-law, Ray, for a number of years. Ray's father, the most traditional of the four grandparents, had strong Jewish cultural interests. Ray explained, "My father sings, and has CDs and tapes of famous chazanim singing cantoral pieces." This last comment prompted

Estelle to elaborate: "We kind of laugh about our parents because they get along famously. We often have both sets of parents here and they are very nice together but they're so different. Like Ray's father was into hazan [cantorial] music and my dad listens to K.D. Lang."

Estelle's comment might not seem especially significant. It's the kind of remark that gets lost in an interview; it did at the time. We see now what it reveals about family structure, especially when contrasted with the situation at the Wallace family. At the Lombards, both sets of grandparents are "often" in Ray and Estelle's home, in Estelle's telling, and it seems that they bring a continuous flow of Jewish capital with them. Their presence is part of a larger network of relationships in which family members enrich one another's lives. Thus, as we learned in our follow-up interview, when Ray's sister was serving as Canadian high commissioner to Australia, the whole family went to Canberra to make the first ever Seder at the Canadian embassy there. Even when geographically dispersed, the family members have been closely connected to one another.

Lombards: Two Children

Just as the older members of the family system feed it with Jewish content, so do the younger ones. It might seem trivial, but because there are two children in the family—one three years younger than the next—the family continued to be connected to Jewish institutions and peak Jewish moments longer than would have been the case if there had been just one child, as at the Wallaces. When the older child's exposure to Jewish educational and social stimuli declined during his years in a public high school, his younger sister was preparing for her Bat Mitzvah and was deeply involved in her Jewish school. By the time the younger sister got to high school, her older brother (living at home while at university, as is the case for many Toronto families) was enrolling in Jewish studies courses at university and preparing an application for Birthright. Thus, the structural composition of the household contributed to an enriched Jewish environment over an extended period of time.

Relationships

Family structure is only one part of what accounts for the differences between these two families. The quality and nature of the relationships between family members is no less important. Olson and his colleagues identified two dimensions of such family relationships that cut across many frameworks for analyzing family dynamics: *cohesion* and *adaptability*. They define cohesion as "the emotional bonding members have with one another and the degree of individual autonomy a person experiences in the family system" (Olson et al. 1979, 3). This dimension expresses the degree to which family members share values and behaviors that are in sync or are aligned with one another or allow for individual members to express differences and act in divergent ways from one another. As Olson and Gorall (2003) elaborate: "When cohesion levels are very high, there is too much consensus/emotional closeness within the family. At the other extreme, family members 'do their own thing,' with limited attachment of commitment to one another" (518). Balance is seen in families that are able to moderate both separateness and togetherness.

In Olson's model, adaptability is defined as "the ability of a marital/family system to change its power structure, role relationships, and relationship rules in response to situational and developmental stress" (Olson et al. 1979, 8). This dimension refers to the extent to which family members are able to change over time. Again, to elaborate, "in a rigid relationship, one individual is in charge and is highly controlling. Roles are strictly defined, and rules do not change. At the other extreme, a chaotic relationship has erratic or limited leadership. Roles are unclear and often shift from individual to individual" (Olson and Gorall 2003, 519). Balance is seen in families that are able to manage both stability and change.

As Olson and his colleagues argue, these dimensions of cohesion and adaptability capture and integrate a multitude of dynamics in the ways that families function as systems. His team has integrated these characteristics into a framework—the Circumplex Model—that underpins quantitative instruments for the analysis of family dynamics. In our work, we use these constructs in order to parse out distinct but interactive relational qualities within the family system.

Wallaces: Rigidity and Low Cohesion

With regards to the dimensions of cohesion and adaptability, the differences between the Wallaces and the Lombards are no less instructive than are the differences in their family structures. As we have already noted, the three members of the Wallace family are pursuing three independent religious trajectories. For Adele, that independence is a matter of principle. She is highly invested in her own religious and spiritual exploration beyond Judaism, and she's committed to her son finding his own way in life too. As she explains: "I always felt that I want to find the most effective way to have [Sam] know about his heritage and then he could do whatever he wants with it. I'm comfortable with that."

For Dave, independence is less a matter of principle than of personality. On the one hand, as he elaborated, "it was very important to maintain my connection to my heritage, to my historical heritage. People died because they were Jewish. I can't give up on that." On the other hand, he is uncomfortable participating in Jewish life as a member of a group. He prefers to do his own thing: "I also got a little turned off by the practice of religion, to say the least. I only joined a synagogue when Sam was old enough to go. I didn't really feel it was worthwhile."

Thus, Dave expresses disappointment now that he notices how much the family's Jewish life has thinned out. He sees it as an unfortunate coincidence. For Adele, it does not come as a surprise. She had not planned to sustain the family's Jewish culture once her son reached Bar Mitzvah. That was a task she left to her husband and son.

For his part, their son, Sam, is not himself the kind of young person who tells his parents much about his religious life. That accounts for his parents' surprise when during the interview he shared that his experiences learning karate have been as formative of his outlook on life as his Jewish education at DJDS had been. This interview seemed like the first occasion that Dave had heard his son talk about these matters.

Dave expressed disappointment when he heard Sam describe how he thinks of himself as a Jew, but in many ways his son's views are an exquisite composite of the disparate dispositions and ideas to which he has been exposed at home: "If someone just asked [about my religious orientation], I would probably say 'Jewish.' But I'm not into the worshipping part. I like religion because it gives you the ethical stuff, but I'm fine getting that from whichever way my parents seem to want me to get it from—whichever religion. I'm proud of being Jewish. The words don't mean much to me. I'm not into prayers or davening."

Dave blamed himself for the decline of Jewish life in the family: "I guess I'd have to say I dropped the ball. . . . I think that's probably my fault it didn't sink in. I should have taken you to shul more." In reality, Dave's lack of attention, and the absence of cohesion in the family, is only part of the story, at least in terms of Olson's model of family dynamics. It becomes apparent from Dave's account of his religious outlook that his worldview and his behaviors were set many decades earlier when he left his parents' home. It is unlikely that they would change in late middle age stimulated by his son's experience in elementary school or in order to support those experiences. After a brief flourishing when their son was younger and the family started observing Jewish rituals in a more routine fashion, the family has reverted to former patterns. That was part of the reason they had not visited Israel during Sam's Bar Mitzvah year. Adele had very much wanted to go, but Dave preferred not to because of what he called "his attitude toward Israel." That was something about which he had not been prepared to compromise at the time. In Olson's terms, this is a family that exhibits limited adaptability.

Symbolic of the family's Jewish trajectory and its reversion to an earlier point of stasis were the decorations on the Christmas tree in the family's home at the time we visited to conduct a last interview with them. We made reference to the tree in chapter 2. The tree serves an essentially social function, a neutral—post-Christian—meeting place. As Sam explains, "we don't even think about it as a Christian ritual. We set up a tree and we make it look nice and give people gifts." Among the stars and cards decorating the tree are Chanukah dreidels that Sam made in elementary school. It is as if the Jewish interlude during Sam's childhood years has been reduced to one more decorative supplement of the family's ecumenical religious culture.

Lombards: Adaptability and Cohesion

Just as the trajectory of the Wallace family's Jewish life is strongly marked by both the dimensions of cohesion and adaptability (at least in terms of their limited presence), so the changes observed at the Lombards seem strongly related to these same dynamics, if in a different direction.

As we have seen, the Lombards joined a synagogue because they thought it would enrich their children's experience at school. In turn, as the children aged and moved on from their Jewish elementary school, they were drawn to take on responsibilities at their parents' congregation, reading their Torah portions each year and contributing to special services, things that Joshua, the son, says have become "sort of a nice reoccurring tradition." And as the children have become more Jewishly literate, so have their parents. Having become "somewhat close" to their children's teachers, Ray joined an occasional Torah study group with one of his son's teachers. And then with Joshua signing up for a Jewish studies minor at university (taking a course with one of his father's fellow founding board members from the school), his father in turn signed up for a course at the synagogue on contemporary Jewish identity with the rabbi, someone with whom all members of the family feel close. There is a thick web of relational threads connecting their continually growing interest in Jewish ideas.

Socially, the parents became good friends with the parents of their children's friends, and although all have now outgrown the school, they remain closely connected to these families. Generally, it is noticeable that the Lombard parents and children seem to enjoy spending time together. Even though Joshua was in university when we interviewed them, parents and children were excited to be planning a vacation together. And with the children talking about participating in trips to Israel, it seems that the parents were now considering taking a trip back to the country themselves.

To make clear, the relationships between the parents and children are not suffocatingly close. This is not a case of what Olson calls *enmeshment*, where there is "an overidentification with the family that results in extreme bonding and limited individual autonomy" (Olson et al. 1979, 3). These children seem more than capable of doing their own thing. And the parents evidently have active social and personal lives independent of their children. The point is that there is a holistic, mutually enriching quality to the relationships of different members of the family with one another, especially in relation to Jewish matters. As one member of the family grows so it stimulates the growth of others; personal development is not an independently undertaken project, and it is not limited by predetermined boundaries. That is the mark of adaptability in Olson's model.

Toward the end of our final interview, Ray reflected with satisfaction on the journey the family had taken, and on what had been produced by his investment and involvement in his children's lives: "Thinking about my kids and how I was hoping their lives will be led, so that Bar or Bat Mitzvah would be something that would be important to them and that ultimately they'd marry somebody Jewish and have a Jewish home. It's all, I mean that was all part of my thinking, and getting involved with the school, thinking, that's when you have to start thinking about the future and what you want for your children. So in a way it might not have been as conscious, but it was definitely, definitely there."

Interestingly, while Ray highlights qualities of cohesion and his willingness to get involved, he doesn't mention his own journey. His own adaptability and openness to growth were no less important than his investment in his children's lives. Paradoxically, his focus on enabling his children to grow has resulted in his own growth.

An Unsettling Juxtaposition

The juxtaposition of these two families makes vivid the elements of their structure and functioning as family systems that have mediated the impact of various life course transitions on the content and intensity of their Jewish lives. These two families have journeyed through similar ontogenetic, generational, and historical transitions—in fact, they literally shared a host of personal experiences—but the outcomes have been quite different, as conveyed by figure 4.1. Those differences, we suggest, are a consequence of the parents' age, the number of children at home, the proximity of grandparents, the religious faith of the parents, and the nature of the relationships of family members, their cohesion, and their readiness to adapt as a family. In other words, the differences in the life course of these two families are in each instance a consequence of the many structural and relational elements that compose the family system.

Viewing the accounts of these families through the prism of family system theory leads to two important insights that unsettle conventional accounts of Jewish identity development. The first is that the seven individuals we have looked at most closely so far in this chapter (three members of the Wallace family and four members of the Lombard family) act or think of themselves as Jews in ways that are deeply implicated in the lives of those with whom they live, no matter how close or distant their relationships with one another. Read alongside each other, the interviews with the members of these families reveal the extent to which Jewish identity is forged in the context of the home. In this context, the Jewish self looks anything but sovereign; at most, it is a voting member in a cacophonous family democracy.

Of course, it is conventional to conceive of the emergent Jewish identities of adolescents as shaped in part by the homes in which they're raised; that's a commonplace of developmental psychology. To that effect, we already noted echoes of Sam Wallace's parents' worldviews in his conception of himself as proud to be Jewish, but "not into the worshipping part," and open to "ethical stuff" from "whichever religion" it comes. And, in similar fashion, Josh Lombard's comfort with his non-Jewish friends from high school, his intellectual curiosity about Jewish culture and ideas, and his responsiveness when asked to take responsibility at the synagogue, although attending only very occasionally, all seem to emerge from the relationships and resources we found in the Lombard home.

More unexpected is that the parents in these families also act and think of themselves as Jews in ways that express the relationships and structures in their homes. Dave Wallace might seem stuck—in his own telling—with the behavioral and attitudinal patterns that he attributes to the environment in which he was raised more than fifty years previously, and yet he indicates how moved he was by the High Holiday services at the synagogue the family joined only because they felt they should, now that their son was old enough to attend. Turned off communal prayer for decades, he was recommending the experience to us when we interviewed him. For a few years, while his son was in Jewish elementary school, Jewish practices at home started to become part of his routines—after a long absence. For someone set in his ways, these were tectonic shifts, no matter how short lived. Less dramatically, Estelle Lombard—someone more open to change—found how "everything came together" for her in the context of a synagogue community despite not being comfortable in "the actual services," having not grown up going to synagogue. Today, some of her closest Jewish friends are the parents of children with whom her own children went to school, and who like her have become members of this community. Who Dave Wallace and Estelle Lombard are as Jews at this moment in time, and what they find to be most meaningful as Jews, emerges powerfully from the balance of factors and forces in their immediate families.

A second insight prompted by a family systems perspective relates to the role of intermarriage in shaping the lives of families. Seen through the prism of family systems theory, the religious status of the adults in these families is evidently a significant component of the family structure. In this instance, the fact that Adele Wallace was not Jewish narrowed the Jewish social networks within which her family was embedded. The fact that she was not Jewish also closed off access to potentially enriching Jewish social and educational experiences for her son. At the same time, her refusal to raise her son as Jewish without the institutional support she found at DJDS set the family on a course it would probably not otherwise have taken. Overall, then, Adele's non-Jewish status profoundly shaped the trajectory of her family's life, particularly because, as we have noted, she—and not her husband—was the non-Jewish parent in this family. And yet, viewing her non-Jewish status as one component in a system reveals it as a factor among other structural and relational factors that have been just as significant in shaping the intensity of Jewish life in this home. In this instance, the father's age or psychological fixity, Adele's gender, their only son's indifference to Jewish things, or the family's lower levels of cohesion, might be much more determinant than the fact of the mother's non-Jewish faith. Viewed as an element in a system, intermarriage is less a demographic tsunami, as it is often portrayed, and more an unsettling element in the fragile ecosystem of contemporary Jewry.

The Goldmans: When Less Is More

In the final section of this chapter, we further expand on these claims by looking at the cases of two more families. These families share structural and relational features with those we have just analyzed and, at the same time, are distinguished by structural elements that enlarge our appreciation of the range of elements in the family system that moderate the impact of family life course transitions: in one family there is only one parent, a mother; the other family is conversionary—that is, one of the parents converted to Judaism after marrying.

We suggest that the Jewish trajectories of these families can be depicted as in figure 4.2.

Ruth Goldman was raised in a traditional Conservative family from which she considers herself to be a kind of refugee. Her rebellion, she says, derives from the fact that "I come from a generation where the Jewish God is an old man saying no." Jewishly educated herself, she was committed to her daughter acquiring a similar level of Jewish literacy. As she put it in equally pithy fashion, "cultural ignorance is really dangerous and very sad." She was therefore drawn to DJDS as a school that was at the same time educationally and socially progressive, and also Jewishly pluralistic.

Ruth is a single mother. She never married, and in her thirties she adopted a child of color and brought her to Canada. These structural features of the family have significantly impacted the development of her Jewish life and that of her daughter. Ruth specifically sought out a school for her daughter that would

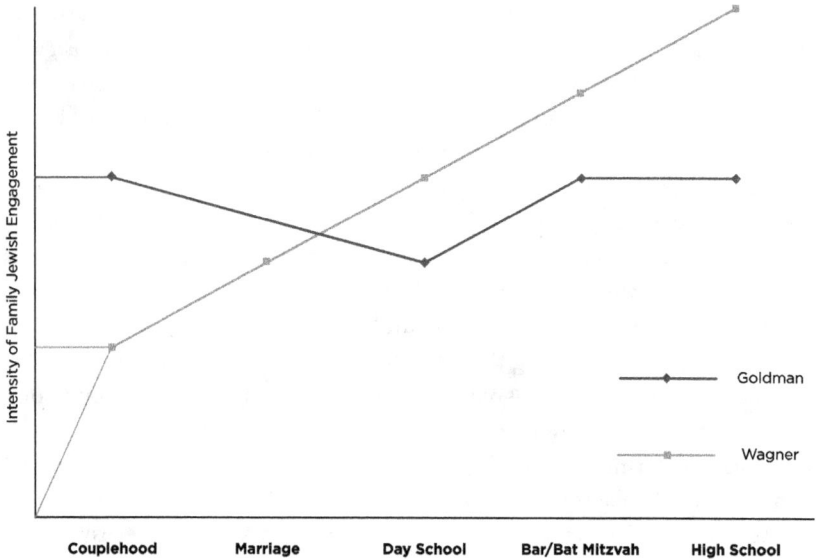

Figure 4.2. The Jewish life course trajectories of the Goldmans and the Wagners

welcome children of color, provide opportunities for her to share experiences with her daughter, and enable her daughter to become Jewishly literate. DJDS met all of these goals, Ruth told us, when we interviewed her for the first time, four months after her daughter had started school.

At our second interview, two years later, Ruth's view of DJDS had changed. She spent a great deal of time detailing her discontent with the school for being insufficiently accommodating of working parents who could not be available to take care of children on days when the school was closed—on the eve of Jewish holidays in addition to the holidays themselves. ("They presume that everyone has an at-home parent or a nanny or both.") Even with these concerns and numerous others about the quality of the academics beyond kindergarten, she still continued to reenroll her daughter, and did so until the end of sixth grade, unlike other families we have described, such as the Kleinmans and the Lowes, who removed their children from the school within the first two years. As Ruth explained, she and her daughter, Dara, stayed at the school above all because of its commitment to diversity. ("There's no other Jewish day school that I would consider . . . that has all this diversity.") In short, they stayed because of the school's affirmation and acceptance of the particular structural features of their family.

As was the case for the Silvers, another single-parent family whose story we recounted in the previous chapter, the school provided a unique place to belong. Ruth had never experienced another Jewish community where she felt so welcomed. Staying within this community for six years meant that as her daughter underwent the experience of ontogenetic change, becoming more of a partner to her mother than a dependent, the two of them were still very much members of a meaningful Jewish community.

In the previous chapter, we described the impact of ontogenetic changes on the two of them: how when Dara was younger, her mother could not go to synagogue as she had wanted because Dara was too tired to get up and dressed on a Saturday morning, and how as Dara aged the two of them would now go to synagogue together. Drawing on family systems theory, we can now locate the source of Ruth's decision to switch to a synagogue closer to home where more of the families of Dara's friends attended. In this family unit of just two individuals, a mother and daughter, the relational qualities of cohesiveness are especially strong, and, it seems, both mother and daughter drive family choices which impact on one another. Having switched synagogues to accommodate her daughter's needs and interests, Ruth then became highly active in the community herself, joining the board of directors—something that has been "a wonderful experience." She then continued to be involved even after her daughter's Bat Mitzvah. Her daughter, Dara, meanwhile, became a youth leader at the congregation, matching and occasionally exceeding her mother's activism.

Previously we also noted the impact of generational change in the Goldman home, and how transitioning out of a day school to a public school meant that neither mother nor daughter stayed at home any more on Jewish festivals, other than Rosh Hashanah and Yom Kippur. Having expressed concern about the many days that she had to take off work for festivals when Dara was at DJDS, Ruth admitted that she now missed the stimulus provided by the school operating according to the Jewish calendar. And yet it is now much clearer why this generational transition did not diminish the Jewish culture of the home, as it did for other families. Both mother and daughter are priming the family's Jewish pump. Like the Wallaces, there may be only one child in the home, but the Jewish culture of this family is not dependent on the child bringing Jewish stimuli into the home from school; both mother and daughter are sources of new Jewish cultural and social capital, and they continue to enrich one another. In this respect, the family much more closely resembles the Lombards.

When Dara left DJDS at the end of sixth grade, she had intended to go back into the day school system for high school. When we interviewed them for the last time, Dara was in eighth grade and had decided to explore options in the public system instead, enabling her to develop her skills as a singer, something at which she excelled. A choice like this might be expected to indicate a decline in the intensity of Jewish life at home, but for the reasons we have just suggested, and for others too, this seems unlikely. Again, the contrast with the Wallace family is interesting. Over all the period in which we followed her family, Ruth remained close with her own mother, someone who had been widowed before the time of our first interview. Ruth seems to be close too with her brother, who has also remained in town, even while she did not agree with his religious traditionalism. Every Friday night, she and Dara celebrate Shabbat at her mother's home. This kind of regularity, and the continuing contribution of older siblings and parents to the family's Jewish life, sustained its steady intensification in the Goldman home. These supports were absent at the Wallaces, where it is no wonder that the family experienced much more of an ebb and flow to their Jewish lives.

While the Goldmans are not an interfaith family, there is one further structural feature that emerges from contrasting them with the Wallaces and is also consistent with other families in our sample. In both cases, there is only one Jewish parent in the home, and it seems to make a profound difference—in structural terms—whether that one parent is male or female. This is consistently the case in seven of sixteen families in our sample, either because these are interfaith or one-parent families. In three families (Kleinman, Ruben-Fine, Wallace) where the Jewish parent is the father, there was a discernable easing off in the intensity of the family's Jewish engagement over the ten years of the study. In four families (Silver, Goldman, Elbaz, and Manning) where the Jewish parent is the mother, Jewish engagement remained relatively stable and even intensified over time.

We have already noted how consistent these patterns are with studies of intermarried families by McGinity (2009, 2014). They are further confirmed by the work of Thompson (2013) and Barack Fishman and Parmer (2008). Certainly, they speak to the continuing, deep influence of gender in shaping family systems and, in turn, their Jewish trajectories. It is surely no coincidence, for example, that while both Joe Kleinman and Dave Wallace attributed how things were turning out in their families to their own lack of time to attend to their children's Jewish identity, none of the mothers spoke in these terms. The mothers, it seems, don't have the luxury of not paying attention to their children.

In accounting for these gendered patterns, there is no doubt much else at play too. To return to the categories of an earlier chapter, it is intriguing that these divergent family life-course trajectories confirm an earlier insight about the different roles of cultural and social capital in the family. There seems to be no obvious correlation between the extent of the Jewish *cultural* capital that the Jewish parent brought into the family system and the intensity of their current Jewish engagement (there are single-parent and intermarried Jewish fathers and Jewish mothers both with and without much Jewish cultural capital).

Yet, there is a striking difference with regards to Jewish *social* capital. None of these Jewish fathers had access to extensive Jewish family networks; they hardly ever spoke about their extended families or of spending time with them. For the mothers, those social networks were palpable and vital. They, their children, and their partners would often spend Friday nights with grandparents, aunts, and uncles, and those relatives were an immediate or symbolic presence in their homes. This difference prefigures a theme in the next chapter where we make explicit the gendered role of family kin-keepers in maintaining ritual, and specifically Jewish ritual, within the home. Gender evidently continues to influence relationships with family members within the home and beyond the home too.

The Wagners: At a Point of Balance between Stability and Change

To fill out this account of the moderating impact of structural and relational factors on life course trajectories, we turn to the case of one more family: the Wagners. When Brian and Anne Wagner met, Brian was not Jewish. He was finding his way into Jewish life. When we asked him in their first interview what attracted him to Judaism, Anne jumped in with a telling insight that foreshadowed many aspects of the story we heard over the course of subsequent interviews. She stated, and Brian concurred: "I think Brian was attracted to the legalistic aspects of it: Talmud, the intellectual aspects of it, and through that he got growing into the other more spiritual aspects. I think his attraction to Judaism came very much through the texts." The couple were married at a ceremony officiated by a Unitarian Church minister who agreed to remove all religious references from the ceremony. Their oldest child, Gary, was born three years later. A couple of years after that, Brian formally converted, having by then become deeply committed to traditional Conservative Judaism.

Just as Brian had traveled a long route from his origins in an atheist family in small town Nova Scotia, so Anne had followed a winding path of her own from her family's involvement in a Reform congregation in Chicago, through participation in a secular Jewish humanistic group in Toronto soon after she first met Brian, with stops along the way in Israel, then Vancouver where she spent her teenage years, and finally in Kingston, Ontario, where during her college years she let Jewish observance take a back-seat: "I feel like I've done a grand tour of Jewish observances and I feel like I've found something in a fairly traditional Conservative synagogue where I feel comfortable. I feel in a place where I'm happy to stay."

As we indicated in an earlier chapter, when they enrolled their son Gary at DJDS, they were one of the most traditional families in the school. They described their Jewishness in the following terms: "We don't work on Shabbat or Yom Tov. We keep kosher, we go to shul, it's a Jewish home. There [are] also Jewish books. And Gary has been nourished on Jewish stories since he was a babe." They were drawn to the school, as Ruth Goldman had been, by the "diversity of the family backgrounds." They were comfortable being much more observant than almost all other families in the school. It was something they sought out. They feared that if they had enrolled at the day school at the synagogue they attended each week, their son would end up with "a very insular view of the Jewish community."

In many respects, the family is a kind of anomaly. Their Jewish life was enriched or extended to only a very limited degree by their experiences at their son's school. As Anne put it in our final interview with them, "I think we've always sort of been of the opinion that most of his education happens at home and we send him to school to reinforce." When Anne says, "at home," she seems to literally mean within their nuclear family of three then four people. With little family in town and no Jewish family on Brian's side, the richness of their Jewish lives was not enriched by grandparents or siblings. Over the course of three lengthy interviews, they hardly mentioned their extended families.

While their relationships and experiences at their Conservative synagogue have been important to them over many years, not least in providing a framework for Brian's conversion to Judaism, the most significant contributor to their Jewish lives has been what they created at home for themselves. Both parents are highly educated in Jewish terms, and yet both are essentially self-taught. Neither attended Jewish schools or institutions of higher learning, other than the one year that Anne spent in the secular Israeli school system where she picked up Hebrew. They have been highly self-sufficient, teaching themselves and taking the odd course here and there. By the time Brian started the conversion process, Anne reported she had "taken him through quite a bit of the Torah in Hebrew so his Hebrew was pretty good." Their self-sufficiency was summed up well by Brian's own description of his conversion process: "I sort of looked on it more like an undocumented resident of a country wanting to naturalize his citizenship. I mean I was living a Jewish life and it was appropriate to regularize it, which is how I looked on it. As a result of the fact that I already was fairly knowledgeable, I didn't go through the usual process. Instead of taking intro to Judaism which would have bored my socks off, I signed up instead for a Talmud class at the shul, which was far more interesting."

Their children (Gary has a brother six years younger than him, born between the first and second interviews) are both products and producers of this family system, a system characterized by great cohesion. In the previous chapter, we noted how as Gary matured he was able to accompany his father on ever longer treks to shul. At the time of our last interview, they were taking a round-trip of six miles each Shabbat, by foot, so as to attend a traditional egalitarian synagogue that advertised itself as a "place for intelligent Judaism," an institution very much aligned with the family's values. We have also previously noted how Gary, age fourteen when we met for the last time, was now studying Talmud with his father. An exceptionally bright young man, he had skipped a year of elementary school, and had found stimulation through the independent extension work his teachers readily provided. He shared his father's great interest in Jewish study; that was why he insisted on continuing on to a Jewish high school rather than an elite public school program at which he had gained a place. Explaining why he wanted to go the Community Jewish High School, he said, "I wanted to continue my Jewish education and a lot of friends go there (from shul and other places)."

Viewing the Wagners through the prism of family system theory, it seems as if their great internal cohesiveness, characterized by their shared intellectual passions, enables them to navigate the family life course with great stability. Much as with the process of Brian's conversion, formally enacted at a time of his own choosing, they determine their own pace through life's transitions. Generational transitions—marriage, their son's Bar Mitzvah, changing schools, and even conversion—have not resulted in dramatic change. The steadily intensifying trajectory of their Jewish lives seems to have been set long ago, with its intensity being fueled by the children's ontogenetic change.

The contrast between the Wagners and the other families in this chapter is striking. The Wagner family structure is unusually lean, with extended family playing a limited role in their day-to-day lives, let alone at peak moments such as Seder night or Bar Mitzvah. Such conditions—similar to those in the Wallace family—might have been expected to result in more ebb and flow or in greater instability. And yet of all of these four families, they seem least affected by life course transitions. They display the least evidence of sudden change. At the same time, in Jewish terms, since leaving their own parents' homes, the lives of Anne and Brian Wagner have changed more dramatically than any of the Wallace, Lombard, or Goldman parents. In Jewish terms, over the course of their adult lives they have journeyed further than others in our sample.

Family system theory helps explicate this paradox. As Wertheim (1975) puts it, cited by Olson et al.: "An ideal, adaptive family system can be conceptualized as one characterized by an optimal, socio-culturally appropriate balance between stability-promoting, 'self-corrective' processes, or *morphostasis* and change-promoting, 'self-directive' processes, or *morphogenesis*." (286).

At the Wagners, thanks in large part to the family's great cohesion, the family members have found an optimal point of balance between stability and change, between morphostasis and morphogenesis. The Wagners resemble the Lombards in that respect, while finding a point of Jewish equilibrium at a different degree of intensity, and while drawing on their own intellectual resources, rather than on those outside the home such as their children's school or the extended family. Less dependent on external resources, generational transitions that might lead to changes in the source or depth of those external resources produce fewer ripples within the home. At the same time, as at the Lombards, the high levels of cohesion and adaptability in the family have resulted in all members of the family system moving in one direction rather than canceling out one other by pushing or pulling in different directions.

A last point, made vivid by the cases of these four families, emphasizes a central claim of family system theory, drawn in turn from family therapy: the developing lives of even the most independent and self-actualized individuals occur within the context of family systems. The choices of these individuals are informed and their life chances are expanded and constrained by other members of the family system in which they are members. Adele Wallace, Ruth Goldman, and Brian Wagner are decidedly strong-willed individuals, pursuing personal journeys that swim against the current of many, if not most, in their communities, and yet those journeys are not lonely odysseys, they are undertaken in the company of fellow travelers, some of whom are not even going in the same direction. Take the example of Ruth Goldman: she has rebelled against the patriarchal Jewish traditionalism in which she was raised; she has chosen to adopt and parent by herself a child of color; and she has raised her daughter as a committed and well-educated Jew. Ruth personifies the self-invention or reinvention made possible by historical changes in opportunities for women over the last fifty years. She is not constrained by her past. And yet observing her choices over time, and the battles she wages, hearing her talk about her family's choices, finally in the company of her daughter, it is evident that who she is—the self she has invented—is a co-creation, forged in her relationship with her young daughter. Who she is the product of home-work.

In the next chapter, we focus on what is probably the most valuable resource in all families for the effective conduct of such work: home-based family ritual. Such rituals serve as the sacred center for Jewish self-formation.

FIVE

"This Is the Way Our Family Is": The Work of Home-Based Family Ritual

It has long been understood that religious commitments and identities are nourished by ritual, understood as "a sequence of activities involving gestures, words, and objects, performed in a sequestered place, and performed according to set sequence" (Webster Dictionary 2016). Ritual provides an occasion to release emotions, communicate values, and display priorities that might otherwise be inexpressible (Price 1984; Turner 1975; Myerhoff 1977). At the same time, through the enactment of ritual, individuals are socialized or habituated into beliefs, values, and commitments (Katriel and Shenhar 1989; Connerton 1989; McLaren 1999).

In Jewish historical and contemporary contexts, the first, *performative* dimension of ritual has been the focus of the study of ritual innovation among Jewish women, at Jewish summer camps, at Jewish weddings, and in Holocaust commemoration (Ochs 2010; Koren 2010; Reimer 2012; Baumel 1995). These studies explore the ways in which ritual serves as a medium to give embodied, public expression to values and commitments shared by specific social groups. The second, *formative* dimension has been applied to the examination of ritual as a vehicle of Jewish collective memory, most famously in Yerushalmi's *Zachor*, and in studies as diverse as Marcus's investigation of "rituals of childhood" in medieval Europe, and Zerubavel's of the formation of Jewish national myths in Israel (Yerushalmi 1996; Marcus 1996; Zerubavel 1995). The emphasis in these studies is on the educational and acculturative force of ritual, bringing, for example, new generations and new immigrants inside a shared circle of values and beliefs.

In this chapter, we supplement this abundant literature by exploring both the performative and formative functions of ritual within the home, drawing on the two major analytical frameworks we have employed in this book: life course analysis and family system theory. Approached in this way, a study of ritual within the homes of our research sample serves as a test case of the complex phenomena we have observed; ritual provides a site within which to better appreciate particular aspects of our study. At the same time, against the backdrop of our study, we can better understand the dynamic functions of ritual, specifically at different phases of the family life course and as an indicator of and contributor to the cohesion and adaptability of the family system. These are dimensions of family ritual that have not been widely examined until now, and certainly not in a Jewish context.

Home-Based Ritual

One can go far beyond Jewish culture to examine the important functions that ritual plays in family life. Literature in the health sciences (e.g., in social work, family therapy, and nursing) conceives family rituals as providing an effective strategy to combat clinical pathologies (particularly alcoholism) and to promote health and well-being (Adelson 2010; Denham 2003; Fiese and Wamboldt 2000; Markson and Fiese 2000). While such pathologies are not the focus of our work, the capacity of family rituals to act as therapeutic tools to protect from alcoholism or asthma and to promote physical well-being indicates by analogy how Jewish family ritual might serve to combat the erosion of Jewish social and cultural capital and promote vibrant Jewish identity and expression.

In this chapter, our interests are focused on what Wolin and Bennett (1984) identify as "family celebrations" from among three broad types of ritual. These experiences, they argue, typically mark holidays (e.g., Passover Seder, Easter dinner, Shabbat dinner) or rites of passage (e.g., Bar Mitzvah) in ways that, usually, are heavily influenced by a family's cultural, religious, or ethnic origins. Family celebrations are distinct, first, from "family traditions," activities that are less culturally specific and more idiosyncratic to the family. Typically, family traditions are also less structured: for example, annual family summer vacations or family birthday customs, where the birthday person gets served their favorite food, or gets whatever kind of party they wish, in a fashion that expresses the uniqueness of the family. Family celebrations also function differently from "family interactions or routines," activities that are the least deliberate and most variable over time. These rituals include dinnertime, bedtime, weekend routines, kids staying up later at night, parents sleeping in, and kids taking care of themselves in the morning, or everyone having the same seat at the dining room table. Even in these commonplace activities, families are expressing, through repeatedly enacting certain behaviors, shared beliefs, and common identity.

As indicated above, in this chapter, we focus on family celebrations. These experiences are, to a large degree, culturally specific to Jewish life. They are highly structured and deliberate, and according to sociologists of contemporary Jewry, they are assuming ever more significance in the sustenance of the Jewish collective (Davidman 2003). As Jewish adults engage less with mainstream

Jewish institutions, such as synagogues and schools, their focus is drawn inward to their own narrow circles of familiarity. The immediate family has become a cocoon of safety and comfort. Within the intimacy of this cocoon, privatized family ritual, away from public scrutiny and often self-created, has become a primary site both for family bonding and for the transmission of Jewish culture across the generations. Home ritual, Cohen (2000) argues, has become "the main source of Jewish meaning" for many Jewish families. And this investment in home ritual "serves to differentiate Jews from most American Christians who, with the exception of Christmas, lack elaborate home-based religious rituals." No wonder that in recent studies of Jewish emergent adults and millennials, interviewees speak of Jewish family holiday dinners (Shabbat, Rosh Hashanah, and Passover) as the essence of how they understand and express their Jewish identity (Cohen and Eisen 2001; Prell 2000). Those frequent and recurrent home-based religious rituals are what set these young Jews apart from their non-Jewish contemporaries.

In our own study, some interviewees have been highly self-aware about the functions that home-based, family celebration rituals perform. Early in their first interview, when their son Elijah was in first grade, Carrie Maybaum reported that "we do Friday night dinners in our family every Friday." The casual insertion of the words "in our family" provides a key to both the performative and formative functions of this particular ritual in their home. Later in the conversation, we learned that Carrie didn't simply mean her nuclear family, but the extended family whose presence added a significant dimension to the experience. Responding to a question about what Jewish practices they observe in their home, she said:

> We do not keep kosher but we have Friday night dinner every week with family. Whether it's my parents—like at my mother's house, my aunt's house, my other aunt's house, Ian's parents' house, his sister's house, every week. Probably twice a year we don't, when something comes up. And now we are at the point where.... Elijah pulls out his own prayer book whether it's a real one or not, he definitely always has one in his hands, sometimes it's just a little notebook with notes in it but that's his prayer book. He sings along, he wants to be part of it and he does it with his cousins, so there's definitely something very nice about it. It's nice, it's really nice!

For the Maybaums, the family's Friday night ritual knits the extended family together, expressing those things that are most important to them. Elijah's maturation—his ability to "pull out his prayer book"—symbolically signals to the family that he is ready to join this intimate circle as an active participant.

As below with the Lowe family, this act of Elijah's is also a performative barometer of the Hebrew literacy of the younger members of the family. That Elijah sings along "with his cousins" enhances the meaning and the joy of the ritual moment. It communicates the profound importance for all those present of the value in family coming together.

This ritual's formative dimension is made explicit when Carrie reports how she responded to Elijah when he asked her, "Mommy why don't I get the challah from the challah program?" The challah program at DJDS enables families, who wouldn't do so otherwise, to consider performing some form of Friday night ritual in their own homes. Carrie explains that she responded: "Because, Elijah, we have Friday night dinner every week and we are always going to have a challah. Sometimes Auntie Patty buys it, sometimes Bubbie buys it, sometimes Uncle Eric buys it, but we don't have to get it from school every time. We are still going to have a challah." With her explanation, Carrie helps Elijah see something that is self-evident to her, that is, the formative outcome of the ritual itself: the family's singular commitment to coming together on Friday night as the essence of what distinguishes the Maybaums as a family.

To look at a further example, we have already had a few occasions to note the ongoing spiritual search of Adele Wallace. Adele is acutely sensitive to the potential significance in the observance of ritual. As she expresses it, "I'm still very committed to finding meaning in the rituals and doing what you're supposed to do, [although] obviously, there are many definitions about what you are supposed to do." We have previously noted how important DJDS was in enriching this family's Jewish life when Adele's own family is not Jewish and when there are few local supports in Toronto in her husband's Dave's family. Under these circumstances, Adele acts with great intentionality in determining how the family celebrates Chanukah and Pesach. She explains, "I really like to use the holidays to stay connected with friends and family, so a couple of weeks ago [at Chanukah] we had two friends over, both parents from the DJDS, for latkes and malt cider. Actually, we had a whole meal in the end." At Pesach, Adele is similarly committed to bringing together whichever few family members of Dave's family live in Toronto. Despite the great religious diversity of these individuals— one family that "doesn't even crack a haggadah" and one with four children in Jewish day school—"we want to connect, not just as family, but performing the ritual and honoring the traditions." Their home-based family celebration rituals are enacted, then, with great intentionality so as to hold together a shrinking family, while at the same time, in Adele's own words, "bringing some joy into our lives." The formative and performative dimensions of ritual are in this way neatly integrated.

Performative Ritual from a Life Course Perspective

The family celebration rituals we have just described and the functions they serve are familiar from previous studies of ritual in the home. These activities readily fulfill the functional characteristics that Wolin and Bennett ascribe to family ritual: they "serve as a window into a family's underlying shared identity," they "contribute significantly to the establishment and preservation of a family's collective sense of itself," and through repetition these rituals contribute to family stability. By delineating boundaries within and without the family, and by defining rules, they enable all members to know that "this is the way our family is" (Wolin and Bennett 1984, 401).

When viewed from a family life course perspective, the performative functions of family ritual assume a fresh and not previously considered dimension. By expressing "who the family is," ritual can serve as a useful indicator of ontogenetic and generational change within the family. The form and content of family ritual sensitively and idiosyncratically mirror a family's values and priorities, more so than publicly performed rituals that may not fully reflect the preferences of all participants. Changes in the form and content of family ritual, choreographed by the family members themselves, thereby indicate deep-seated changes in the family over time. Ritual, for these reasons, provides an exceptionally sensitive and vivid measure of change in the family, and of the ways in which family members may be in tension with one another.

One of the most powerful instances in our study of such change over time and what it indicated was provided by the Richards family and their account of the ritual they employed to observe Rosh Hashanah. In chapter 2, we described how the family headed out to an apple orchard together to mark the Jewish High Holidays, a practice we analyzed at length in our previous book. This practice and its inclusion of a close non-Jewish family friend richly expressed the family's shared discomfort with synagogues, John Richards's religious agnosticism, the generally strong Jewish literacy of both John and his wife Jean, and their openness to meaningful relationships with non-Jewish friends and neighbors. When we revisited the family almost nine years later, we were especially curious to learn whether they were maintaining this ritual.

We learned that the family ritual had changed over the years. When the children were young, in the years following our first interview with them, they continued each year to go apple picking. Melanie Richards, nineteen years old at the time of this last interview, remembered that on the holiday evening, they would announce at a large family dinner that they planned to go apple picking the next day, and "all the other cousins would [say], 'that's a great idea!' and then we'd be joined, normally, by family on both sides."

When the children were a little older, the apple picking turned one year into raspberry picking. Then as the children got older still and became especially busy, stressed by schoolwork, some of them would choose not to go at all. They'd go to school instead or be picked up from school when the family headed out to a local farm. Consequently, as John elaborates, they started to stay closer to home. "The last couple of years we had a little pow wow on Yom Kippur, and we would talk to one another about what we could improve of ourselves. In the house, I think. I can't remember if it was in the backyard or something."

Interestingly, talking with John, Jean, and Melanie, it was surprising how hard they found it to remember the specifics of what they did each year, it had changed so much over time. Some years, members of the family brought a reading with them, something that spoke to them—poetry, often. John remembers bringing a handout one time, a Joni Mitchel song another. One year, Melanie recollects how *tashlich*, the Rosh Hashanah custom of confessing sins at the bank of a river, turned into a water fight among the cousins. Of course, as John notes, it's hard not to forget "going to get apples and throwing them at each other," especially when that's instead of spending time in synagogue. Summing up her own recollection, Melanie reconstructed the major elements of the experience: "I don't remember anything except for not liking synagogue and being forced to dress up, versus.... I remember, we'd do our chat at the apple orchard ... saying sorry to other people in the family, and like personal goals through the year. I mean, always fun family meetings.... I mean it's about family time so, because it's a high holiday you know we are not going to go to school, we are going to have a family time."

The trajectory of this particular family celebration's ritual form—starting out in a local apple orchard and ending up in the family's backyard—and its essentially stable content, enabling family members to take stock of themselves and of their relationships with one another, powerfully convey a shared family identity in which communication and authenticity is valued. At the same time, the ritual's changing form also indicates what has shifted in the family due to ontogenetic and generational changes, with children increasingly pursuing their own Jewish paths. In our conversations with them, the Richards conveyed an impression of being exceptionally thoughtful about their own spirituality, uncomfortable in religious institutions, and deeply committed to marking major moments in the Jewish year as a family, at Rosh Hashanah, Chanukah, and Pesach. As the children aged and gained more independence, with parents reluctant to make them do anything against their will (something about which we'll say more later in this chapter), they had to adjust the ritual so that its valuable content could be expressed in at least some form. From one perspective, sharing their thoughts with one another in their backyard seems a thin substitute for the creative ritual they had performed when their children were younger. This looks like one last contrived effort to sustain some shared values before they finally expire. From another perspective, the ritual still has meaning and does still involve at least some members of the immediate family.

We propose that the evolution of this ritual is reminiscent of a famous Hasidic story included in Martin Buber's (1974) *Tales of the Hasidim*. Buber's punchline echoes a more optimistic reading of what happened in the Richard's home.

> When the founder of Hasidic Judaism, the great Rabbi Israel Shem Tov, saw misfortune threatening the Jews, it was his custom to go into a certain part of the forest to meditate. There he would light a fire, say a special prayer, and the miracle would be accomplished and the misfortune averted.
>
> Later, when his disciple, the celebrated Maggid of Mezritch, had occasion for the same reason to intercede with heaven, he would go to the same place in the forest and say, "Master of the Universe, listen! I do not know how to light the fire, but I am still able to say the prayer." Again, the miracle would be accomplished.
>
> Still later, Rabbi Moshe-Leib of Sasov, in order to save his people once more, would go into the forest and say, "I do not know how to light the fire. I do not know the prayer, but I know the place and this must be sufficient." It was sufficient, and the miracle was accomplished.
>
> Then it fell to Rabbi Israel of Rizhin to overcome misfortune. Sitting in his armchair, his head in his hands, he spoke to God, "I am unable to light the fire and I do not know the prayer and I cannot even find the place in the forest. All I can do is to tell the story, and this must be sufficient."
>
> And it was sufficient. For God made man because he loves stories.

In Buber's (re)telling, the ritual, in its final expression, is a modest recreation of earlier forms, and yet somehow it fulfills its purposes (miraculously, in Hasidic terms). In our last interview with John and Jean Richards, they seemed to be of a similar view. They see that "having a little pow pow" in the backyard is far removed from some of the unforgettable moments they spent marking the High Holidays with their children when they were younger. And yet they believe that there is still value in undertaking some form of family performance that echoes those former experiences, even if weakly.

Life course change of a different sort and with different significance played out for Karen and Adam Lowe. The Lowes are one of the couples we introduced in chapter 1 whose daughter left DJDS after just one year. As uncomfortable as they might have been with the notion, they indicate that Seder night each year served as a performative barometer of the Hebrew literacy of the younger members of the family. The ability of family members to participate in this ritual, while reading in Hebrew, powerfully signaled the extent to which the youngest generation was fulfilling the values of the senior members of the group. At their first interview, during the year after Carla had started at DJDS, Karen explained: "At previous family things at my parents [before transitioning to DJDS], [Carla] was really the only cousin not going to a day school. So, my father would make a point of saying, you know at the Seder or something like that, that, look Brad and Jared know these songs and Carla is singing 'Away in a Manger' or something [laughs]. So now she really gets into it and everything."

Having noted the great significance of what the children's performance meant for other members of the family, we were curious, at the time of our second interview two years later, to see if Carla's withdrawal from DJDS had any ramifications in the context of this ritual. We found that the question sparked a heated disagreement between Karen and Adam about what actually happened, who was responsible, and what it signified:

INTERVIEWER: What's going on at the Seder? Is she competing
    with the other cousins?
ADAM: No, she dropped out this year.
INTERVIEWER: Of what? The Seder?
ADAM: She didn't do the Four Questions.
KAREN: Hold on a second! Hold on a second! First of all, you came
    on way too strong; second of all, she is right. She is not
    the youngest cousin nor is she the youngest cousin that's
    capable. She has a younger cousin that goes to [day school]
    and by definition that younger cousin is supposed to do
    it. She was right. And the more you push her at anything,
    Adam, the more she is going to back away. So you were
    wrong actually. So let's not use that as an example.
ADAM: I'm not. It doesn't matter. You still participate in the Seder
    the way you can. She just dropped out of the Seder.
KAREN: No, she didn't. She went over to help Maddie.
ADAM: Not really.
KAREN: Yes, Adam. But it's already to the point on my side of the
    family anyway where she will be the only grandchild that is
    not going to a day school.

The emotion generated by this interchange makes evident the performative significance of the family Seder, and the implications of what life course analysts would call generational change: change in the status of individual family members, in this case, from Jewish day school student to student in a non-Jewish school. The consequences of this change raised doubts about what it means to be a member of this particular family. Soon after this change had occurred, Karen and Adam were evidently struggling to come to terms with its significance for the wider family.

Visiting the family again, eight years later, when Carla was sixteen, we made sure to probe again on this issue. As had happened at the Richards', by the time of the third interview, the family seemed to have found a new point of equilibrium in relation to this particular ritual. Expectations had shifted, as indicated by the changed tenor of the conversation.

> INTERVIEWER: How are they at the family Seders?
> KAREN: Our kids are very good participants.
> ADAM: Having said that . . . .
> KAREN: Although they don't read in Hebrew.
> ADAM: Right they don't read in Hebrew so there's a lot of English. Thank God for Birkat Hamazon that they learned at Camp Shalom so they can. . . .
> KAREN: Do it off by heart.
> ADAM: They know it phonetically, but you know. . . .
> KAREN: It was an issue with my dad, but . . . regardless our kids are not intimidated, and they're not embarrassed by the fact that they can't do it in Hebrew. They're happy to do it. I think the issue we had at the beginning was my father is very, uh, what word do you want to use?
> ADAM: He likes tradition.
> KAREN: He likes tradition you know, and his girls went to day school, and I am the only girl that didn't send her kids to day school, and actually I'm one of six girls because his brother had three girls as well. So I'm the only one of six girls that didn't send their children to day school. But having said that, our kids, and I'm not just saying this, our kids are very well-behaved, and I can't say that about everybody's kids. They sit there, they listen, they talk, and they participate. It was only at the beginning. Although I had to have a discussion with my dad: "Don't put them on the spot like that, and don't . . . They're not embarrassed, so don't make them feel embarrassed. They want to do it in their own way. . . .

They're willing to do it, and they want to do it, so just let
them do it."

The interchange is once again fabulously rich in ethnographic terms. The
issue of Hebrew literacy is evidently still freighted with significance within
the family, as is further clarified, now that it is apparent that Karen is the only
member of her generation in the family whose children don't attend day school.
While not avoiding the issue, and evidently still somewhat uncomfortable with
it, Karen introduces "good behavior" as an additional criterion for evaluating
the quality of participating in this ritual. In terms of this criterion, her own children hold their own. In her eyes, this restores the value of her children's contribution to the ritual. It re-establishes them as family members, one might say. At
the same time, Karen has also moved to diminish her own discomfort by trying
to limit her father's control of the ritual, something she was able to do even
more fully at the most recent Seder before our final interview, the first Seder
she ever held in her own home rather than at her parents' home: "So, when they
came here I said, now listen, this is my … this is our Seder. This is the way we
do it, and I think it was the most relaxed Seder we ever had." Whether Karen's
father was quite as relaxed as she was, we can't know. In her own eyes at least,
a change in the location of the ritual brought about by an ontogenetic change
in the family (her parents' aging and move from their own home) provided an
opportunity to adjust the ritual's content and ultimately what that content meant
for some members of the family. As at the Richards family, changes in family
ritual serve as an expression both of more deep-seated changes in the family and
of sustained commitment to certain values. In this instance, multiple generations
of the family still find meaning in coming together to exchange stories about
Jewish history, to sing, and to feast together.

The plasticity of ritual, and its capacity to express continuing significance
despite ontogenetic and generational changes in the family, is far from inevitable. In some families, the ritual simply does not evolve; its meaning becomes
ever less compelling as a consequence of constant, unchanging repetition.
Overall, we found few instances of such a pattern; at the Stern family, about
which we'll say more below, and at the Richards's family where John and Jean
had trouble sustaining their children's interest in Friday night rituals. John
blamed himself for not having done enough to make this experience suffi-
ciently appealing to his aging children who preferred instead to stay out with
their non-Jewish school friends. It was a theme he returned to a few times
during the course of our last interview, given that this was, as he explained,
"the one Jewish tradition they tried to enforce" at home. This was something
that troubled him:

I think that I could have done a better job of nurturing the beautiful traditions involved in Judaism, like you know sitting down at the Shabbat dinner and just talking as a family. I think I could have nurtured that a little bit better .... It's hard to even get the kids to have some appreciation for the tradition, you know. It's like we will sit down and we will still cut the bread and we have fourteen- and sixteen-year-olds and they are still kind of not paying attention.... We have nice Shabbat dinners prepared where there's effort that goes into bringing the family together. And its beautiful traditions. And Jean will light the candles and sing. And the boys wouldn't even be focused on it and then we will say the blessing over the wine and we will start to cut the bread, and they will be kind of, they don't relish the moment.

It's difficult to account for the diminishing appeal of Friday night routines in the home. Melanie Richards attributed the problem to being compelled to participate in this one ritual (in contrast to the laissez faire status of other Jewish traditions in her parents' house). "I mean having to come home every time and being forced to [be there], it doesn't make you appreciate Shabbat as a sacred thing." It seems also that—unlike their Rosh Hashanah practices—the ritual never changed over the years. It was increasingly out of sync with children's lives and with the broader agnostic Jewish orientation of the family. To this extent, this particular family celebration ritual suffered from the kind of rigidity that—as we saw in the last chapter—Olson and his colleagues identify as an over-abundance of morphostasis in the family system, a lack of adaptation to changes among family members.

In other families where rituals quietly faded away, we more commonly found a contrary dynamic, what Olson would call a surfeit of morphogenesis—too much change: the families were altered so much (and the ritual they once performed did not possess such ultimate significance) that after a certain point in time there was less and less reason to observe the ritual at all or at least not with the same regularity. We noted in a previous chapter how, for example, the Manning family, when the children were still at DJDS, made Friday night dinner each week, replete with the blessings and challah brought home from school. This was an enjoyable family ritual that expressed the cultural competence of the members of this interfaith family, something that all family members celebrated. Yet, when all of the children had left Jewish day school and were old enough to spend time with friends further from their own backyard, Sharon and Ed felt that it was no longer worthwhile to compel their children to "come inside" to celebrate Shabbat in this way, and certainly not every week as they had once done. A similar pattern played out at the Kleinmans' following a different form of generational change: parental divorce. At the time of our first interview, Michelle and Joe Kleinman were excited to narrate how they were gradually taking on more Jewish traditions at home, such as Shabbat ritual on Friday, which, they said, they had "become pretty good at doing" the more their daughter Sandy brought home from school. Yet, as we previously described, following Sandy's withdrawal from DJDS and even more so following Michelle and Joe's divorce, Sandy and Joe ceased observing any Shabbat ritual at home.

The demise of family ritual in this case is consistent with the broader research literature on the impact of divorce on family life. For example, Pett, Lange, and Gander (1992) report how even in cases of late-life divorce (after age fifty), offspring testify that the impact of the divorce was keenly felt in the disrupted practice of traditions such as Christmas, birthdays, vacations, and Thanksgiving. Evidently, ritual's performative function in expressing "this is the way our family is" changes when the composition of the family changes.

Formative Ritual from a Family System Perspective

Usefully, the literature on family ritual and divorce points also to another dimension of ritual we had previously identified: its formative function. There is evidence that maintenance of ritual and of regular routines in divorced and remarried families has the effect of fostering better adaptation in children, providing them with a sense of security and stability of family life (Guidubaldi et al., 1986; Henry and Lovelace 1995). Ritual, in these terms, functions not as a barometer of family life course change, but rather as a medium for supporting the cohesive and adaptive features of the family system (Eaker and Walters 2002). This is an aspect of ritual we encountered in almost every family we interviewed.

Friday night at the Stern family provides a strong instance of this function. As we will explore more fully in the next chapter, when we visited the Sterns for the last time, we found that their youngest son, Jayden, eighteen at the time, was more critical of his parents' religious orientation than any of the other teens in our sample. And yet, each Friday night—despite his frustration with the unchanging routine from week to week ("we haven't changed it for the last eighteen years")—he still agreed to join his parents for Shabbat dinner, often bringing along his non-Jewish girlfriend. When we asked the family what they do each Friday night, Rhonda—Jayden's mother—answered, "it's just dinner." Jayden commented: "compared to somewhere else where there's more singing, and dancing, this is very rigid and boring." The response of Phillip—Jayden's father—was succinct but revealing: "just being together." This last description provides an effective account of the ritual's formative function: the meal—the same chicken and challah each week, and the routine of bringing family members together around the same table—works to keep Jayden connected to his parents despite his cynicism about their religious practices. Intriguingly, the parents reported that although Jayden's older brother had been just as critical of their Jewish commitments when he lived at home, once he had moved out of the house he made a point of coming home "every Friday night." This limited ritual has helped keep the family members together in a more than loosely connected system, even while Jayden expresses frustration about the ritual's unchanging form.

This pattern of home-based family ritual binding together members of the family was most vivid among the single-parent families in our sample. In these instances, ritual didn't just hold the family together, it enabled child and parent (actually mother and child in all three cases) to create a distinct family culture, a gendered pattern we noted in the last chapter. In chapter 3, we described at length the Jewish journey taken by Joyce Silver alongside, and to some extent inspired by, her daughter Ruby. Home-based family ritual fuels that journey, and Ruby's role as an active agent in those rituals enriches the Jewish culture of their home.

In response to a question in their first interview, about what her Jewish life is like, Joyce responded, "Yeah. I mean I light candles on Fridays, not every Friday but most. I don't shut down for Shabbos but I do like to mark it as a special time. So, I don't light candles maybe exactly at 7 o'clock but we come back or go up to the cottage or light candles up there or have a moment here, it happens not often, but often enough." As with other families we've mentioned, Friday night provides an opportunity to engage in some form of Jewish ritual at home or wherever the family happens to be. This is commonplace in almost all of the families in the sample. It is striking then that a little later in the interview, when she returned to this question about her Jewish life, Joyce elaborates:

> My home life is very much *talking* about all the things that I had when I was a kid, and you cook the same food and we build the Sukkah out here. We don't do it the kosher way but we do it and have fun, and Ruby, I'm thrilled that she knows. Like we lit candles on Friday night and her friend Tina was over and they did the long blessing of the wine which I don't know. I mean I can hum along with it but I never really learned it and it gives me great joy that Ruby knows the blessings. That's where she excels, not in the Hebrew writing but she loves the study of the Torah and loves the prayers, so it's wonderful. I get such joy out of it. We *talk* a lot about that— the relationship to God. And I believe in God. It's in my own kind

of Jewish-Buddhist way, but it's there. So I bring that into our home. [Emphasis added]

A strong theme in our interviews with Joyce and Ruby is how much they talk to one another, about their relationships, about what's important to them, about Israeli politics, and about their work. As Ruby aged, she became more and more of a soul mate to her mother. It is therefore powerful to see in this additional account of Joyce's how the Jewish content that Ruby infuses into their rituals at home is a stimulus to deep conversation, prompted by the cultural richness that Ruby is able to add to Joyce's practices. In our previous book, we analyzed this same narrative to highlight how much the family's Jewish life was enriched by the cultural capital that Ruby brought home from school (Pomson and Schnoor 2008). Now, we are able to observe more fully the consequences of her doing so. Mother and daughter might possibly have found another time to talk about these important matters, but it is also likely that the distractions of day-to-day life would have gotten in the way, as Joyce's first comments indicate; ritual provided a meaningful space in which those conversations could occur with some regularity.

Unlike at the Mannings' where the rituals became less frequent as the children aged, at the Silvers', as Ruby aged, her ritual role expanded, and the conversations in the house expanded too. As we noted in chapter 3, by the time of the last interview, Ruby's enriched cultural competence meant that she was able now to lead the family Seder. In turn, that stimulated even more conversation, the hallmark of this family's distinctive culture.

> RUBY: The last two years I invited, each year I honor one of my friends who is not Jewish to come to a Seder and like they loved it.
>
> JOYCE: They loved it. And we invited Linda, who is Malaysian and Irish Catholic combinations, she is interesting. We invited her Malaysian mother and Irish Catholic father and her sister and they loved. They loved it a little too much. Like he wanted to talk about you know,
>
> RUBY: Everything!

The Kin-Keeper in Family-Based Ritual

Our analysis of the formative function of ritual in the Silver family culture reveals an aspect of how ritual comes to perform this constructive work through the agency of what scholars have called a "kin-keeper." According to Fiese and colleagues (2002), a kin-keeper is a family member who assumes responsibility for maintaining kinship ties and organizing family gatherings.

Typically, this role is played by someone—almost always a woman—in the generation between grandparents and children (Leach and Braithwaite 1996). These women tend to be aged forty to fifty-nine. Before this age, it was the woman's mother who took the leading role. After this age, the woman is ready to pass on the responsibility to the next generation. These patterns help clarify, for example, the decline of ritual at the Kleinmans', as described above. In the absence of his ex-wife, Michelle, Joe Kleinman's home ritual with his children dramatically decreased. Michelle was the family's kin-keeper, as were other mothers we have described in this chapter, such as Adele Wallace and Jean Richards. In the emphatically gendered family system, it is less likely that men will step up to perform this role.

While the literature on the kin-keeper phenomenon emphasizes how ontogenetic change—the process of aging—accounts for changes in which family member performs this role, our data point to an additional dynamic: the changing cultural competence of particular family members. In these situations, it is not only middle-aged individuals who play the role of kin-keeper; it can be teens or young adults too, if they possess greater cultural competence than other members of the family. To take up categories we have employed in previous chapters: in conventional sociological accounts, the kin-keeper is viewed as drawing on extensive resources of *social* capital in order to hold the family together. She binds the generations. In a few of these families, it seems that the kin-keeper's influence derives from a different resource, from her possession of relatively rich *cultural* capital compared to other members of the family. This seems to account for the role Ruby Silver has assumed in her home, as the family member capable of making the "long blessing" for Kiddush or of leading grace after meals. This phenomenon also echoes a comment of Yael Reinhart, who, we saw in chapter 3, argued that she brings most of the Shabbat "momentum" into the house when she's home from university. Her cultural competence certainly does not exceed that of her highly educated parents, but enriched by the additional dose of enthusiasm she unquestionably brings, her presence is what helps make Shabbat ritual at home happen despite the busy lives of family members.

In the Elbaz family, there is an especially acute instance of a younger person serving as kin-keeper of Jewish rituals in the home. Rachel Elbaz argues that her daughter, Orli, started to play this role almost as soon as she started kindergarten at DJDS, for reasons closely related to specific circumstances in the family. As she elaborates:

> RACHEL: ... And the minute that she came home [from kinder-
> garten], and whether it was Tu B'Shvat or Chanukah or

whatever, she was our leader.... Without Orli's contribution, ... it would have been very difficult, it would have been
very....

INTERVIEWER: Not too much going on here?

RACHEL: Very. It would have been ... with a heck of a lot less joy
because it would have been up to me to be the educator. It
would have been up to me to try teach the songs which, as a
foregone conclusion, is going to be ... (giggle), I can't sing,
you know for me to try to, you know.... And then remem-
bering that there is the father who doesn't know anything, so,
not only is he neutral, at times he's pushing back.... When he
married me, and we were both living in Morocco, I was very
secular and then we are in Toronto. It's one thing to be secular
and living [in a close knit traditional community], and it's
another thing to be secular and living in [an open] non-Jewish
environment, with a non-Jewish father who is celebrating
Christmas and running an Easter egg hunt every year. So they
are two very different things. Single, secular in traditional
Morocco with children, and non-Jewish father in Canada....
If we stayed in Morocco it would have been, you know, you
can kind of go with the flow of things and Shabbat meals
are just natural, very similar whether you do or don't do the
blessing.... Here, obviously, you have to make the effort.

Rachel's last comment serves as a helpful starting point for highlighting the
role of the kin-keeper in sustaining the formative aspects of ritual. As she says,
"You have to make the effort." Preserving ritual requires effort in every family.
In this particular family (where the mother has a strong secular identity, along
with her knowledge of traditional Moroccan Jewish culture, and where there is a
non-Jewish father), sustaining any kind of Jewish religious ritual requires a great
deal of effort. And, as Rachel indicates, the effort required is further predicated
on the prevailing norms in the broader society. In Morocco, marking Shabbat
is part of the broader, traditionalist communal culture, for secular Jews too. In
North America, it calls for a countercultural effort within the family setting, and,
in turn, that requires some cultural competence. It also calls for other personality traits, she claims, such as being prepared (and able) to sing. These are
qualities that her extrovert and highly capable daughter, Orli, possesses in abun-
dance. Moreover, as Orli herself reveals later in this final interview when she was
eighteen years old, she also possessed a deep affection for ritual. Unprompted,
she offered the following:

I have always thought Havdalah was really beautiful. My best friend from DJDS, Yael, I think her family made me fall in love with it. I was always there with her, and so I was at her house for Saturday nights, and they would do this celebration, just with the light, and all the ritual. I love the ritual, I love the songs, and they pass around a bowl of angels, and that's the angel that will protect you for the week. They are like little pages with angels on them and it says like Hope or Harmony or Peace or whatever and that's the angel that will bring you whatever that thing is, that week or whatever.

Orli may be a lot younger than a conventional kin-keeper, but she can play this role with aplomb because of the particular characteristics of the family system in which she lives. As her mother reports, because of Orli's enthusiasm and evident pleasure with this ritual, if they have people over on a Saturday night they will "do Havdalah," a remarkable phenomenon given Rachel's avowed secularism.

Circling back to Rachel Elbaz's account of ritual, her reflection contributes to our investigation of ritual in the home in one further respect, by returning us to an argument we made at the start of the chapter. Family ritual, she appreciates, has both an expressive and educative dimension; it is both performative and formative. As Rachel infers, a first criterion in terms of what the worth of a family ritual can be judged is emotive, whether, in her terms, it nurtures "joy." In and of itself, that's reason enough for family members to observe a ritual, as many of the practices we've described in this chapter indicate, whether on a Friday night with extended family, on Rosh Hashanah in an orchard, or on Chanukah with friends over hot latkes. Who participates and how joy and meaning are produced are sensitive indicators of the ontogenetic and generational moment within a family's life course. The ways in which the family chooses to observe a ritual may also reflect a historical moment—for example, their infusion of feminist and other personalized practices on Seder night or their inclusion of non-Jewish guests. Ritual reveals aspects of relationships and values that might not be otherwise readily expressed.

Rachel's comments also point to the other dimension in ritual we have highlighted, what she calls its educational dimension, and what until now we have called its formative function. Anthropologists are accustomed to describing ritual as doing cultural work, through embodying, socializing, entertaining, and instructing (Beck 2003). In the context of the family, and of family systems, we have seen in this chapter how rituals also perform home work. They hold families together, and they communicate values from one generation in the family to another. They make clear who this family is. Sustaining ritual can be hard work, especially when forces unleashed by family life course changes complicate or erode what makes the ritual compelling or accessible.

Finally, as we have just seen, and perhaps what has been the most unexpected finding generated by our study of family celebration rituals, the work of sustaining family ritual need not only be carried out by older members of the family, especially when those young people (young women, to be precise) have cultural and social competencies that others in the family lack. In our next chapter, we take a close look at who these young people in our study are.

SIX

"I'm My Generation": Talking with Jewish Teens at Home

In the preceding chapters, we have pointedly taken a view of the family as our "unit of analysis." We argued that we can see more clearly who people are and what moves them when we view them within the context of their family relationships and their family life course trajectory. To put it succinctly, we have argued that ours is a study of people as family members. More than once we contrasted this position to a stance that sees the individual self as sovereign and that seeks, in methodological terms, to locate the individual's story through one-on-one interviews to find out who they *really* are.

In this chapter, we take a different tack while continuing to affirm the utility of a family system and family life course orientation. When we first met them, the children who had originally prompted this study were either in fifth grade, the frontier year of DJDS, or they were new to the school, in kindergarten or first grade. When we concluded our final round of interviews, the "children" were either in their first year of university or were in ninth or tenth grade of high school. They were between thirteen and nineteen years old. All were teenagers.

The data gathered in that final round of interviews offer a special chance to investigate and understand the lives of Jewish teens. These interviews are rich with indications of how these young people talk about themselves as Jews, about their relationships with their friends and families, their perception of their Jewish education, and their future plans. We suggest that these data are unusually valuable, first because they offer an opportunity to view the lives of teens against the backdrop of and in the context of their families, and second because until now there has been relatively little research into the lives of Jewish teens, especially when compared with the generational cohort that preceded them, those typically conceived as "emergent adults" (Arnett 2004; Wuthnow 2007).

In the context of the Jewish community, the slightly older, emergent adult population has been extensively studied both in terms of its birth cohort and its birth period (Cohen and Kleman 2007b; Ukeles, Miller, and Beck 2006; Greenberg 2006). Its members have been submitted to research and evaluation as alumni of programs such as Birthright Israel and Masa Israel Journey, as participants in emergent communities or social justice programs, as new Jewish leaders, and in terms of their relationship to Israel (Chertok, Sasson, and Saxe 2009; Rosov Consulting 2015; Chertok and Samuel 2008; Cohen et al. 2011; Wertheimer 2011; Cohen and Kelman 2007a).

By contrast, little is known about Jewish teenagers and in particular those who are teenagers in the second decade of the twenty-first century. Kosmin and Keysar's longitudinal study of Conservative high school teens stands out as an exception, as do two studies undertaken by the Cohen Center for Modern Jewish Studies (Kosmin and Keysar 2000; Kadushin, Kelner, and Saxe 2000; Sales, Samuel, and Zablotsky 2011), and two studies by Bryfman (Bryfman 2009; Bryfman 2016).

In the last few years there has been a surge of interest in more effectively engaging Jewish teens. Jewish educators and community leaders have become increasingly concerned that this age group is falling between the cracks in the period between Bar Mitzvah or Bat Mitzvah and university. Children under the age of thirteen are well served by a plethora of programs and experiences that are designed to prepare for them for this rite of passage. Once they make it to university, they are regaled again by any number of efforts to "engage" their attention and activity. The years in between have been sparsely resourced by comparison. To address this phenomenon, a national effort—a Funder Collaborative—of fourteen foundations and federations has come together to expand and deepen Jewish teen education and engagement in ten communities across the United States. Millions of dollars are being invested in this initiative (Informing Change 2015).

While this programmatic effort starts to gain traction, and attracts millions of dollars of funding, little is known about today's Jewish teens. In research terms, concern with the teen population has resulted in one investigation of the educational and communal programs that serve this age group (BTW/Rosov Consulting 2013); the two explorations of this population's needs and interests by Kadushin and Sales, cited above; and most recently, two studies initiated by members of the aforementioned Funder Collaborative (Woocher 2014; Bryfman 2016). Our study, although narrow in scope and geographically limited, opens a valuable window on the thoughts, feelings, and commitments of this age-group. Although the animating intent of this study had a different focus overall, it nevertheless provides a valuable opportunity to understand better this demographic group.

Researching Teens—Methodological Concerns

In recent decades, research on teens has overwhelmingly taken place independent of children's own homes and free of family influences. The goal has been to hear teens' voices in spaces not constrained by their families (Way 1998). As Bryfman (2009) argues, in the broadest terms, this methodological stance reflects an effort going back to Gilligan's groundbreaking study of women's lives to "focus on subjects' own perceptions of the world" (Gilligan 1982). The intent has been to privilege the voices of teens, especially those who are not typically heard. Yet, as we will show, studying teens at home, and in conversation with their parents, turns out to be more of an opportunity than a limitation. Far from being silenced in this setting, the teens make themselves heard in the contexts where they express themselves every day, in the course of ceaseless negotiations and conversations, and through silences too. There is a different kind of authenticity to these interviews because they occur in the very place where an important part of the teens' lives plays out.

In a paper about a study of family food choices, the authors report how important it was to find an interview location that "provided privacy to allow teens to speak freely without being overheard" (Bassett et al. 2008, 123). Their concern derived from a perception that for too long those charged with the care of children and teenagers spoke for them too. The researchers wanted to create a space where teens could speak for themselves. Christensen (2004) reports a similar concern in a study of child health and self-care in Denmark. He went out of his way to find interview spaces that reflected his commitment to redressing imbalances in child–researcher power relations. These positions are consistent with those of Smith (2005) in his landmark study of religion in the lives of American teens. Smith describes the great lengths to which his research team went in order to find places to interview teens where their parents were not physically or symbolically present. His team feared that if the teens were interviewed with their parents around, the teens would censor their own responses, or simply not have an opportunity to speak for themselves. The solution in that study was to interview teens in the meeting rooms of public libraries or in coffee shops.

The concerns of these researchers stand in sharp contrast to our own situation. When we first interviewed their parents, the youngest of the children in our study were still in kindergarten or first grade. When we visited their family homes to interview their parents, usually during evening hours, the children were often already in bed. Not only did we not hear the children's voices, we didn't even see them. When we visited their families a couple of years later, when they were in second, third, or sixth grade, we were often introduced to the children before they disappeared to another part of the house. If we were fortunate, we held short conversations with the children while their parents stood on the sidelines. At that point in time, few of the young people stayed in the room for the entire length of the interview.

When we visited their homes for the last time, the research situation was entirely different. Although some of the teens were completely absent from their family homes for the evening, or were away at camp for the summer, in most cases the teens were present together with their parents for the major part, if not all, of the interview. In a few cases, where the teens were eighteen or nineteen years old, they proved more talkative than their parents. The children had become the interview's center of gravity.

For sure, there were occasions when the parents contradicted their children or simply preempted their contribution by answering a question that had been directed to their child rather than to them. These, no doubt, are the kind of dynamics about which Smith was concerned, of children being pushed to the side and losing their voice.

Take the following instance where a mother inserts her own view into the interview and ends up talking about her fourteen-year-old daughter as if she wasn't there. It's striking and not surprising that the daughter's responses are so terse compared to the lengthy excursus of her mother. There is no doubting where the balance of power lies in this conversation, and perhaps in this family.

> INTERVIEWER: Okay and when did you start going there
> [a new school]?
> DAUGHTER: In grade 7.
> INTERVIEWER: And before?
> DAUGHTER: With DJDS
> INTERVIEWER: Okay that long. Okay, I didn't know that.
> MOTHER: If I can jump in here, I think that we intended to stay at DJDS and then we accompanied a friend of hers to an open house at Pine Crest and it was a jaw dropping experience for both of us.... I don't know if you recall this but she was very happy at DJDS. It was a small class but she had outgrown it. It was like she was ready to leave. It has been a cocoon and a very safe place and she was ready to fly.
> INTERVIEWER: Dara?
> DAUGHTER: Yea.
> MOTHER: (laugh)
> INTERVIEWER: I thought maybe you didn't agree.
> DAUGHTER: Well no.
> INTERVIEWER: No?
> MOTHER: No. School fell apart (laugh).
> INTERVIEWER: School fell apart?
> (Laughter)

In a further example, a mother offers a different, alternative account that seems intended to override what her fourteen-year-old son had shared. Evidently, she wants the interviewer to leave with her version of events, repeatedly amending her son's responses.

> INTERVIEWER: So, I understand you're at Belmont now, grade 8. Remember back in the old days when you were back at Paul Penna? It was a while ago I guess. How was your time there at Paul Penna, what would you say about it?
> SON: I dunno, it was good at first.
> MOTHER: It was great at first.
> SON: I liked it, but eventually it just reached a point. I couldn't really focus. It was just really easy.
> INTERVIEWER: It was too easy for you?
> SON: Yeah. I just needed a change. I liked it there, until a point.
> MOTHER: I think he liked it until that last year. I don't think he disliked it, I think he just was ready for a change. I don't think he ever disliked it there.

As disconcerting as these examples might be, they are not typical of our experiences in most interviews, especially not in cases when the children were older. Older children, we found, were comfortable contradicting or calling out their parents for what they perceived to be inaccurate responses. They and their parents were equally likely to amend and challenge one another's account. Essentially, they were engaging in the give and take of conversation. For example, in the following instance, a daughter readily inserts herself into her mother's words.

> INTERVIEWER: Okay. Any major, significant changes in the family?
> MOTHER: Yea, and so I guess the big shift in terms of the family was my mother moved in with us.
> INTERVIEWER: Oh, okay.
> MOTHER: Almost a year ago, before my dad died but it was inevitable.
> DAUGHTER: He wasn't, they weren't living here. Like he was living at Sunrise Terrace. So, he felt like she was going to come home. But she was in an apartment.
> INTERVIEWER: So, is your mother here now?
> MOTHER: Yea, she lives in the basement.
> DAUGHTER: Actually has her own apartment.
> (Laughter)
> FATHER: Very organized.

DAUGHTER: It's clean.
MOTHER: Bright.
DAUGHTER: And warm. So, if I had a choice I would be there.
(Laughter)

In a further, sparky, example, the power balance between parents and child is far from skewed in the parents' favor. The mother may try hard to communicate her own version of events, but she does not drown out the voice of her sixteen-year-old daughter.

INTERVIEWER: So, it sounds like you're pretty happy with what
     you have with your Jewish identity.
DAUGHTER: If I could, I'd be a little bit more observant of the laws
     of kashrut.
INTERVIEWER: Why can't you?
DAUGHTER: Well I came down ... you know what my brother had
     for the breakfast buffet [on holiday]!
MOTHER: That was Rueven not me.
DAUGHTER: I said my brother.
MOTHER: That was outside the house.
DAUGHTER: I know but ...
MOTHER: We don't have bacon buffet here.
DAUGHTER: Okay. Excuse me.
MOTHER: I had a BLT yesterday.
DAUGHTER: Yeah, you did.
MOTHER: But I didn't cook it.
DAUGHTER: You ate it on the plate, and you ate in the house.
MOTHER: But I didn't make you eat it. By the way, you're eating
     non-kosher chicken.
DAUGHTER: But there's a difference.
MOTHER: It's either kosher or not kosher.
DAUGHTER: But there is a difference ....

We share these excerpts to convey the kind of authenticity in these interactions that comes from their being conducted when both parents and child were together. At times, they are more like conversations where it is not clear who is driving the interaction. In the last excerpt, the interviewer fades into the background leaving mother and daughter to contest their narrative. Certainly, it is inaccurate to suggest that these children are silenced when interviewed together with parents. Their voices are heard, albeit differently from in a one-on-one interview, and in ways that open a window on the dynamics of the family system at a point in the life course where teens are trying out different ways of speaking for themselves and are testing a shifting balance in their relationships.

A last point is worth emphasizing in relation to these methodological issues. Far from resulting in self-censorship, these conversations have resulted in children expressing views that genuinely surprised their parents. As we have already asserted, the interviews were opportunities to learn about how these young people thought about themselves as Jews and their relationships to other Jewish people. They were also occasions to observe the reactions of parents to these expressions and to gain insight into parents' relationships with their children around these issues.

In a previous chapter, we already noted Dave Wallace's disappointment at hearing his nineteen-year-old son—a graduate of seven years of day school education—articulate limited enthusiasm or interest in his own Jewishness, especially when compared to other aspects of his life. The interview, it seems, brought to the father's attention a phenomenon that had taken shape over a number of years. Observing Dave's surprise and disappointment was as instructive in understanding the family system in this particular home as the account provided by his son.

In a different example, Karen Lowe appears unsettled by her daughter's responses. She jumps into the conversation to seek reassurance. She may possess the most powerful voice in the conversation (even while apologizing for inserting herself into the talk) but that doesn't prevent her daughter Jordy (the eleven-year-old sibling of our primary interviewee Carla) from replying forthrightly and disarmingly, a case of speaking truth to power, one might say. Jordy's responses certainly resonate with her father, a point to which we'll return below.

> INTERVIEWER: How important is it to you that you would marry a
>   Jewish person?
> JORDY: Not very important.
> INTERVIEWER: No. Why not?
> JORDY: Uh, Judaism doesn't matter that much to me.
> INTERVIEWER: Does it matter a little bit to you?
> JORDY: Yeah.
> INTERVIEWER: In what way does it matter to you?
> JORDY: That I get to go to camp.
> (Laughing)
> . . . .
> KAREN: So, let me ask you, not to take over this.
> JORDY: Okay.

KAREN: If someone said to you, Jordy what does being Jewish
    mean to you?
JORDY: I don't know.
KAREN: You wouldn't have an answer?
JORDY: Yeah.
KAREN: What do you think being Jewish means to Daddy and I?
JORDY: Umm I don't know. It's hard to define.
KAREN: Okay, but as we're raising you. Do you feel like … ?
JORDY: Well, Dad doesn't really believe in God and stuff like that.
ADAM: You have a fine point in that.
JORDY: (laughing)
ADAM: I believe in the transcendence of a higher being. Do I
    believe in a God in a throne with a white beard and judge's
    people? I don't believe in that sort of God.
INTERVIEWER: Is that being Jewish, according to your Dad?
JORDY: No. Is it?
ADAM: It is actually.

As this conversation demonstrates, the family home is a most authentic setting in which to interview young people about their lives and their outlooks on the matters that are most important to them. It is in their homes that their views about what it means to be Jewish are powerfully forged. In their homes, they test out their own ideas in the cut and thrust of debate with their parents. These are compelling methodological reasons, we suggest, for why it makes good sense to ask both teens and preteens about profound questions within the family setting.

Teens: Considerably Different from One Another

Reflecting on what we learned from these interviews about the teens as an age cohort, the first phenomenon to note is how diverse the lives and the Jewishness of these young people are. They might all have attended the same parochial Jewish day school at one point in time, but it is hard to detect evidence of this common denominator other than in a broadly progressive orientation to Judaism and to society in general, characteristics that bear the mark of the same downtown values their parents generally exhibit. Since leaving the school—in some cases in second grade and in others after eighth grade—their lives have followed different trajectories.

Some teens mix almost exclusively with Jewish friends even while they attend public schools; others prefer to stay away from crowds that are "too Jewish." A small minority of them are quite religiously observant, and one even attends synagogue daily. Others hardly ever attend, if at all; a couple of them "can't bear the idea" of going. Of those still school-age, one goes to a Jewish parochial school, a couple go to nonsectarian private schools, and the remainder attend public schools, commonly in special programs for the arts or for gifted students. Most frequently, they characterize themselves as agonistic, atheist, or secular. Some though—exclusively the religiously observant—characterize their religious orientation as progressive. None employ denominational identifiers such as Reform, Conservative, Orthodox, or even Renewal. This may be as much a mark of their age-cohort's indifference to labels (Frazer 1989) as it is a consequence of the post-denominational Jewish institutions with which their families are connected, starting with the elementary school they all once attended. Their indifference to (and perhaps discomfort with) denominational labels confirms further why so few of them marked their Bar Mitzvah or Bat Mitzvah in a denominationally affiliated synagogue.

The following sketches convey the variety of Jewish identities and expressions that some of them articulate:

Dara Goldman, age fourteen, says that she "always liked being Jewish," and now that she attends public high school she "misses Hebrew." She leads a service for young children at the traditional egalitarian synagogue that she and her mother attend every week. According to her mother, "she knows how to daven [pray], she reads Hebrew beautifully, she has a natural gift for *layning* [chanting Torah], and she reads Torah a number of times a year."

Melanie Richards, age nineteen, is an alumna of March of the Living, a travel program that takes Jewish teens to Holocaust sites in Poland and then on to Israel. Her grandparents are Holocaust survivors, and she continues to be interested in better understanding that aspect of her family's past. She's uncomfortable socializing at university with people who are, what she calls, "too Jewishy." That's why she never went to Jewish summer camps either. She resents being compelled to participate in Jewish rituals, whether on Friday night, Passover, or the High Holidays. She hates going to synagogue.

Gary Wagner, age fourteen, is a year ahead of his age-group at his parochial Jewish high school, and relishes the opportunities he has to argue about Talmud with his teachers. He attends morning services every day at a local synagogue rather than at his school where he is bemused by the nonegalitarian services. As he puts it: "The idea of separation [of genders] doesn't make sense to me."

Lisa Ruben-Fine, age fifteen, doesn't say much about her own Jewish life. It does not seem important to her. In ninth grade, at the age of fifteen, she comes across as a mature young woman, the stable force in a somewhat unsettled family who "gets" both her divorced parents and what is important to them. She is especially insightful about her non-Jewish mother's needs and relationships.

Ruby Silver, age eighteen, has been dating a Jewish young man a few years older than her for the last four years. She is very comfortable with who she is Jewishly and shares her Jewish interests with non-Jewish people in her life, such as the friends who she and her mother invite to Seder, or with classmates at school where she presented a final project about the State of Israel's journey to independence. She is taking a minor in religious studies so she can study Judaism from an academic perspective.

Sam Wallace, age eighteen, is attracted by the moral core of Judaism but not more than by the values he finds when practicing karate. He's proud of being Jewish but has no patience with "the worshipping part" of it. He explains: "I like religion because it gives you the ethical stuff, but I'm fine getting that from whichever way my parents seem to want me to get it from—whichever religion."

Yael Reinhart, age eighteen, recollects having been "the most religiously Jewish" in her DJDS class. She argues that at home she "brings a lot of the Shabbat momentum. I like Shabbat and I think probably ... I would like to do things for Shabbat more than my siblings do." While her parents define themselves as postdenominational Jews, she says that she identifies herself as "Havurah," reflecting an extremely meaningful experience she had at the summer institute of the National Havurah Committee, a pluralistic, nondenominational Jewish network.

Orli Elbaz, age eighteen, is a member of a progressive youth movement. She considers herself a humanistic Jew. She doesn't believe in God. She is very much attached to Jewish culture. She elaborates: "I love ritual. I love song; stuff like that. Pesach also, because of the Seder. I also love Tu B'Shvat because there is order, tradition.... Family is important to me so I try to make it somewhat of a priority."

Jayden Stern, age eighteen, is looking forward to being able to leave home and not observe any Jewish practices anymore. He says: "I'm sick and tired of that whole family thing." He continues: "I understand that religion is like my parents' thing. They like bring it toward you, but whether I would actually take it upon myself to actually try to practice those beliefs; well, I would be practicing *their* beliefs, not mine."

Sandy Kleinman, age fifteen, identifies herself as an atheist or secular Jew. An indicator of her thin Jewish social network is that she reports having only ever been to one Bar Mitzvah or Bat Mitzvah. She wonders whether the reason she doesn't feel a strong bond with other Jews is because she doesn't know much about the religion: "Saying that somebody is Jewish, it means something to me, but I don't really know all of what it means because I don't know what exactly being Jewish means."

Between fourteen and nineteen years in age, these young people convey a range of understandings of what it means to be Jewish that include ethnic, social, cultural, and religious points of reference. The "everyday religion" they live [in Nancy Ammerman's [2007] phrase] is situated first and foremost in the family homes where most of them still reside, rarely beyond the home. The most common exception is among the handful who talk positively about the summer camps they attend where they experience a Jewish culture in tune with their diverse Jewish identities. Only two of them are active in Jewish youth organizations in their local community.

As individuals who had spent between one and nine years at a Jewish day school, and who voluntarily joined an interview alongside their parents that was explicitly interested in their families' Jewish lives, it is not surprising that all are comfortable to some degree with identifying themselves as Jewish. And yet a few do convey a strong feeling of detachment and even alienation from the Jewish community. It's noticeable that the few who live away from home, to study at university, do not describe engaging in much if any Jewish activity in places other than their own homes. As we have observed with regards to their parents, family provides both the context and content for their Jewish identity.

Teens: Overwhelmingly Similar to Their Parents

While these teens talk about their Jewishness in ways that are quite different from one another, it is striking just how similar they sound to their own parents, both in terms of what they say, and how they say it.

Only one teen, Jayden Stern, seemed to be openly defiant of, or cynical about, his parents' Jewish outlook. As he says, "I don't really see myself as Jewish. I more think of it as my parents are Jewish. I'm my generation, which is pretty uncaring about religion."

And yet despite mocking his parents' unchanging religious rituals ("We do the same thing every Friday. We haven't changed it for the last eighteen years") and despite his complaints about being dragged to synagogue on the High Holidays, this young man nevertheless respects his parents wish that he sit down to dinner with them on Friday nights. He even brings his non-Jewish girlfriend along who seems to enjoy the experience far more than him. It is hard to know, therefore, what to make of his promise that once he completes his high school coursework he intends to get as far away as he can, to a university on the other side of the country. We don't know if this is a case of adolescent bravado or a genuine desire to forge his own divergent path.

With the exception of Jayden, this group of teens expresses views that sound very much like those of their parents. They often say things that one could have imagined their parents saying. Sandy Kleinman's humanism, Yael Reinhart's intellectual postdenominationalism, Gary Wagner's intellectual traditionalism, Ruby Silver's strong Jewish communal sensibility, and Orli Elbaz's progressive Jewish sensibilities hue close to templates established by their parents. Though nuanced differently, or expressed in a tone that reflects their own generation's sensibilities, they essentially affirm many if not most of their parents' Jewish values.

As we have already indicated, we do not think that this isomorphic tendency is an artifact of the fact that the interviews took place at home where children suppress their own divergent views or parrot what they hear the parents saying. In fact, as we will see shortly, there are certain issues about which the teens decisively part ways from their parents.

If these young people resemble their parents, we believe that there is an authenticity to this resemblance. So much so that in some instances the teens seem to express views that reflect a more honest rendering of the ideas their parents express.

Take the example of the Richards family. Both parents express disappointment that their children know less about Jewish culture, and feel less comfortable with Jewish culture, than they do. And yet they understand why, for example, their son was so resistant to celebrate his Bar Mitzvah in shul. As John Richards, the father, explained, "I think that part of the thing is he smelled the hypocrisy ... he knew that he could push our buttons on it because we were [ambivalent ourselves]." John recognizes that he suppresses his own ambivalence out of respect for his father, a relatively observant Holocaust survivor. In the course of our last interview with the family, he explained to his daughter why he goes to synagogue on the High Holidays despite his discomfort: "Well I mean, you know, I am fifty years old, grandpa is eighty-eight.... I spend some quiet time with him. I don't, I don't even like the religious Jewish part of it, like sitting, and you know Beth Israel. I shut that off to just be with grandpa for an hour."

An atheist himself, John is comfortable that he hasn't forced observance on his own children. Giving them choices is an extremely important value for him: "I'd be hypocritical if I was forcing you guys to go to synagogue." And yet, as we saw in the last chapter, he blames himself that his children choose not to engage in Jewish practices outside of the home: "I think that I could have done a better job of nurturing the beautiful traditions involved in Judaism, like you know sitting down at the Shabbat dinner and just talking as a family more. You know I think I could have nurtured that a little bit better.... As for the other Jewish stuff, I am okay with it. I am okay that they are not into going to synagogue and stuff but I would like them to have a, I think I could have nurtured a better connection to their roots you know?"

His daughter, Melanie, does not share his regrets or his ambivalence. She sees her preference to lead a fully "integrated" (non-Jewish) life as a direct consequence of how she was raised. Her religious skepticism is an outcome of the very questions and doubts she heard her own parents raise. Her Jewishness is expressed almost exclusively within and with family. When family members aren't around, she does not see a strong reason to identify or engage as a Jew. For her parents, her lack of Jewish interest and engagement outside of the home is hard to hear, but they don't challenge her on it, in large part because they feel the same way themselves. She expresses without compromise and hesitation many of the very same things they feel.

A similar, perhaps even more dramatic instance of children's honest rendition of their parents' views and values is evident in the Wallace home. As we have already noted, Dave Wallace expresses disappointment with what he learns about his son during the interview. He berates himself: "I think that's probably my fault. It didn't sink in. I should have taken you to shul more." But eight years previously Dave himself spoke at length of his own discomfort in synagogues and other public Jewish settings:

> When I moved to Toronto and started to live on my own, I had
> nothing to do with the synagogue. I used to daven on my own
> on Rosh Hashanah and Yom Kippur.... I never considered it was
> worth paying to pray and thought I could certainly do fine on
> my own. Why should I pay someone to allow me to pray when I
> could do it at home, you know? But on the other hand, I always
> had a certain, well because of where I grew up, there was always
> a certain feeling, not better, but it felt more familiar to go to a
> synagogue.

Listening closely, we find that Dave's son Sam thinks and acts in ways that are in fact a synthesis of his parents' own views. The following extract from an interaction between Sam and his parents reveals vividly how they occupy similar ground despite his father's expressed disappointment. The conversation begins with the mother, Adele, an educator herself, seeking to understand better the opinions expressed by Sam.

> ADELE: So, would you say culturally and historically that you have
>   a Jewish heritage?
> SAM: I know I do.

ADELE: (Laughs) And does that mean anything to you? What
would you say if I said, "Oh, you're Jewish! What does that
mean?" Let's pretend I'm from Mars or something.

SAM: To me, it's not an important part of me. It wouldn't change
my actions in any way.

ADELE: It shaped the fact that you're here, of course.

DAVE: Would you say it's a stronger influence on you? Would you
say it's as strong an influence on you as what you've learned
at karate?

ADELE: That's an interesting question.

SAM: They teach me much the same sort of things. The things that
I think are important are being taught there as well.

DAVE: And they're similar to some of the things you think you
learned at DJDS?

SAM: I guess so.

DAVE: Good.

INTERVIEWER: What about your core identity? Does karate have a
stronger place for you?

SAM: I wouldn't really place it above it, if I was to rank it.

DAVE: But, that's important.

SAM: It's important. Karate is important to me. Being Jewish is
important to me, but not because of the culture, history,
worship part. It's. . . .

INTERVIEWER: So what else is there?

DAVE: (Laughs) Culture, history, worship—what else?

SAM: Well, after that, there is what I could find anywhere, but
given through Judaism. There's the Golden Rule. There's the
commandments. Don't hurt someone else. Don't let anger
consume you, which is a message in a lot of stuff that we
went through when we did go look at the Bible.

ADELE: So, universal and, as you say, we chose Judaism as the
vehicle. That's interesting.

SAM: And that works quite well.

ADELE: Well, that's interesting. Can I extrapolate from that? Are
you saying then. . . . I guess that's what you said earlier,
Sam, about—that they taught ethics. That's interesting. You
wouldn't normally say that about a school, I don't think.

DAVE: I certainly don't remember learning ethics from my
education, but then it was so long ago.

ADELE: How does that compare with University Heights High
    School?
SAM: University Heights was just a school.

Conveying nostalgia for his own youth, when his experience of Jewish
community was centered on the synagogue, Dave seems to have wistfully hoped
that his son would turn out differently. Sam, however, is both a child of his
own time and of the home that his parents have made. And in the course of
dialogue with his parents, he reveals an understanding of Judaism that, it turns
out, is quite close to their own: a view of Judaism as, above all, providing individuals with an ethical system. The conversation expresses an honest search
for common ground. Intriguingly, even surprisingly, at eighteen years old, Sam
connects his understanding of Judaism in part to what he learned at his Jewish
elementary school, a deep learning about life that he contrasts with what he
learned at the elite non-Jewish private high school he subsequently attended.
As he says dismissively, "University Heights was just a school." Given the many
hours that his mother invested as a volunteer at DJDS, and given her own search
for meaning in the world's religious systems, it is no wonder she is so satisfied
with what this conversation reveals.

To return to our earlier argument, we do not think that continuity such
as this between parents and children is an artifact of our interview methodology, that is, interviewing parents and children together, in their homes. We
propose, instead, that this continuity is consistent with one of the central findings of Christian Smith's study of the religious lives of teens in the United States.
Smith writes: "The majority of US teenagers tend to be quite similar to their
parents, when it comes to religion. They tend to share similar beliefs, tend to
be situated in the same general religious traditions, and tend to attend religious
services with one or both of their parents" (2005, 68). In the concluding chapter
of his study he reports: "Contrary to many popular assumptions and stereotypes,
the character of teenage religiosity in the United States is extraordinarily conventional. The vast majority of US teens are not alienated or rebellious when it
comes to religious involvement. Most are quite content to follow in their parents'
footsteps" (260).

Smith characterized this conservatism as surprising in that it confounded
popular perceptions of teens as rebellious and deviant, or as departing dramatically from their parents' practices. The teens in our study conform to a similar
pattern, and, in the context of our study, seeing these teens as members of
family systems, there is even less reason to be surprised. Children, we have
seen, shape their families' Jewish norms and practices with what they bring
into their homes, and they in turn are profoundly shaped by what is already

there, formed across the generations. If anything, it is surely significant when teens actually free themselves from the orbit of their families' values and priorities. As we will see in the next sections, when such a fracture occurs it is worth taking note.

Differing from Their Parents: Upbeat about Their Jewish Education and Experience

We now explore some specific ways in which the teens do indeed differ from their parents while at the same time strongly resembling their peers. These patterns reflect, we believe, different family life course dynamics: on the one hand, the conservative influence of microsocial forces at home and, on the other, the disruptive macrosocial forces in the culture and society outside the home. While being raised within particular family systems at home, these teens have also experienced institutional influences outside the home that did not directly touch their parents; they have also grown up in a different cultural era from their parents. Such differences are reflected in two patterns that consistently distinguish the teens from their parents even while these two patterns seem also to contradict each other.

The first such pattern can be characterized as the remarkable degree of satisfaction these young people express with their Jewish education and the security with which they communicate about who they are as Jews. When the teens in our sample talk about their Jewish selves, it is with confidence and comfort rather than with awkwardness or ambivalence.

The teens talk positively about the Jewish content of the day school they attended for between one and nine years. If they left DJDS before the end of middle school, it was rarely if ever because of boredom with or alienation from the Jewish aspects of the school. Typically, it was because of social issues, because of specific family circumstances, or because of concerns about the academic quality of the school. Consistently, the teens look back positively on their Jewish education, and this, in turn, seems to have contributed at least in some way to their feeling good about their Jewish selves.

The following recollections about their experience at DJDS convey well the tenor of these reminiscences. The tone is generally positive, albeit mixed with adolescent complaints about restrictions or repetitiveness. These memories frequently spill over into equally upbeat expressions of how the teens express their Jewishness.

> LISA RUBEN-FINE, AGE FIFTEEN: "It was really great. The best part about it was probably the sense of community, and

everyone who's kind of very loving. I had a really nice school class. We were very close, so, that was a good part about it.... I thought [Jewish studies] was very interesting. By the end of it, I was almost fluent in Hebrew, yea. Sometimes we all got a little bit annoyed when we had to wear the Kippahs at lunch. That part, I don't know. But I liked Hebrew class and bible study and everything."

YONI WEINSTEIN, AGE FOURTEEN: I don't think I was ever really involved with the Jewish studies at school.... I wasn't really involved. I like learning Hebrew and all. I liked learning songs when I was little.... I guess when I was little I was more enthusiastic about Jewish studies. Now, I don't know. It's changing. I don't really get involved in congregations.

ORLI ELBAZ, AGE EIGHTEEN: Well, it definitely informed my entire Jewishness. Like a lot of people are Jewish but they don't know what that means.... I was like fortunate, I guess, to learn what that meant.

DARA GOLDMAN, AGE FOURTEEN: So, like, we got a good background and foundation of biblical Hebrew but our conversational Hebrew was, you couldn't really talk to someone who was fluent without embarrassing yourself because you had no idea what you were saying. I know a lot of people didn't really like doing tefilla. I mean, I personally liked it but a lot of people didn't like doing this.... I always liked being Jewish. And I guess I just made it better because we had a specific subject in Hebrew, like Hebrew binder, and we would make it into three things: Hebrew writing and then the Torah biblical stuff and then holidays.... And as you got older they still made it fun.

JOSHUA LOMBARD, AGE EIGHTEEN: Yea, we went through a lot of Hebrew teachers over the course of our time there, but who we had for grade 7 and 8 ... probably left the biggest impression on me in terms of Jewish studies as well. He [the grade 8 teacher], you know, he did a lot of Hebrew in like the Hebrew language, but we focused a lot on the sort of culture and sort of Torah aspect of it. We analyzed the portion of the week heavily and he, he left a pretty big impression and we sort of kept in touch after.

INTERVIEWER: Sounds like a positive impression

JOSHUA: Oh yea, yea.

In our sample of sixteen teens, there are really only two exceptions to this pattern. First is Sandy Kleinman a fifteen-year-old who left DJDS after kindergarten and who, since then, seems to have had very little exposure to Jewish experiences outside her own family. As we have already noted, Sandy did not have a Bat Mitzvah herself and only one of her friends marked such an event. The other exception is Jayden Stern, someone whose cynicism and rebellious rhetoric was referenced earlier in this chapter. It is noticeable that Jayden's critique extends to his experience of Jewish day school.

> JAYDEN: Not the best. It's not my favorite school. I liked the people.
> I didn't like, you know, the religious aspect.... The preaching
> to you over and over again, the whole Jewish thing. You're
> supposed to find your Jewish identity, they preach to you. But
> it's like they're forcing it down your throat. Because it's kind
> of not letting you spread your wings, and figure your own
> stuff out.... I mean parents force you to go to the school, and
> then you're learning the same stuff in Hebrew over and over
> again that can't be used outside of that class. So, unless I went
> to CHAT or some other Jewish high school, I wouldn't use
> any of that.... I mean after a while it's repetitive. Just goes
> in one ear and out the other. It's kind of more pushing you
> against it because it's continuously being there.

Jayden's comments are noteworthy first for being so different from the views expressed by the great majority of the teens. Second, they further confirm the close interrelationship between the teens' expressed Jewish identity and their experience of Judaic study and learning. His estimation of the limited worth of his Jewish school experience is tightly wrapped up with his discomfort Jewishly. Finally, these reminiscences underline how—with just a couple of exceptions— the formative Jewish educational experiences of this group of teens were so different from those of their parents.

When we first interviewed the parents, at a time when their children were starting Jewish elementary school, we asked about their own Jewish education and the relationship between their experiences of school and the school choices they made for their children. Consistently, the parents complained of having suffered through a Jewish education that they characterized as polarizing, homogenous, and uniform. Repeatedly they reflected on the lack of joy, inclusiveness, and diversity in their own Jewish educational experiences and how that contrasted with what their children were savoring at DJDS, as conveyed by the following examples:

> JOE KLEINMAN: I went to afternoon school maybe for a year or
> two but I hated it, it wasn't very good.... It was boring after

a whole day of school. I mean it was like one little classroom mixed with probably kids of different ages. It wasn't fun it was just like more school, I mean I didn't mind school but it wasn't fun.

RUTH GOLDMAN: I don't know how much I learned or if I learned anything, but I had to trek off to school, to Hebrew school after, it's just the way it was. I don't recall it is as being particularly good or bad it was very different then.... I come from a generation where sort of the Jewish God is an old man saying no.

KAREN LOWE: I resented having half my day in Hebrew with teachers that were *shlichim* that had absolutely no teaching ability whatsoever, and I felt like I wasted half my day, and I didn't like that, and I didn't want that. And also it really is a narrow way of forcing rich Jewish kids who, for the most part, I found had no sense of discipline, might have had academic discipline, but had no respect for their teachers whatsoever, and I didn't want that environment for my daughter.... I didn't want her world to be too narrow, I didn't want her only to be friends with Jewish kids.

DINA FUNK: I went to Torah Academy and Torah Academy was ... how many *psukim* [verses] can you memorize? I did well there but I didn't think it was a good education.

The contrast between these generally negative and alienating experiences and those of the children is consistent with a contrast between how the parents remember their own Bar Mitzvah or Bat Mitzvah and those that their children experienced. For the parents who celebrated one (most commonly the fathers) the experience required submitting themselves to a meaningless ordeal in Religious School that only saw release in the party that came at its climax. As Sandra Reinhart, an otherwise keen participant in Jewish matters, tells it: "I think the general attitude was pretty poor so we kind of picked that up." The parents' depiction of this ordeal and of their misbehaviour in the Religious School classes they were required to take by way of preparation is consistent with autobiographical and scholarly literature that has depicted the problematic features of this rite-of-passage, and especially of its yoking of afterschool Jewish education to the prize of a Bar Mitzvah weekend in the spotlight (Schoenfeld 1987; Aron 2010).

In an earlier chapter, we already noted evidence of a generational shift in the fact that most of the teens do not seem to have suffered in the same way. On the contrary, with so many of them having been active collaborators in the design of their Bar or Bat Mitzvah, outside the framework of the synagogue, they were proud of what they produced. In three homes, when during the interview we were discussing their Bar or Bat Mitzvah, the teen went to get a copy of the personalized siddur they had designed for the event so as to proudly share what they had made.

The event itself too was remembered as enormously positive. Some of the adjectives applied to it were: "joyous," "meaningful," "glorious," "an adventure," and "cool." One story, of Ruby Silver's Bat Mitzvah at an egalitarian/liberal congregation, communicates how such positive sentiments were associated with this experience.

> It was good. I remember my Torah portion went well, and then—I always tell this story—and then I began my Haftorah, and like half-way through I just kind of lost my place and so there was, like, I don't know where I am, like (laugh). And Rabbi Rafi was like feel, feel through it. I was literally like no, no, I can't. Everyone in the audience trying to find something, no-one knows what's going on. My grandfather who I guess is the only one who fully speaks Hebrew he was like well enough to find where I was. He called it out. It was nice to be—why I tell the story—it was nice to be in a congregation with a rabbi like that who I wasn't afraid, like, I am really lost, like I said, I remember saying.... Yea. I didn't stop or get nervous; I did all that I could because of my personality, my friends. I didn't feel like I was being judged or anything, but it was also nice to have him there knowing that he wouldn't feel disappointed and that was a nice kind of feeling. I think it was great. It's an interesting age to celebrate, definitely, it's a little awkward but it was fun, it was nice.

We suspect that positive Jewish experiences such as this are related to, and were formative of the teens' comfort with their Jewishness. The upbeat quality of these experiences surely helps explain the teens' comfort in talking positively about themselves as Jews in ways that distinguish them from their parents, at least when we first interviewed the parents.

Differing from Their Parents: Profoundly and Publicly Comfortable in Their Skins as Jews

The teens' comfort with who they are as Jews sees its strongest expression in their ease with displaying their Jewishness in front of their non-Jewish friends and acquaintances, and with including those friends in Jewish rituals. Melanie

Richards, for example, communicates how special her Bat Mitzvah was, in part because so many of her non-Jewish friends had never attended one before. She then continues to describe other noteworthy occasions when she celebrated meaningful Jewish moments with those friends:

> My Bat Mitzvah felt really special because for so many people it was the first Bat Mitzvah they'd have ever been to and, like, I loved it.

> I remember, I think I was in grade 5, we had a huge Chanukah party and for years you [her mother] were the latkes lady because you came in and made latkes for everyone. So, kids would ask, it would be, like, oh my God it's the latkes lady. And so we had, I think it was grade 5 or 6, we had a big Chanukah party here [at home] and so all my friends came over. And for years after, they'd say, when are we making latkes? And we made latkes one time and it wasn't even Chanukah just because it was fun. And we made them here. So, like sharing that type of stuff.... And sharing I mean it's all the great stuff. During Passover, everyone has matza. A few of my [non-Jewish] friends have even been invited to different Seders. I mean ours is full capacity.

What is ironic in Melanie's case is that she seems more comfortable performing her Judaism—"sharing" it is the word she uses—for and with her non-Jewish friends than with Jewish peers who, as we mentioned above, she finds too "Jewey." It seems almost as if the act of sharing is more meaningful than the content of what is being shared. Melanie is not alone though in her comfort with disclosing her Jewishness in this way. We previously mentioned Joyce and Ruby Silver's custom of inviting a non-Jewish friend to their Seder each year. Ruby Silver indicates a similar unselfconsciousness when bringing her Jewish interests to her public school classroom.

> I remember like in high school all my classes were so, like Judaism wasn't really discussed until we talked about it in history. Then in grade 12 history I got to write a final project. I got to choose a topic, any topic to do a presentation on, it was one of three projects actually and I did the independence of Israel as my topic. I said I really want to do this. Like, we hadn't had time to go into the details in class.... I loved my presentation and it was awesome to put a little bit of my opinion especially because it's Israel. There is so much craziness going on there, I feel like just like some history that it wasn't so complicated; it was a nice story when it began and it was kind of talked about it in my class, and some people were like oh my gosh like I had no idea how that started.

Ruby continued to describe another incident in her public school classroom, this time regarding the Holocaust:

> Actually, they had a Holocaust survivor come to speak to us in Grade 10 and this was the most influential Jewish moment of high school.... He came to speak to the Grade 10s. And we went back, we had drama after that so your homeroom kind of like everyone is really close and we had a discussion about it and every single person was crying. Because I think that so many people don't necessarily know the details of the Holocaust or small things just because they didn't go to Jewish school and obviously it was emotional for me as well. It was really nice and also comforting to see that like it affects people who aren't Jewish around you and then it became like, Joseph was sitting with me as well. And then they kind of started asking us about our, I guess kind of connections to Judaism which was really nice and that was probably like.... It was a very emotional day but it was nice to do that, and I think especially because of the school I went to everyone was so open to emotions and learning about everything that goes on in the world.

Such self-confidence in displaying and sharing their Jewishness contrasts sharply with how the parents describe themselves as Jews. When Joyce Silver was herself in high school she was rebelling against being Jewish. Unlike her daughter, when she was a teen she went to great lengths to hide her Jewishness outside the home. As we have seen previously it took many years to comfortably resolve how she thought of herself as a Jew.

When we interviewed the parents for the first time, specifically about their reasons for enrolling their children at DJDS, many were evidently still wrestling with this "Jewish question." Half tongue-in-cheek, Karen Lowe described herself as a self-hating Jew, reacting in her own parenting choices to the bifurcated world in which she grew up where you either mixed entirely with Jews or you were beyond the pale. With a different biographical backstory, Michael Ruben was struggling with similar issues, "I'm also not one hundred percent comfortable in a Jewish environment.... I went to Upper Canada College and I had a really kind of schizophrenic childhood, so I'm not entirely comfortable in a WASP environment although I probably am more.... I mean I spent most of my time with gentiles and have for a long time, although my closest friends are all Jewish."

In our previous book, we highlighted a common denominator among the parents: their discomfort with denominational and suburban Judaism, and how they came together at DJDS, feeling comfortable within its walls as "a community of difference" (Pomson and Schnoor 2008). These families were drawn to the school in the first place because it provided them with the rare experience of not being judged for who they were as Jews, whether because their partner was not Jewish, because they were a gay couple, because they had children much later in life, or because they were financially challenged. The school was the first Jewish institution that enabled them to feel comfortable about their Jewishness and if or how they fit within the Jewish community.

By contrast, their children—teenagers when we interviewed them for the last time—did not seem to exhibit the same kind of angst about their Jewish identities. The Jewish was not in competition with other aspects of their lives. Sometimes it was present, sometimes not. If it was not present too much, it wasn't a problem. Unlike their parents, they didn't feel the need to justify themselves before earlier generations of more observant family members. And they didn't feel burdened by the kind of "survivor guilt" that characterized their parents' and grandparents' generations in a community with an exceptionally high proportion of Holocaust survivors (Bialystok 2000).

Thus, while Joshua Lombard experienced no discomfort being the only Jewish boy in his high school class, and while he amused his family because "most of his friends in high school had names beginning with Zee," he was nevertheless planning to major in Jewish studies at university, he read Torah at synagogue at least once a year, and looked forward to going to Israel on Birthright. His strong Jewish identity did not conflict with his deep integration within a network of close non-Jewish friends. Carla Lowe revealed that "I feel so home at camp, and I feel so comfortable there, and it's far, far, more observant than I think any household I will ever live in." And yet she also explained how pleased she was that she hadn't attended a Jewish school since she was in first grade, even though that actually meant choosing a different school from most of her camp friends. As she put it, in a Jewish school, "I think there would be subjects that would be pointless." Her skepticism about the worth of Jewish learning and her distaste for the ghettoized character of Jewish social life did not clash with the fact that her best friends were the young Jewish people she met at camp. In a strikingly different example, we saw earlier in this chapter how Sam Wallace knew clearly and could talk eloquently about what he valued most about Judaism ("the ethical stuff" and a "sense of right and wrong") and what he didn't ("the worshipping part"). His certainty, and articulacy, about such things surprised but eventually reassured his parents particularly given his lack of participation in Jewish activities outside the home. These teens— and their peers—were comfortable with who they were as Jews and they knew what they liked most and what they liked least about being Jewish. In their easy weaving of what they saw as the more and the less positive, their outlook couldn't be further from the uncertainty and discomfort articulated by their parents.

There seem to be a number of reasons for these differences between the parents and the children. We have already highlighted the different quality of their experiences in and with Jewish institutions outside the home. Undoubtedly, parents and children had very different experiences of Jewish education. Some parents still seemed to bear the scars of those times. The teens have also come of age in an era where multicultural values are much more deeply embedded in society, where public schools celebrate and affirm the different traditions of diverse families, and where Jews are much more confident about their places in Canadian society. Consequently, these teens have little reason to feel self-conscious about their Jewishness even in contexts when many non-Jews are present. This contrasts with their parents' and grandparents' generations who were uncomfortable about publicizing their Jewishness in places of work and in other non-Jewish settings (Weinfeld 2001). Lastly, the Jewish institutions with which the teens were familiar and of which their families are members tend to affirm the legitimacy of different ways to be Jewish. For example, if they marked their Bar or Bat Mitzvah in a synagogue, that institution was typically inclusive of non-Jews, both women and men equally, and of gay couples. These are the outstanding features of the Jewish school they attended. The teens do not therefore feel the same compulsion or revulsion about having to conform religiously. Absent such pressure, they identify much more fully and readily as young Jews than did or do their parents.

Reflecting on these differences, one of the fathers, Adam Lowe, put it like this: "We grew up one generation removed from the Holocaust. And we spoke about Judaism in hushed tones. They grew up in a very pluralistic society.... You [gesturing to his children] don't have that, and you don't have the guilt from the Holocaust generation."

Differing from Their Parents: A Weak Commitment to Marrying Jewish

Against the backdrop of such strong and consistently positive feelings about their Jewishness, and of their comfort exhibiting their Jewishness in front of others, it is striking that the teens part ways with their parents in one more significant way. Not one teen was committed to the notion that if they choose to marry, it should be to a Jew.

Of course, a significant minority of the parents in this sample are themselves intermarried; in five of the sixteen families who continued to participate in this study for ten years there is a non-Jewish parent or partner. And, as we just noted, this fact is part of why those intermarried parents who were themselves raised as Jews feel so uncertain about their own Jewishness. They came of age in an era when to "marry out" was regarded as a significant defection from the Jewish community (McGinity 2009). It is striking then that on the issue of inter-marriage even when they seem to agree with one another, the parents subtly but consistently part ways with their children.

Toward the end of our interviews with the families, we asked the teens: "If you see yourself settling down one day ... how important is it to you that your partner or spouse be Jewish?" In some families, this question provoked the live-liest discussion between parents and children, indicating a decisive fissure between the generations.

In their thinking about these matters, the teens' outlook is remarkably uniform, reflecting—we suggest—the historical moment in which they live and the generational life course phase in which they're situated. The normative stance of the teens is well communicated by the responses of Sandy Kleinman and Melanie Richards, two teens raised in very different home environments: one where there is a thin Jewish social network and where parents and grand-parents are intermarried; and one where that social network is thick and exten-sive, and includes Holocaust survivor grandparents. The two teens approach this question with very similar assumptions.

> SANDY: It [settling down] wouldn't be about religious background.
> It's more about what the person's like, and I guess what they
> believe in. More, what kind of person they are, and not what
> kind of religious thing they belong to, or whatever. I guess
> their ethics, what they think is right and wrong. And I think
> that's more important to me than what they identify with.
> Yeah.
> MELANIE: It's not, it's not a top priority at all, I mean the grandpar-
> ents would be happy but ... it's all about people and I think,
> like, it depends. It's not whether they are Jewish or not; it's
> whether they are a nice person.

Melanie's next comments indicate, however, the difference in the Jewish cultures and networks in her and Sandy's homes, even while they do not moderate the shared assumptions that the two of them share.

> MELANIE: For me, I mean, and who knows, I mean maybe I will
> end up with a Jewish guy, we'll see, but I think that a lot
> of Jewish values are not just Jewish values, they are values

that ... can be shared amongst anyone, and my kids will still
know about their grandparents being Holocaust survivors
even if I don't have a Jewish husband. Like, I can still take
them back to Hungary, take them to Israel and, we'll see.

The default position for all of the teens is that religion is a secondary matter
when it comes to committed personal relationships. The first consideration
is compatibility with another person, and that person's values, not whether
they're Jewish. If a partner is Jewish, that's a bonus. What matters is whether
she or he supports continuing those parts of Judaism that their partner defines
as important.

When teens expressed sentiments like these during an interview in
which their parents also participated, subtle generational differences became
apparent, even when parents seemed to agree with their children. We suggest
that those differences partly derive from teen discomfort with any hint that
their parents might be exerting even a little pressure on them about their life
choices. Perhaps they reflect the relative immaturity of teens, most of whom
have not yet left home. Most profoundly, they probably derive from a distaste
for what teens perceive as tribalism: the notion that some people might be
more compatible (let alone more desirable) than others because of their ethnic
or religious identity.

Where precisely teens and parents part ways is well demonstrated by
conversations at the homes of two teens who, as we have already shown, display
robust and positive Jewish identities: the Lombards and the Lowes. What makes
these conversations so interesting is that there is a great deal about which parents
and teens agree. Yet, at a certain point (a different point in each case) they end
up disagreeing.

At the Lombards', our research team got lucky. Joshua's sister, Lara, two
years younger than him, joined the conversation alongside Joshua, himself a first-
year university student by this time:

> INTERVIEWER: So, Joshua do you see yourself getting married one
> day?
> JOSHUA: I guess, yes.
> INTERVIEWER: How important is it for you for your spouse to be
> Jewish?
> JOSHUA: I don't. I don't think it's quite as important as maybe
> it was to you [turning to his father]. But, I mean, I see the
> value in it for sure and I think it holds a certain amount of
> importance in my head.
> LARA: I agree with what he said.

INTERVIEWER: So, have you succeeded in that? [In Ray's previously
expressed hope that his children would ultimately marry
somebody Jewish and have a Jewish home]

(Laughter and Chatter)

INTERVIEWER: What did you say?

RAY: She said "love conquers all."

INTERVIEWER: Oh.

RAY: I remember. I realized a few years ago that I never told them
that that was something important to me.

LARA: Oh, you told me. I got very mad.

RAY: That's when I told you. And she got really angry that it's
important to me that she would get married to somebody
Jewish. And Lara got very upset. Joshua didn't say anything.

JOSHUA: I don't even remember this conversation.

RAY: (Laugh) See? And then, Lara, now why were you angry?

LARA: Because I don't think that's something you should, you
don't really have to say, I don't know. That's my choice, not
yours.

RAY: Well, yes, of course. It's your choice.

LARA: And just knowing that I have that sort of pressure at the
back of my mind from you is not a great feeling.

INTERVIEWER: Did you also have a feeling that that's what you
want?

LARA: I think it would be a great asset but it's not required, I don't
know.

RAY: You didn't like my....

LARA: I don't like the way....

RAY: I think you felt like I was being somehow negative about
everybody else who wasn't Jewish.

LARA: Yea.

RAY: And I don't think that was my intention.

Lara's sentiment that "love conquers all" and the emotion that accompanies
her response indicate that her starting point is similar to that of Sandy's and
Melanie's, even if stated less sharply. Joshua's position is closer to his father but
not fully in sync with it either. Both children see the advantages in finding a
Jewish partner—"it would be a great asset"—but such pragmatism is different
from their father's normative stance. Given how much else parents and children
agreed about in these final interviews, this point of difference seems a significant divergence.

In the conversation at the Lowe home, those differences surface again, precisely when parents and daughter seem to have agreed on what in their case is a more liberal stance on this issue. The conversation starts in familiar fashion, with the teen articulating a perspective we've heard from her peers. It ends up surfacing a nuanced difference between parent and child.

> INTERVIEWER: Okay. If you were to settle down with someone?
> CARLA: Hold on. My views on stuff like this have more to do with North American culture and society than it does with Shtetl matchmaker stuff.
> KAREN: Meaning?
> CARLA: Meaning, if I want to get married or not, that decision-making process is most likely going to have nothing to do with Judaism.
> INTERVIEWER: Okay. What about the religion of that person that you might want to be with? How important would it be for you for that the person be Jewish?
> CARLA: Unless I'm going to procreate, I don't think it's important. If I'm involved with someone, I just want to be with someone who makes me happy.
> INTERVIEWER: If you were to possibly procreate with someone down the line ... it would be?
> CARLA: Well I don't think that's likely. I don't want kids. (Laughing)
> INTERVIEWER: Okay.
> CARLA: Well, even if I were, the one thing I took away from Jewish studies is that if the mother is Jewish, then the child is Jewish.
> INTERVIEWER: Correct.
> CARLA: So, even if my partner, husband, whatever, isn't Jewish he has to at least respect my religion, and respect that our kid will be raised Jewish. He doesn't have to convert, but just get ready to live the Jewish lifestyle.
> INTERVIEWER: So that's important to you, sounds like.
> CARLA: To an extent. I don't expect you guys to sit shiva if I don't marry a Jew.
> ADAM: I expect you to name him Alef like Natalie Portman.
> KAREN: My parents said they would sit shiva for me if I married someone non-Jewish.
> INTERVIEWER: Right. And how do you feel about your kids?

KAREN: I would not do that to them.

INTERVIEWER: Do you have a preference?

KAREN: Do I have a preference? (Sigh) I would say yeah. No.
    I don't know.

INTERVIEWER: So, you guys are pretty much on the same page?

ADAM: But, if you marry Jewish, good. I mean post-Holocaust,
    there is still the guilt that people died.

KAREN: Pack your bags and put on the guilt.

CARLA: Here's the thing. Not all Jews are like us. There are so
    many Jewish people whose parents tell them that they have
    to marry Jewish. I know a lot of people at camp. We're best
    friends, so we talk about everything. And we got to this
    topic one night, and I was like ... we were talking about
    what our parents thought if we marry Jewish. And I was the
    only one whose parents didn't really have a preference. So,
    I'm not too worried.

KAREN: I wouldn't say we don't have a preference.

CARLA: Well obviously you want me to marry Jewish but it's not
    the end of the world.... You're not going to forbid me.

This long extract allows us to pinpoint where parents and children part ways. On the one hand, Adam and Karen celebrate that they are more open-minded than their own parents' generation. They wouldn't "sit shiva"—that is, respond as if their daughter had died—if she were to settle down with a non-Jewish partner. Parents and daughter have both left what Carla calls "the Shtetl" (the Jewish village of yore). But it seems that their open-mindedness is nevertheless uncomfortable, especially for Karen. This is indicated first by her hesitation ("Do I have a preference? [Sigh] I would say yeah. No. I don't know."), and then by her correction ("I wouldn't say we don't have a preference"). Karen's position isn't quite the normative stance of Ray Lombard, but it is a principled position; she does evidently have a preference. And this position is significantly different from that of Carla whose starting point is that her partner "make her happy" whatever his or her faith. She reads differently what it means that her parents "won't forbid her" from marrying someone who isn't Jewish.

Our close reading of these conversations highlights an apparent paradox. These teens—certainly because of the historical era in which they have traversed adolescence and perhaps because of the Jewish education they have experienced—are proud of who they are as Jews. They're comfortable with their

Jewish literacy and with displaying their Jewishness in public places, unlike many of their parents. At the same time, their pride as Jews does not imply a commitment or even a preference to marry Jewish. If anything, it's possible that their confidence as Jews has undercut any concern about raising their own children as proud Jews while living with or married to a non-Jewish partner. They are ready to admit—pragmatically—that it might help to marry Jewish, but they don't see a principled reason for doing so. What appears to be quite paradoxical is best understood through the lens of historical change. As members of a generation that has experienced a more positive and more intensive Jewish education than most of their parents, and as young people more proud and less ambivalent about their Jewishness than their parents, they do not see endogamy as a necessary requirement for raising a Jewish family. This idea of a natural connection between endogamy and Jewish continuity that most parents hold, is not an idea this generation feels has special importance, although, to be clear, none of their parents condemn intermarriage; a sizeable minority of them are married to non-Jews themselves. But some do conceive of intermarriage as a challenge. And, for those parents, marrying a Jew is more than just a preference. For most of their children it does not seem to be even that.

Lenses for Viewing Individual Lives

Having highlighted the extent to which teens and parents agree with one another, and having dismissed the possibility that such agreement is an artifact of interviewing parents and teens together, and having also emphasized the relative diversity among the group of teens in this study, it is noteworthy to find what these teens share with one another and how what they share sets them apart from their parents. The teens' comfort with and celebration of who they are as Jews, on the one hand, and their discomfort or distaste for the notion that they should marry Jewish, on the other, seems at first glance paradoxical. When viewed through the lenses of a life course perspective and of family systems theory, these positions take on a different hue.

As we have endeavored to highlight, these apparently inconsistent positions reflect the interplay between some of the historical forces we identified in a previous chapter and generational changes within family systems where adjustments in one part of the system set in motion changes in other parts of the family system. These children have come of age at a time when there has been a historic change in attitudes to intermarriage within the Jewish community and when at the same time some of those liberal Jews who are most comfortable with those changes have turned to Jewish parochial, albeit inclusive, schools to educate their children. In this chapter, we have shone a light on what the coincidence of these circumstances and choices has meant for the children.

To put it succinctly, it has resulted in a generation for whom the categories of universalism and particularism are no longer incompatible. These young people celebrate Jewish difference and at the same time are not especially concerned about sustaining the social structures that have traditionally maintained that difference.

In previous chapters, we have argued, by drawing on family systems theory, that when making educational choices for their own children, parents set in motion changes in their own lives too. In this chapter, we have set aside a consideration of what those changes mean for parents and what they imply. In the next chapter, our last, we return to a discussion of these changes and what they mean for both parents and children.

SEVEN

Home Work: Reflections on Studying Families for Ten Years

During our work on this study, over more than a decade, colleagues and friends have often asked us how things were turning out with "those Toronto families." Many of our associates were familiar with our previous research with these same families. They wondered, as we did when we reached the end of that earlier project, what would become of the Jewish lives of these families once their children withdrew from or graduated the Jewish day school that had contributed so much to the Jewish vitality of their homes during a particular period of time. Could we discern longer-term impacts for children and parents of Jewish day school education that outlived a direct connection with the school? Were there any lessons in the continuing trajectories of these families about how best to sustain the Jewish engagement of families during their children's teenage years?

In this chapter, we take stock of what we have found. In doing so, we view our work as constituting what Robert Stake (2005) calls a form of "collective case study." We have had the good fortune that sixteen families have been willing to open their homes to us over a ten-year period. Those sixteen cases are both similar and dissimilar to one another. Above all, they share one distinct characteristic: during the course of one particular academic year, all of the children attended the same Jewish day school. Underlying our methodology, then, is the assumption that the study of sixteen families, and not just of one or two, will, as Stake puts it, "lead to better understanding, and perhaps better theorizing, about a still larger collection of cases." While we are aware that our understanding might be sharpened further, and our theorizing made more reliable, if our sample included 116 families and not just 16, we are also encouraged by how—through paying close attention to these particular stories, and to how those stories have been told and retold over an extended period of time—we have been able to discern the ways in which home-made cultures "speak themselves," to adapt Kohler-Riessman's phrase (Kohler-Riessman 1993). Listening carefully to *how* these individuals tell their stories as well as to *what* stories they tell, we gain a special insight into the everyday Jewish lives of parents and children as they are constructed in their homes.

Beyond Unpredictable

This case study methodology, we believe, has a humanizing effect on the study of Jewish lives. Quantitative studies of hundreds or thousands of individuals, especially studies with retrospective designs that associate outcomes today with factors from the past, tend to objectify the lives of human subjects. Such studies are constructed to identify the influence of particular variables or interventions on the ways things have turned out at the present time. Thus, the Pew Research Center's (2013) *Portrait of Jewish Americans* concludes: "Whatever the causal connection, the survey finds a strong association between secular Jews and religious intermarriage. . . . Married Jews of no religion are much more likely than married Jews by religion to have non-Jewish spouses. Jews who have non-Jewish spouses are much less likely than those married to fellow Jews to be raising children as Jewish by religion and much more likely to be raising children as partially Jewish, Jewish but not by religion, or not Jewish at all" (9). These are robust conclusions based on the analysis of a sample of almost 3,500 individuals. Yet, even if unintentionally, they reify these outcomes as inevitable. They do not help account for the trajectories that individual lives take, or, to be precise, the specific and often idiosyncratic reasons why a particular interfaith family chooses to raise its children as practicing religious Jews and another does not.

Having had the opportunity to look closely at the lives of the individual members of sixteen families, both interfaith and inmarried, over a period of decade, we have been struck again and again by the unexpected and personally distinct ways in which their lives develop. We started this book by recounting how, when we first met them, the families of Sandy Kleinman and Carla Lowe seemed embarked on similar trajectories of Jewish engagement, stimulated by their daughters' Jewish school. A year later, when both families withdrew their children from the school, albeit for different reasons, those trajectories did not look all that different. Yet, ten years later it was hard to believe that the experiences of the Kleinmans and the Lowes had so much overlapped at one point in time. There were few resemblances between the families' Jewish lives by the time their children had become adolescents. In one home, there were rich conversations—even arguments—about what it meant to be Jewish, the children attended Jewish summer camp, and the extended family came together in an ongoing cycle of home-based rituals. In the other home, there were intense conversations about politics and values, but rarely if ever with Jewish content. There was almost no interaction with an extended Jewish family, there was no obvious contact with educational or public Jewish institutions, and there was very limited if any observance of Jewish rituals at home.

In previous chapters, we explored the reasons behind the different trajectories of these two families. Here our point is to highlight how unexpected such divergent outcomes were. As we have noted on numerous occasions, when we went to visit many of the sixteen families in the sample for a last time, sometimes eight years after we had previously met them, we were genuinely surprised by the course their lives had taken. We simply could not have predicted the interaction between certain common phases in the life course of each family (such as Bar or Bat Mitzvah, school transition, and the death of older family members) and certain aspects of the family system in their homes (such as family size, the proximity of the extended family, and the particular religious faith of the parents). Each family was creating its own unique story through the interactions and expressions of family members.

The following examples demonstrate how particular *family life course phases* have resulted in surprisingly different outcomes within different family contexts.

Staying in a Jewish School—In most instances, spending close to the maximum possible time (between seven and nine years) at DJDS seems to have been associated with the development of more extensive Jewish social and cultural capital for both children and parents, in line with previous studies of the outcomes of Jewish schooling (Cohen and Kotler-Berkowitz 2004; Cohen 2007). Moreover, our data also provide evidence of the multidirectional causation of such outcomes (from home to school, from school to parent, and from school to child). And yet our sample also includes at least one case where the longer a child stayed in school, the more disaffected he became because, he complained, "it's like they're forcing [Judaism] down your throat." In another case a child's attendance at Jewish day school over a period of nine years seems not to have made any discernable difference to the intensity of Jewish life in a home already well-resourced with Jewish social and cultural capital. Such exceptions highlight why we cannot reliably conclude that Jewish day school attendance over many years is associated with consistent outcomes.

Divorce and Separation—There are similarly unpredictable consequences to the experience of divorce, typically assumed in life course literature to be associated with what Bengsten and his colleagues call the disruption of "religious transmission" (Bengston et al. 2014; Tanaka 2009). In one family, the divorce of two Jewish parents seems to have resulted in the almost complete disappearance of Jewish ritual from the father's home. As we suggested in the last chapter, this case seems to be a paradigmatic instance of family ritual being disrupted by the departure of a female family kin-keeper. In another family, where there was a Jewish father and a non-Jewish mother, Jewish conversation and practice were dramatically diminished in both parents' homes following their separation, a result of the non-Jewish mother having previously been the main driver of Jewish activity in the home. And in a third case, where a Jewish mother separated from a non-Jewish father, divorce served to reset the Jewish balance in the home. As the mother vividly reported, the synagogue provided a sanctuary during this period of transition, and connected mother and children with the broader Jewish community. Retrospectively, each trajectory possesses its own internal logic; none was predictable at the start of our inquiry.

In similar fashion, *features of the family system* that are typically associated with particular predictable consequences seem to have resulted, on a case by case basis, in surprisingly diverse outcomes.

Intermarriage—As we noted in earlier chapters when exploring the phenomenon of intermarriage, the consequences of this feature of the family system for the Jewish lives of families was almost completely unknowable in advance, even when taking into account the gender of the Jewish parent in these instances. In our sample, we found families where a non-Jewish partner supported or even drove forward the Jewish engagement and education of children; families where the absence of Jewish relatives, on one side of the family, meant that parents and children lacked the stimulus and support for Jewish experiences; and families where a Jewish parent possessed sufficient social and cultural capital to sustain the intensity of Jewish life at home with limited assistance from a disinterested non-Jewish partner. Such differences were mirrored in their diversity among families where both parents were Jewish, making it difficult to establish any general rules about the impact of intermarriage or inmarriage on the Jewish lives of specific families in this sample.

One-Child Families—In the course of exploring the impact of family system characteristics on the Jewish lives of families, we noted the previously overlooked impact on the family's Jewish culture of the number of children in the home. In a couple of notable instances, we found that the presence of more than one child in the family prolonged the interaction between parents and other Jewish parents or between parents and Jewish institutions, in contrast to families where there was only child. Yet, as with so many other features of the family system, this was not a phenomenon that resulted in predictable outcomes. There were at least a couple of instances of parents who also withdrew younger children from Jewish schools when they withdrew their older children. In these cases, the educational choices made for older siblings overwhelming determined the experiences of other members of the family, and not vice versa. Far from sustaining the flow of Jewish stimuli into the family, these younger siblings missed out on those stimuli themselves.

These examples vividly confirm a commonplace: while sociologists can identify what *typically* occurs in hundreds of cases, it is not possible to predict in what ways a *particular* family's Jewish life might take shape as a consequence of family life course forces or family system features. Applying generalizations to the anticipation of what will likely happen in the case of one family is tendentious at best. By the same token, it is equally problematic to make generalizations or draw general conclusions from the case of one family or even sixteen families about what would happen in most other cases. The accumulation of sufficient instances of a phenomenon doesn't produce a general rule (Kahneman 2011).

And yet, returning to Stake's basic premise for case study work, it is still reasonable to propose that as a consequence of the study of a limited number of cases, we can see things more clearly that were previously opaque. A case makes clear the qualities of a phenomenon. A series of cases sharpen that clarity further. As Flyvbjerg compellingly argues, cases help develop a nuanced view of reality, buttressed by what he calls "the force of example" within given fields or in relation to different social phenomena. They make contributions to scientific understanding without establishing general rules (Flyvbjerg 2006).

In this spirit, we review the "nuanced view of reality" we have acquired from the findings in each of the proceeding chapters, from chapter 2 to chapter 6. We then paint a picture of what comes into view when these separate snapshots are pieced together.

Learnings: Insights into Jewish Self-Formation, Home Work, and the Study of the Family

The Dynamic Qualities of Jewish Social and Cultural Capital—In chapter 2, by taking up the sociological categories of social and cultural capital, we were able to schematically chart the relative intensity of the Jewish lives of the families that participated in this study. In mapping the Jewish capital of the families, we found that fewer than half of them possessed both high Jewish social capital and high Jewish cultural capital. We confirmed thereby that this sample of individuals constituted an unusual group of day school families. They were ready to pay more than $10,000 a year to send their child to an all-day private Jewish school, and yet many were ambivalent about their relationship to Jewish community and culture.

Of broader significance, and pointing to the dynamic quality of capital over time, we noted that the families with higher Jewish *social* capital and lower *cultural* capital at the start of the study were among those whose Jewish lives intensified most over the course of the study. It seems that over time, as Lareau (2011) has demonstrated in a different context, social capital can be translated into increased cultural capital; extensive Jewish relationships seem to be associated with ever deeper Jewish literacy and cultural engagement (as previously proposed by Cohen and Veinstein 2011). By contrast, other than in one outlier case, cultural capital was not readily translated into social capital. Being knowledgeable about

Jewish matters does not seem to stimulate or nourish extensive Jewish social relationships. Indeed, there is evidence that Jewish capital is not always something that an individual or a family consistently accumulates or that remains inert over an extended period of time. In some cases, we observed how both social and cultural capital may have been higher in the distant past but had declined by the time of our first contact with the family. Capital, it seems, does not resist decay without supporting social systems. It erodes even within the same generation in ways not previously noted in either Bourdieu's or Putnam's influential formulations (Bourdieu 1986; Putnam 2000).

The Long View: Seeing (Jewish) Change Differently from a Life Course Perspective—In chapter 3, we saw what is revealed by applying a life course perspective to the analysis of interview data accumulated over the course of a decade. This perspective makes visible the interplay between processes of ontogenetic change, generational change, and historical change, or what some scholars refer to as the intertwined forces of biographical time (age), generational time (cohort), and historical time (period).

The family life course perspective dramatically alters our appreciation of what might stimulate change in the Jewish lives of families, and of how change often does not occur at a single moment or as the consequence of a single turning point. While, of course, generational transitions such as divorce, Bar and Bat Mitzvah, school transitions, or extended stays in Israel can be associated with personal growth and even transformation, Jewish change might also occur, less dramatically, as a consequence of ontogenetic processes such as the physiological maturation of children or the physical decline of parents and grandparents. Even harder to discern at any given moment, change might also be enabled by macro-social phenomena, historical changes in the broader culture or society, such as the normalization of interfaith relationships, changes in the status of women, the personalization of rites of passage, and the normalization of parochial Jewish education. These broader changes don't determine specific outcomes, but they do create circumstances that enable lives to develop in ways that would not otherwise have been possible.

Close reading of interviews with the same individuals over a period of years reveals how cautious researchers must be about soliciting interviewees' perspectives, at a single point in time, about what brought them to the present moment. Individual interviewees find it hard to discern those changes that occur at such a slow pace that they don't notice them occurring or that play out at a historical register that they are not aware of living through them. As a result, they can end up attributing too much retrospective influence to the "critical moments" in their lives. The life course perspective not only widens the analytical frame to include both microsocial and macrosocial forces, it also extends the longitudinal range of our expectations. Overall, it enables a radical correction in how to conceive of the processes and pace of Jewish self-formation.

Family System Theory and the Deep Structure of Jewish Self-Formation—In chapter 4, we came to grips with the puzzle of why some families change more than do others when exposed to the common stimuli identified by the life course perspective. We asked why do the same historical, generational, or ontogenetic shifts stimulate lasting changes in the lives of some families but not in the lives of others? We addressed this question by drawing on family systems theory, and in particular on one variant of it that takes account of—on the one hand—aspects of family structure, such as family size, the number of parents in the home, proximity of grandparents, parental religious faith, and gendered family patterns, and—on the other hand—the quality and nature of the relationships between family members, particularly in terms of family cohesion and adaptability.

Family system theory underpins the primary insight of this book: when individuals act or think of themselves as Jews, they do so in ways that are deeply implicated in the lives of the family members with whom they live, no matter how close or distant their relationships with one another. Jewish identity, for the members of our sample, is forged at home. Family provides the context and content for their Jewish lives. And, in these terms, as we expressed it previously, the Jewish self looks anything but sovereign. At most, it is a voting member in a cacophonous family polity.

A secondary insight derived from our application of family system theory relates to the role of intermarriage in shaping the lives of families. Whether or not the adults in a family share the same faith is evidently a significant contributor to the content of the family system. Yet, seeing intermarriage as one component in a system reveals it as one factor among other structural and relational factors that might be just as significant in shaping the intensity of Jewish life in the home. Viewed as an element in a system, intermarriage is less a demographic tsunami, as it is often portrayed, and more an unsettling element in the fragile ecosystem of contemporary Jewry. This finding underlies how important it is for Jewish communal policy-makers to employ a nuanced view of how family systems function. Rarely does one feature of the system—even intermarriage—result in a definite set of outcomes.

Family Ritual: A Sacred Site for Home Work—In chapter 5, by zooming in on both the formative and performative dimensions of home-based family rituals, we gained an appreciation of the extent to which ritual can serve as a useful barometer of ontogenetic and generational change within the family. As we have argued, because the form and content of family ritual so sensitively and idiosyncratically mirror a family's values and priorities—more so than publicly performed rituals that may not fully reflect the preferences of all participants—changes in the form and content of family ritual, choreographed by the family members themselves, indicate deep-seated changes in the family over time.

At the same time, in almost every family we interviewed, ritual functioned not only as a barometer of family life course change but also as a medium for supporting the cohesive and adaptive features of the family system. Ritual is the special site in which the work of forging "who families are" is carried out. In many instances, ritual doesn't just hold the family together, its most common-place function, it also enables children and parents to create a distinct family culture. If the family home is where the Jewish self is most fully formed, then home-based ritual is its sacred center.

In an additional insight, our cases revealed an important variation on the role played by those family members who assume responsibility for maintaining family rituals, what scholars call "kin-keepers." While the literature on the kin-keeper phenomenon emphasizes how ontogenetic change—the process of aging—accounts for changes in which family members (typically middle-aged women) perform this role, our data point to an additional possibility: who kin-keepers are can be determined by the changing cultural competence of family members, and not only their age. In certain situations, it is not only middle-aged individuals who play the role of kin-keeper, it can be teens or young adults too (usually women), if they possess greater cultural competence than other members of the family. This finding was in evidence on a few occasions in our sample as a consequence of the children's Jewish day school education.

Paradoxical Teens: Proud Jews with no Special Commitment to Marrying Jewish—Although, as we have repeatedly emphasized, the family served as unit of analysis for this study, in chapter 6 we analyzed the data gathered in the final round of interviews so as to investigate and understand Jewish teens. Our last round of interviews was rich with indications of how young people talk about themselves as Jews, about their relationships with their friends and families, their perception of their Jewish education, and their future plans. These data are unusually valuable first because they offer an opportunity to view the lives of teens against the backdrop and in the context of their families and, second, because of the general paucity of research into the lives of Jewish teens, especially when compared with the generational cohort that preceded them, those typically conceived as "emergent adults."

We found that while teens talk about their Jewishness in ways that are quite different from one another, it is striking just how similar they sound to their own parents, both in terms of what they say, and how they say it. This isomorphism is consistent with one of the central findings of Smith's study of the religious lives of teens in the United States (Smith 2015). At the same time, these teens do differ from their parents in two noteworthy ways. On the one hand, they are much more comfortable in their Jewish literacy and in displaying their Jewishness in public places than their parents. On the other hand, their pride as Jews does not imply a commitment or even a preference to marry Jewish. Not one of the teens was committed to the notion that if they choose to marry, it should be to a Jew. To express these findings in more paradoxical terms: these teens have experienced a more positive and more intensive Jewish education than most of their parents, they are more proud and less ambivalent about their Jewishness than their parents, and at the same time, they are less committed to a norm of Jewish endogamy. In this respect, their talk blurs the categorical distinction between universal and particular commitments employed by Wertheimer (2010), for example, to study an older cohort of Jewish young adults. Because of the coincidence of historical changes they have experienced, these teens have a special appreciation for Jewish culture, and at the same time they are deeply committed to the notion that Jews are just like everyone else.

Methodological Questions

In a final section, we offer some thoughts on the big picture that emerges from the piecemeal insights we have just gathered. First, we address three methodological questions with which we have wrestled, and with which we have been challenged when reflecting on our findings. These challenges derive from one common epistemological source: the geographic, demographic, and diachronic situatedness of our data.

Ironically, the selfsame characteristics that make case studies so compelling—their singularity and situatedness, what Flyvbjerg calls their "force of example"—are precisely what can invite their dismissal. Their specificity in terms of place, time, and content can make them seem irrelevant to a broader set of phenomena. When we have shared our emerging work over the past few years, colleagues have sometimes questioned its usefulness in these terms. We introduce these critiques and address each in turn.

These Families Are Canadian and They Have Chosen to Send Their Children to Day School. Doesn't That Make Them an Idiosyncratic if Not Sui Generic Sample?

As we recounted in chapters 1 and 2, the parents in this study constitute an opportunity sample. They are connected to one another almost by coincidence. It so happens that at one time their children all attended the same Jewish day school in downtown Toronto. After that one year, their lives (and specifically their school choices) changed in profoundly different ways. Some remained at the school for just one year. Two or three stayed for the following eight years and played prominent roles as volunteers.

We make no claim that these families are somehow representative of Jews in North America; no single group associated with any single institution, no matter how pluralistic, would be. Nevertheless, the very features that make this group so unusual are precisely what make it so interesting. On the one hand, these families have constructed highly personalized Jewish lives. They display liberal values, and demonstrate relatively low levels of traditional Jewish engagement. In large part, the parents, most of whom are public school graduates themselves, are advocates of the public school system. Their profiles align quite closely with the secularizing trends highlighted in the 2013 Pew study of Jewish Americans. On the other hand, for some period of their lives (longer for some, shorter for others), the parents chose to enroll their children in a private Jewish all-day school. These choices place them somewhat outside of mainstream Jewish trends. Precisely because of these peculiarities, many Jewish families in North America—both more liberal and more conservative—will see reflections of themselves in the lives we have described.

We are inclined to believe that even if somewhat by chance, we have gained access to a fascinatingly diverse group of families, some of whom are today marginally engaged in Jewish life, while others have become leaders of Jewish institutions. As we have argued in this chapter, the insights we have gleaned are significant, we suggest, for the broader Jewish community and for those who study contemporary Jewry.

There Are Only Sixteen Families. How Robust Are Insights Based on the Study of So Few People?

Conventionally, sample size in qualitative research is determined by data saturation. Sampling continues until no new information is forthcoming or nothing new is heard (Cresswell 2012). In our case, where data have been collected from an opportunity sample rather than a purposive sample, the relevant criterion is less *how many* individuals were interviewed and more *how much* was it possible to learn from the sample (Guest et al. 2006). In terms of this criterion, we have been fortunate, first, in terms of the composition of the sample, and second, in the willingness of interviewees to talk frankly about their lives.

In terms of sample composition, the families that agreed to participate in this study over an extended length of time were unusually diverse in their family structures and in their religious orientations: there were six families where one of the adult partners was not Jewish, one family where one of the partners converted after marriage, and nine where both partners were Jewish at birth.

The sample includes four one-parent families, two blended families (following divorce or separation), and a further ten with two parents who had been married or partners since before their children were born. In terms of Jewish identification, the sample included families ranging from those who did not define themselves as Jews by religion to those who were traditional Conservative Jews. Overall, there were probably only two obvious sociological types missing from the sample: same-sex couples and religiously Orthodox families. Our original sample had included a same-sex couple, but they did not remain involved after the first round of interviews. And in terms of the Orthodox, there simply are not any such families at DJDS. (A different study is needed to explore the extent to which our findings are echoed among adults who live in highly traditional structures, and in what Boyarin calls nonliberal communities [Boyarin 2013].)

As for how much it was possible to learn from this sample, it will be obvious by now that we have been showered with empirical riches. Again and again, the great majority of those who we interviewed were willing to respond with seriousness to our questions and wanted to engage us in conversation. In just one case, one of the parents declined to participate in the study (staying in the kitchen and other parts of the house) while the remaining family members joined an interview. Just a couple of families took part without having very much to say for themselves. These families are referenced and quoted in the preceding chapters but aspects of their life stories are not recounted to any great length.

Overall, from within this sample, there emerged about fourteen families whose stories we have really come to know in all of their richness over many years. We have homed in on these stories at different points of analysis, in part because these narratives were revisited over time, but also because they were challenged or confirmed by other members of the family, or were simply recounted with care and investment. Our understanding of how Jewish life takes form at home is all the richer for the generosity and loquacity of these individuals. Reflecting on these rich and often intense stories, we don't feel as if we have somehow overlooked important factors or forces that forge Jewish culture and commitment at home.

The Children Are Still Relatively Young.
Isn't It Too Soon to Say How They Will Turn Out?

One of the most profound insights provided by the family life course perspective is that a family's life story is never complete. Each new life phase brings a new set of experiences and meanings, as new generations take an active role in shaping a family story, as family members age, and as the broader sociocultural context continues to evolve.

It is true that by the time we completed our last interviews, many of the teens were still living at home, conducting their lives within the close orbit of their families. We do not know yet to what extent these young people will sustain active Jewish lives once they move out of their parents' homes. We have already noted that those who were living away from home by the end of our study were less Jewishly active than when surrounded by family. Yet we also do not know how much will change if and when these young people create families of their own. If we get the opportunity, we will need to interview them when they are in homes of their own, and perhaps have children of their own. And so it goes.

Our work has not been directed toward a particular terminus. We saw in the last chapter how those teens who stayed at DJDS for more than one or two years drew on what they gained there—culturally and, especially, socially—to a degree that surprised us. Their Jewish day school education continues to be relevant to them in a variety of ways. Their school experience has also enriched the lives of some of their parents in unusually long-lasting ways, in terms of the institutions with which they have become connected and who their friends are today.

To reiterate, the education that these young people experienced has not delivered a set of fixed or predictable outcomes. This particular school has nurtured a group of literate and culturally empowered young Jews; knowledgeable enough, for example, to design their own Bar and Bat Mitzvahs, and able to communicate reasonably well in Hebrew. At the same time, this particular school has not isolated its graduates from non-Jewish society. These young people are completely comfortable in non-Jewish settings. They're comfortable displaying their Jewishness in front of their non-Jewish friends, whereas at a similar age many of their parents had been anxious about displaying their Jewishness. This is an unusual, perhaps unprecedented, mix. Quite what it will mean in the long-term is decidedly uncertain.

Conclusion: Home Work—A New Approach for Studying Jewish Families and Jewish Self-Formation

For the past couple of decades, sociologists of contemporary Jewry have been focused on the possibility of uncovering "the Jew within," and of better understanding "self-created individuals," engaged often in building a "congregation of one" (Cohen and Eisen 2000; Arnett and Jensen 2002). This sociological paradigm, focused on the internal landscape of the individual, is contingent on the assumption that adult self-formation involves "breaking away from family, home and community," "almost to give birth to oneself" (Bellah et al. 1985; Baumeister 1991).

Over much of this same period, we have been engaged in studying the lives of smart, independent-minded adults and young adults navigating their ways through life, each in their own distinctive fashion. Our study began, in our first book, with an interest in the "long and winding road" that adult Jews take in choosing schools for their children and then in how they interact with the schools they choose. Over time, as the lives of the families in our study took divergent trajectories, and prompted also by the repeated reference to family when people responded to our questions, we became aware that we needed a new theoretical framework to make sense of how people were talking with us. When our interviewees talked about themselves as Jews, they conceived of themselves as mothers, sons, daughters and fathers. Family—as we have noted earlier in this chapter and at the start of this book—provided both the context and content for who they were as Jews. Their Jewish lives were strongly centered within home-based family rituals and interactions. It was these encounters in the field that encouraged us to turn to a life course perspective and to family systems theory. These analytical frameworks are sensitive to the quality of the family as both organism and system.

Taking up these frameworks does not imply giving up the notion that individuals have the capacity to create themselves anew. As we saw in chapter 4, the family system framework has space for individuals like Ruth Goldman and Adele Wallace, strong-willed individuals, pursuing personal journeys that swim against the current of their communities. However, the family-system framework means paying attention to the "fellow travelers" in whose company these individuals create and recreate themselves, those whose lives are deeply implicated in their own, and who enable them to be who they choose to be.

Coming to the end of this study, we are convinced more than ever that we cannot properly understand the Jewish lives of individuals without viewing them within the contexts of their families. To put it more precisely, we think that to fully appreciate who adults are as Jews we must pinpoint where they are, at the present moment, in relation both to the life course of their families and to the characteristics of the family systems in which they are situated. These frameworks provide the longitudinal and horizontal axes within which to locate their constantly developing identities as Jews; their family selves.

This study has convinced us that the time is ripe to reengage with the family as a unit of analysis, no matter how fragmented or open-sourced its form. Moreover, at a historical moment, when, in most Western democracies, public and parochial religious institutions struggle to draw together communities of like-minded individuals, family is one of very few social institutions in which people do continue to find meaning and purpose for nontransactional reasons. That too is confirmed by our study. The home is a site where people continue to come together without extrinsic purposes; just because. At such an historical moment, it seems especially urgent to understand the continued valence of the family as an institution in people's lives, not least because what family means, and what families look like, is profoundly different from earlier periods (Boyarin 2013). The forms that family takes have changed. Its significance may be greater than ever.

Of course, scholars, therapists and educators have long known that who one's family is makes a difference to one's life chances and to one's cultural dispositions. These are commonplaces of sociology, economics, psychology, and many disciplines besides. Such commonplaces convey a sense that earlier generations overwhelmingly determine the prospects of later generations within the same family. Our modest study shows, however, in textured fashion that such influences are not unidirectional. Children's lives are certainly shaped by their parents' experience. But, in turn, parents' lives are shaped by their children's interests, choices and experiences, and—critically—by the choices *they* make for their children. The fabric of their lives is colored by structural and relational features of the family system to which children contribute as much as do the parents themselves.

The family system exerts a powerful force field. It strongly contributes to who we are as individuals, and not only as family members. Given the existence of such forces, it is no wonder that fourteen- to eighteen-year-old children so much resemble their parents—no matter the turbulence of the teenage years that seems to spin children beyond the parental orbit. As we have signaled, we are intensely curious what will happen if and when the young people in our study form families of their own. Our assumption is that they will not be "home alone"; they'll continue to be part of an expanded family system even if it is not physically proximate. But we cannot predict who and what else they will bring with them. And we cannot predict what new family systems will emerge from the collision or integration of previously independent systems and structures. As the life course perspective confirms, such systems are always in flux.

The Promise of a New Field: Family as a Unit of Analysis

These conclusions, and our experiences over the last ten years, prompt us to propose a new direction for the study of contemporary Jewry—one that reclaims the family as a unit of analysis; positions it within a multigenerational, life course context; and employs a qualitative research sensibility. We propose, in other words, nothing less than a new interdisciplinary field within which to conduct the study of Jewish lives.

To unpack (and to review) the elements of this field: First, as our findings show, there is great value in conceiving of the family as a unit of analysis in the study of contemporary Jewry. Studying individuals uncoupled from the family systems in which they are embedded, no matter how loosely, risks losing sight of the most significant features of who they are as Jews. The home is where the plurality of Jews today experience Jewish life, and homes comprise more than just collections of individuals. As we explained in chapter 1, one of the most telling insights of systems theory is that in systems, such as the family and the family home, the sum is greater than the total of the parts. Paradoxically, we gain a thicker and broader sense of the formation of the individual self when we move the family to the center of our sociological focus and displace a notion of the sovereign self.

Second, this study also demonstrates the rich accumulation of insight, and the dramatic adjustment of vision, that comes from researching the same group of people over an extended period, in real time. These insights are a special consequence of employing a cohort-based, life course perspective, a research orientation rarely employed in the social-scientific study of contemporary Jewry. We previously noted how studies of Taglit-Birthright alumni are a rare exception to this general rule, and yet how, at the same time, the Birthright research pays limited attention to the families of alumni and does not directly gather data from their family members. If Jewish social scientific research and those who fund it have the patience (and sufficient resources) to wait and see how lives develop over time, we may see things that we miss with a relentlessly retrospective perspective.[1] The challenge is to let enough time pass for an individual's "Jewish skin to grow," to return to an image employed by one of our interviewees, Ed Manning. It is not just that things look different from a long view; a research stance that is attuned to the emergent qualities of data is more sensitive to the unexpected twists and turns that lives take. It is less likely to smooth over the consequences of those twists and turns than a view that looks back from the perspective of where people have ended up today.

The last element of a new interdisciplinary field suggested by this study is what we called above a qualitative research sensibility. By that we mean a sensitivity to the content of what people say, the ways in which they talk, with whom and in what context, and not primarily how often they say or do such things. We have found it tremendously rich to create space in our interviews for family members to drive forward the conversation. The interview participants took us to the emotional places that were important to them, and not only to the predetermined checkpoints from where we had thought to observe their lives. This research stance we have come to appreciate is both inductive and semistructured. We came to interviews with specific research goals, but not so structured that people couldn't give expression to their own renditions of themselves.

Such an open-ended, interview-based methodological approach would once have produced unmanageable reams of interview transcripts. Today, increasingly sophisticated research software exists to enable the organization of great quantities of qualitative data and its cross-sectional and diachronic analysis. Such resources enable the explorations of patterns across the individuals in large research samples and over time within the interview data gathered from a single individual. These technologies make possible an inductive research orientation that does not reify identity categories before data are gathered but instead seeks out patterns and commonalities in the native language that research participants themselves use. This is what we were referring to earlier in this chapter by a more humanistic research orientation.

Our study of sixteen families makes us wonder what we might learn if we brought the same methodological orientation we have employed here to the study of 616 families. We believe that, if we were to bring a family life course orientation to the cohort-based study of hundreds of Jewish families, our sense of what matters, or what makes a difference in Jewish life, would be dramatically redirected from the additive and often atomized contribution of specific programmatic interventions to the more fluid interplay between individuals and those with whom they are most closely connected, and their interacting life experiences.

To be clear, what we are proposing is more than the design of a single project, ambitious as such a project might be. We're suggesting a realignment of research priorities (or at least an openness to an additional lens with which to examine Jews) toward a family-focused, life course structured, qualitative endeavor. These research priorities could come together in a single project (a longitudinal, cohort-based study of hundreds of Jewish families). In their constituent parts, these priorities would also transform assumptions of what Jewish social scientific research should look like and what else we would need to know to properly understand the dynamics of Jewish life.

Practical Implications: Family as a Unit of Engagement

Concluding a project that has occupied our own lives for over ten years, during which we have experienced significant family life course changes of our own, we are grateful to have had the opportunity to make explicit a different way of thinking about Jewish self-formation. At the same time, we wrestle with the implications of this study for those policy-makers and practitioners who work with Jewish families and Jewish teens, especially those who were encouraged by the findings of our previous book, which identified the contribution of Jewish schools to adults and not just to children. Ten years later, what are the implications for our earlier conclusions?

In mapping the Jewish worlds of our subjects so close to their homes, we have indicated that what matters most for the vitality of Jewish life in twenty-first century North America is the thickness of home-made Jewish cultures and relationships. In doing so, we implicitly diminish the promise of Jewish interventions and experiences beyond the home. Their force pales in comparison to what we have depicted as a kind of forge in the home. And yet as we have seen in a great many instances, the family system is enriched by social and cultural capital that individual members import from institutions beyond the walls of the home. The family system is far from self-sufficient.

The most significant implication of this finding is that the providers of Jewish experiences for teens and for adults must take account of and engage with the immediate families from which their participants come. They must consider the unexpected consequences of their efforts once their educational "products" are integrated into powerful and frequently idiosyncratic family cultures. For example, they should consider how having provided students with strong literacy skills, those young people might prefer to use these skills to design their own Bar or Bat Mitzvah ritual within the intimacy of their families rather than display their competence in a conventional, public synagogue performance. Educators must also be alert to the sources of resistance in the home to the outcomes they hope to produce. Think back for example to Carla Lowe's (somewhat incorrect) assumption, articulated in a nighttime conversation at camp, that her parents were fully comfortable with her marrying someone not Jewish. That surely was a conclusion, formed at home, that conflicted with the intent of her counselors at camp.

To argue that Jewish self-formation is first and foremost home work does not discount the potential of being informed and inspired—"schooled"—beyond the home. What it means, more likely, is that the providers of Jewish educational experiences and interventions ought to think of their work within a different paradigm, one we liken to the flipped classroom where it is understood that learning can be acquired independent of the classroom and yet where the classroom continues to play an important facilitative role. The flipped classroom concept is inspired by a recognition that contemporary information technologies enable learners to become much more fully enriched by new concepts and content outside their college or school classrooms than during class time, or at least independent of their "instructors" (Berrett 2012; King 1993). The classroom, in this model, is a place for review and for meaning-making; it supports and scaffolds learning that starts elsewhere in the students' life. Our work suggests that this might be a useful paradigm for Jewish education writ large.

Recognizing how profoundly people's Jewish lives are formed within the home points toward a model of Jewish education in which the deepest learning, and the most profound meaning-making of what it is to be Jewish, is recognized to occur beyond the influence of Jewish educators, within the walls of the home. Yet, at the same time, Jewish educators have an important facilitative role to play in challenging conclusions reached elsewhere, nuancing those conclusions, enriching them with additional learning that can deepen their meaning, and so on. Home work in the flipped classroom does not supplant school work. It does call for conceptualizing a different form of educational intervention. This may indeed be the next unexplored frontier for Jewish education.

A different implication of our work concerns who is conceived as the client in Jewish education. Just as we proposed reclaiming the family as a "unit of analysis" in research terms, so there is a case for thinking of the family as a "unit of engagement" in education terms. This is an argument that has been made with greater and lesser persuasiveness over the last twenty years, at least since the Whizin Institute for Jewish Family Life emerged in the 1990s as a hub for Jewish family education (Bank and Wolfson 1998). The notion spread rapidly that Jewish educational institutions, and especially synagogues, should offer programs and hire educators to engage parents and children together. Educating parents and children in this way empowered and engaged parents instead of leaving them outside the classroom door where they might obstruct or interrupt their child's Jewish growth.

In recent years, the heat behind this conception of family education has dimmed. Instead, stimulated by the emergence of the PJ Library program—a multimillion dollar initiative that sends free Jewish children books to participating families every month in the expectation that parents and children will "share Jewish ideas and inspiration together"—there has been more interest in exploring how to bring resources into the home so that families can design their own Jewish learning and experience. Our work suggests that this has indeed been an appropriate move, and one worth taking further beyond preschool and the early elementary grades. What if PJ Library was succeeded by a library that sent new learning apps to the families of tweens and teens that prompted then to engage in cool, and educational, activities together? Providing fuel for the forge that is the home would introduce resources to the point of greatest potential impact.

A Last Word

Having spent ten years studying this group of families, and having developed an analytical framework to explore their lives, we have been able to understand with unusual clarity why their lives have taken the trajectories we have observed. Yet, at the same time, we are now more uncertain than ever about what the next ten years will bring for them. That uncertainty is what makes the study of human lives in formation so enriching, so exciting, and so humbling.

Notes

1. The two of us, along with our colleague Helena Miller, are engaged in a project in the UK, supported by the Pears Foundation, which, currently, may be the only truly longitudinal, large scale, family-focused life course study in the Jewish community. Since 2011, when they started high school, we have been "following" a cohort of more than a thousand Jewish young people all born at the turn of the millennium. If we can maintain the sample, we are hoping to stay with them until they have children of their own. During the high school years, we have been surveying the students and their parents every two years, and we have been interviewing a sub-sample of 150 families (children and parents together) at the same intervals. The original goal of this project was to try to discern the contribution of Jewish schooling to the developing lives of children and parents. As the richness of the data has become evident, and as the children have found their voices during the course of our conversations with their families, so the research goals of the project have become more ambitious. As happened in Toronto, we have moved beyond studying school to researching life as families live it.

APPENDIX: THE PARTICIPATING FAMILIES

Rachel Elbaz is mother of Orli and a younger sibling. Orli was in fifth grade when we first interviewed her mother. At that time, Rachel was sharing a home with her non-Jewish husband, from who she had separated. Rachel spent many years living in Morocco, where she met her husband, a freelance writer. She is passionate about Sephardi culture. For a time, during the period of her divorce, she attended synagogue quite regularly with her children. She is enthusiastic about her secular Jewishness and has encouraged her children's involvement in progressive Jewish youth movements in which they have become highly active.

Joanna Fine and Michael Ruben are the parents of Lisa and one older sibling. Lisa was in first grade when we first interviewed her parents. Lisa left DJDS in sixth grade for a private girls' school. Her parents separated when she was two years old. They continued to live close to one another in a multicultural midtown Toronto neighborhood. Joanna was not raised Jewish and had explored converting when Lisa was younger. Michael, a screenwriter by profession, describes himself as an atheist "not one hundred percent comfortable in a Jewish environment."

Dina and Harry Funk are the parents of Amos and two younger siblings. Amos was in senior kindergarten when we first interviewed his parents. He stayed at the school until sixth grade and then transferred to another Jewish day school. Dina had been deeply involved at DJDS. She serves as a cantor at a local congregation.

Ruth Goldman is the single mother of Dara, an adopted child of color. Dara was in senior kindergarten when we first interviewed her mother. She left DJDS at the end of sixth grade for a local public school. Ruth was raised in a traditional Conservative home but felt uncomfortable with the religious conformism of her community. Today, she and Dara spend most Friday nights with Ruth's parents and siblings. They are actively involved in a traditional egalitarian congregation near where they live in midtown Toronto.

Joe Kleinman is the father of Sandy and a younger sibling. Sandy was in senior kindergarten when we first interviewed her parents. She left DJDS in first grade for a public school. Joe and his ex-wife, Michelle, had both attended the early grades of Jewish day school. They divorced when Sandy was in second grade. Joe now lives with Liesha, a non-Jewish woman, in the working-class south-western suburbs of Toronto. Joe, a human rights lawyer by profession, describes himself as a cultural Jew.

Ray and Estelle Lombard are the parents of Joshua and one younger sibling. Joshua was in fifth grade when we first interviewed his parents. After graduating DJDS in eighth grade, he continued to a competitive public school and is now studying at a local university. Neither Ray nor Estelle had received an intensive Jewish education themselves, being raised in liberal Jewish families. Ray was a founding board member at DJDS; and the school was pivotal in their intensifying Jewish engagement. Today, they are active community members at a traditional egalitarian congregation near where they live.

Karen and Adam Lowe are the parents of Carla and a younger sibling. Carla was in first grade when we first interviewed her parents. She left DJDS in second grade for a private school. Both parents had attended Jewish day school during the elementary grades. They have been longtime members of a Conservative synagogue they rarely attend. Karen and her two children are passionate about the overnight Jewish summer camp they attended more than twenty years apart. Over the ten years of the study they lived in the same comfortable midtown neighborhood.

Sharon and Ed Manning are the parents of Max and two younger siblings. Max was in senior kindergarten when we first interviewed his parents. He stayed at DJDS until the end of fifth grade, transferring to a local public school. Sharon was raised in a non-observant Jewish home. Ed is not Jewish, and despite his great curiosity about Jewish matters and despite raising his children as identifying Jews, he has not been interested in converting. The family became members of a popular liberal synagogue, where Max prepared for and celebrated his Bar Mitzvah. They moved house since we first met them but stayed in the same multicultural midtown neighborhood.

Carrie and Ian Maybaum are the parents of Elijah and a younger sibling. Elijah was in first grade when we first interviewed his parents. He left DJDS for public school at the end of fifth grade. Carrie's grandparents had been founders of one of the largest Conservative synagogues in Toronto and her parents continued to be active there. Raised in a Jewish home, Ian describes himself as a spiritual individual who rarely has time to attend synagogue because of his restaurant business. The family lives in midtown Toronto close to a great many of their relatives with whom they gather most Friday nights.

Sandra and Donald Reinhart are the parents of Yael and two younger siblings. Yael was in fifth grade when we first interviewed her parents. She graduated from DJDS at the end of eighth grade and continued to a public school for the arts. She is now studying at a local university. Following a journey of Jewish exploration over the course of their adult lives, including extended stays in Israel, the couple and their children have taken on an observant Jewish lifestyle infused with a Jewish renewal spirit. The family live in the downtown core.

Jean and John Richards are the parents of Melanie and two younger siblings. Melanie was in fifth grade when we first interviewed her parents. She had been in the school from first to fourth grade. One of her younger siblings attended the school for three years, from senior kindergarten to second grade. Today, Melanie attends college at an Ontario university away from home. Jean and John both have Holocaust survivors in their extended families. They became members of a Toronto Conservative congregation, which John attends reluctantly a couple of times a year to keep his father company. The family prefers to create their own Jewish rituals at home. They lived in the same midtown home over the course of the study.

Joyce Silver is mother of Ruby, who was in fifth grade when we first interviewed her mother. Ruby graduated DJDS in eighth grade and continued to a public school for the arts. She is now studying at a local university. Joyce was raised in a nonobservant Jewish home against which she rebelled following her parents' divorce. She never married Ruby's father, a non-Jewish man. Since Ruby's birth, she has become progressively more engaged in Jewish life, climaxing with a spell on the board of DJDS. She is not a member of a synagogue.

Rhonda and Phillip Stern are the parents of Jayden and one older sibling. Jayden was in first grade when we first interviewed his parents. He stayed at DJDS (reluctantly) until graduating eighth grade. He now attends a large public high school. Both Rhonda and Phillip had been raised in liberal Jewish homes. They became more interested in traditional Judaism after spending a five-month period in Israel. They continue to be involved in Israel-related matters at the Community Federation. They are active in a liberal downtown congregation and keep a kosher home. They lived throughout the study in the downtown core.

Anne and Brian Wagner are the parents of Gary and one younger sibling. Gary was in senior kindergarten when we first interviewed his parents. He graduated DJDS early and continued to a Jewish community high school. His mother had been raised in a nonobservant Jewish home in the United States. His father is a Jew-by-choice who converted a couple of years after Gary was born and is enthusiastic about Jewish learning. Today, the family is religiously observant, and attends a Conservative synagogue at least one a week. The family lives in the northern suburbs of the city in a highly concentrated Jewish neighborhood.

Adele and Dave Wallace are the parents of Sam. Sam was in fifth grade when we first interviewed his parents. He graduated DJDS at the end of sixth grade and continued to a competitive private school. Dave was raised in an observant Orthodox Jewish home, but has not been religiously observant for many years. Adele expresses a profound attraction to Jewish people, tradition and culture, but is not Jewish. She has been a spiritual seeker most of her life, and is most comfortable with Bahai culture. The couple are members of a downtown congregation which they enjoy attending on the High Holidays. They live just north of the downtown core.

Carolyn and Zev Weinstein are the parents of Yoni and a younger sibling. Yoni was in senior kindergarten when we first interviewed his parents and attended the school through to the end of eighth grade. Carolyn is the daughter of a Reform rabbi and became more involved in her local liberal synagogue as her children aged. Zev is a Hebrew speaking secular Jew with little patience for synagogues and ritual. They lived in the same midtown Toronto home throughout the study.

BIBLIOGRAPHY

Adelson, J. I. 2010. "Contemporary Family Systems Approach to Substance Abuse." *Forum on Public Policy: A Journal of the Oxford Round Table*, Spring: 15.

Ammerman, N. T. 2007. "Introduction: Observing Modern Religious Lives." In *Everyday Religion: Observing Modern Religious Lives*, edited by N. T. Ammerman, 3–18. New York: Oxford University Press.

Arnett, J. J. 2004. *Emerging Adulthood: The Winding Road from Late Teens Through the Twenties*. New York: Oxford University Press.

Arnett, J. J., and Jensen, L. A. 2002. "A Congregation of One: Individualized Religious Beliefs among Emerging Adults." *Journal of Adolescent Research*, 17 (5): 451–467.

Aron, I. 2010. "Supplementary Schooling and the Law of Unintended Consequences: A Review Essay of Stuart Schoenfeld's 'Folk Judaism, Elite Judaism, and the Role of the Bar Mitzvah in the Development of the Synagogue and Jewish School.'" *Journal of Jewish Education* 76 (4): 315–333.

Aviad, J. 1983. *Return to Judaism: Religious Renewal in Israel*. Chicago: University of Chicago Press.

Bader, C. D., and Desmond, S. A. 2006. "Do as I Say and as I Do: The Effects of Consistent Parental Beliefs and Behaviors on Religious Transmission." *Sociology of Religion*, 67 (3): 313–329.

Bank, A., and Wolfson, R., eds. 1998. *First Fruit: A Whizin Anthology of Jewish Family Education*. Shirley and Arthur Whizin Institute for Jewish Family Life.

Barack Fishman, S. 1995. *A Breath of Life: Feminism in the American Jewish Community*. Waltham, MA: Brandeis University Press.

———. 2001. "Women's Transformations of Public Judaism: Religiosity, Egalitarianism, and the Symbolic Power of Changing Gender Roles." *Studies in Contemporary Jewry* 17: 132.

———. 2004. *Double or Nothing? Jewish Families and Mixed Marriage*. Waltham, MA: Brandeis University Press.

Barack Fishman, S., and Parmer, D. 2008. "Policy Implications of the Gender Imbalance among America's Jews." *Jewish Political Studies Review*, 7–34.

Baumeister, R. F. 1991. *Meanings of Life*. Guildford: Guildford Press.

Baumel, J. T. 1995. "'In Everlasting Memory': Individual and Communal Holocaust Commemoration in Israel." *Israel Affairs*, 1 (3): 146–170.

Bassett, R., Beagan, B. L., Ristovski-Slijepcevic, S., and Chapman, G. E. 2008. "Tough Teens: The Methodological Challenges of Interviewing Teenagers as Research Participants." *Journal of Adolescent Research*, 23 (2): 119–131.

Bechhofer, S. 2011. "Day Schools in the Orthodox Sector—A Shifting Landscape." In *International Handbook of Jewish Education*, edited by H. Miller, L. Grant, and A. Pomson, 729–747. Dordecht: Springer.

Beck, A., ed. 2003. *Cultural Work: Understanding the Cultural Industries*. London: Routledge.

Bellah, R. N., Madsen, R., Sullivan, W. M., Swidler, A., and Tipton, S. M. 1985. *Habits of the Heart: Individualism and Commitment in American Life*. Berkeley, CA: University of California Press.

Bengston, V. L., and Allen, K. R. 1993. "The Life Course Perspective Applied to Families Over Time." In *Sourcebook of Family Theories and Methods: A Contextual Approach*, edited by P. G. Boss, W. J. Doherty, R. LaRossa, W. R. Schumm, and S. K. Steinmetz, 469–504. New York: Plenum Press.

Bengston, V. L., Elder, G. H., and Putney, N. M. 2006. "The Lifecourse Perspective on Ageing: Linked Lives, Timing, and History." In *The Cambridge Handbook of Age and Ageing*, edited by M. L. Johnson, V. L. Bengston, P. G. Coleman, and T. B. L. Kirkwood, 493–501. Cambridge, UK: Cambridge University Press.

Bengston, V. L., Putney, N. M., and Harris, S. 2014. *Families and Faith: How Religion is Passed Down across Generations*. New York: Oxford University Press.

Benor, S. 2012. *Becoming Frum: How Newcomers Learn the Language and Culture of Orthodox Judaism*. New Brunswick, NJ: Rutgers University Press.

Berrett, D. 2012. "How "Flipping" the Classroom Can Improve the Traditional Lecture." *The Chronicle of Higher Education* 12: 1–14.

Bertalanffy, L. Von. 1968. *General Systems Theory*. New York: George Braziller.

Bialystok, F. 2000. *Delayed Impact: The Holocaust and the Canadian Jewish Community*. McGill-Queen's Press-MQUP.

Bourdieu, P. 1986. "The Forms of Capital. (Trans. R. Nice)." In *Handbook of Theory and Research for the Sociology of Education*, edited by J. C. Richardson, 251–528. New York: Greenwood Press.

Boyarin, J. 2013. *Jewish Families*. New Brunswick, NJ: Rutgers University Press.

Boyatzis, C. J. 2003. "Religious and Spiritual Development: An Introduction." *Review of Religious Research* 44 (3): 213–219.

Brodbar-Nemzer, J. 1986. "Divorce and Group Commitment: The Case of the Jews." *Journal of Marriage and the Family* 48: 329–340.

Broderick, C. B. 1993. *Understanding Family Process: Basics of Family Systems Theory*. Thousand Oaks, CA: Sage Publishers, Inc.

Broderick, C. B., and Schrader, S. S. 1981. "The History of Professional Marriage and Family Therapy." In *Handbook of Family Therapy*, edited by A. S. Gurman and O. P. Kniskern, pp. 5–35. New York: Brunner/Mazel.

Bronfenbrenner, U. 1979. *The Ecology of Human Development: Experiments by Nature and Design*. Cambridge, MA: Harvard University Press.

Bryfman, D. 2009. *Giving voice to a generation: The role of the peer group in the identity development of Jewish adolescents in the United States*. Unpublished Ph.D thesis, New York University.

Bryfman, D. 2016. *Generation Now: Understanding and Engaging Jewish Teens Today.* New York: Jewish Education Project.

Buber, M. 1974. *Tales of the Hasidim: Later Masters.* New York: Schocken.

Buckley, W. 1967. *Sociology and Modern Systems Theory.* Englewood Cliffs, NJ: Prentice Hall.

BTW/Rosov Consulting. 2013. *Effective Strategies for Educating and Engaging Jewish Teens: What Communities Can Learn from Programs That Work.* San Francisco: Jim Joseph Foundation.

Bynner, J., Butler, N., Ferri, E., Shepherd, P., and Smith, K. 2000. The Design and Conduct of the 1999–2000 Surveys of the National Child Development Study and the 1970 British Cohort Study. Centre for Longitudinal Studies, Cohort Studies, Working Paper, 1.

Charles and Lynn Schusterman Philanthropic Network. 2014. Inclusivity. https://www.schusterman.org/inclusivity.

Charme, S. 2009. "Tradition Versus Egalitarianism in the Thinking of Jewish-American Adolescents." *Journal of Jewish Education* 75 (1): 4–18.

Cherlin, A. J. 2010. *The Marriage-Go-Round: The State of Marriage and Family in America Today.* New York: Vintage Books.

Chertok, F., and Samuel, N. 2008 *Justice, Justice Shall They Pursue: Young Adult Interest in Long-Term Jewish Service Options.* Waltham, MA: Maurice & Marilyn Cohen Center for Modern Jewish Studies, Brandeis University.

Chertok, F., Sasson, T., and Saxe, L. 2009. *Tourists, Travelers, and Citizens: Jewish Engagement of Young Adults in Four Centers of North American Jewish Life.* Waltham, MA: Maurice and Marilyn Cohen Center for Modern Jewish Studies, Brandeis University.

Christensen, P. H. 2004. "Children's Participation in Ethnographic Research: Issues of Power and Representation." *Children & Society* 18 (2): 165–176.

Clandinin, D. J., and Connelly, F. M. 2000. *Narrative Inquiry: Experience and Story in Qualitative Research.* San Francisco: Jossey Bass.

Cohen, E. H., and Cohen, E. 2000. *The Israel Experience.* Jerusalem: The Israel Institute for Israel Studies.

Cohen, S. M. 2000. "The Utility of Long Interviews in the Study of American Jews." *Contemporary Jewry* 21: 3–22.

———. 2007. "The Differential Impact of Jewish Education on Adult Jewish Identity." In *Family Matters: Jewish Education in an Age of Choice*, edited by J. Wertheimer, 34–56. Waltham, MA: Brandeis University Press.

Cohen, S. M., and Eisen, A. 2000. *The Jew Within: Self, Family and Community in America.* Bloomington, IN: Indiana University Press.

Cohen, S. M., and Kelman, A. Y. 2007a. *Beyond Distancing: Young Adult American Jews and Their Alienation from Israel.* Jewish Identity Project of Reboot.

———. 2007b. *The Continuity of Discontinuity: How Young Jews Are Connecting, Creating, and Organizing Their Jewish Lives.* New York: Andrea and Charles Bronfman Philanthropies.

Cohen, S. M., and Kotler-Berkowitz, L. 2004. "The Impact of Childhood Jewish Education Upon Adults' Jewish Identity: Schooling, Travel, Camping and Youth Groups." *United Jewish Communities Report on the National Population Survey 2001–01*, Report 3, Available at www.ujc.org/njps.

Cohen, S. M., Landres, J. S., Kaunfer, E., and Shain, M. 2007. Emergent Jewish Communities and Their Participants. Pamphlet S3k. Synagogue Studies Institute and Mechon Hadar.

Cohen, S. M., and Veinstein, J. 2011. "Jewish Identity: Who You Knew Affects How You Jew—The Impact of Jewish Networks in Childhood Upon Adult Jewish Identity." In *International Handbook of Jewish Education*, edited by H. Miller, L. Grant, and A. Pomson, 203–218. Dordecht: Springer.

Coleman, J. S. 1994. "Family Involvement in Education." In *Parents, Their Children, and Schools*, edited by B. Schneider and J. Coleman, 23–37. Boulder, CO: Westview Press.

Connerton, P. 1980. *How Societies Remember*. Cambridge, UK: Cambridge University Press.

Coontz, S. 2006. *Marriage, a History: How Love Conquered Marriage*. New York: Penguin.

Cooperman, A., Smith, G. A., Hackett, C., and Kuriakose, N. 2013. *A Portrait of Jewish Americans: Findings from a Pew Research Center Survey of US Jews*. Washington, DC: Pew Research Center.

Copeland, S. 2011. "Israel Travel Education." In *International Handbook of Jewish Education*, edited by Miller, H., Grant, L., and Pomson, A., 497–513. Dordecht: Springer.

Creswell, J. 2013. *Qualitative Inquiry and Research Design: Choosing among Five Approaches*. London: Sage Publications.

Davidman, L. 1991. *Tradition in a Rootless World: Women Turn to Orthodox Judaism*. Berkeley, CA: University of California Press.

———. 2003. "Beyond the Synagogue Walls." In *Handbook of the Sociology of Religion*, edited by M. Dillon, 261–275. New York: Cambridge University Press.

———. 2007. "The New Voluntarism and the Case of Unsynagogued Jews." In *Everyday Religion: Observing Modern Religious Lives*, edited by Ammerman, N., 51–67. Oxford: Oxford University Press.

Davie, G. 1994. *Religion in Britain Since 1945: Believing without Belonging*. Oxford: Blackwell.

Denham, S. A. 2003. "Relationships between Family Rituals, Family Routines, and Health." *Journal of Family Nursing* 9 (3): 305–330.

Denton, M. L. 2012. "Family Structure, Family Disruption, and Profiles of Adolescent Religiosity." *Journal for the Scientific Study of Religion* 51 (1): 42–64.

Diamond, E. 2000. *And I Will Dwell in Their Midst: Orthodox Jews in Suburbia*. Chapel Hill, NC: University of North Carolina Press.

Dillon, M., and Wink, P. 2007. *In the Course of a Lifetime: Tracing Religious Belief, Practice, and Change*. Berkeley, CA: University of California Press.

Eaker, D. G., and Walters, L. H. 2002. "Adolescent Satisfaction in Family Rituals and Psychosocial Development: A Developmental Systems Theory Perspective." *Journal of Family Psychology* 16 (4): 406.

Ecclestone, K. 2007. "Lost and Found in Transition: The Implications of 'Identity,' 'Agency,' and 'Structure' for Educational Goals and Practices." Keynote presentation to *Researching transitions in lifelong learning conference*, University of Stirling, June 22–24, 2007.

Edgell, P. 2006. *Religion and Family in a Changing Society*. Princeton, NJ: Princeton University Press.

Elder, G. H. 1974. *Children of the Great Depression: Social Change in Life Experience*. Chicago, IL: University of Chicago Press.

Elder, G. H., Johnson, M. K., and Crosnoe, R. 2003. "The Emergence and Development of Life Course Theory." In *Handbook of the Life Course*, edited by J. T. Mortimer and M. J. Shanahan, 3–19. New York: Kluewer Academic-Plenum.

Ellison, C. G., Walker, A. B., Glenn, N. D., and Marquardt, E. 2011. "The Effects of Parental Marital Discord and Divorce on the Religious and Spiritual Lives of Young Adults." *Social Science Research* 40 (2): 538–551.

Evans, K. 2002. "Taking Control of Their Lives? Agency in Young Adult Transitions in England and the New Germany." *Journal of Youth Studies* 5 (3):245–269.

Fader, A. 2009. *Mitzvah Girls: Bringing Up the Next Generation of Hasidic Jews in Brooklyn*. Princeton, NJ: Princeton University Press.

Fiese, B. H., and Wamboldt, F. S. 2000. "Family Routines, Rituals, and Asthma Management: A Proposal for Family-Based Strategies to Increase Treatment Adherence." *Families, Systems, & Health* 18 (4): 405.

Fiese, B. H., Tomcho, T. J., Douglas, M., Josephs, K., Poltrock, S., and Baker, T. 2002. "A Review of 50 Years of Research on Naturally Occurring Family Routines and Rituals: Cause for Celebration?" *Journal of Family Psychology* 16: 381.

Fingerman, K. L. and Bermann, E. 2000. "Applications of Family Systems Theory to the Study of Adulthood." *International Journal of Aging and Human Development*, 51 (1): 5–29.

Flyvbjerg, B. 2006. "Five Misunderstandings about Case-Study Research." *Qualitative Inquiry* 12 (2): 219–245.

Frazer, E. 1989. "Feminist Talk and Talking about Feminism: Teenage Girls' Discourses of Gender." *Oxford Review of Education* 15 (3): 281–290.

Gans, H. 1958. "The Origin and Growth of a Jewish Community in the Suburbs." In *The Jews: Patterns of a Social Group*, edited by M. Sklare. Glencoe, IL: Free Press.

Geffen, R. M. and Gerstenfeld, M. 2010. *How the Status of American Jewish Women Has Changed over the Past Decades: An Interview with Rela Mintz Geffen*. American Jewish Committee, Jerusalem Center for Public Affairs, 190–200.

van Gennep, A. 1960. *The Rites of Passage* (trans, B. V. Minika and G. L. Caffee). London: Routledge.

Gerrity, E. T. and Steinglass, P. 2003. "Relocation Stress Following Catastrophic Events." In *Terrorism and Disaster: Individual and Community Mental Health Interventions*, edited by R. J. Ursano, C. S. Fullerton, and A. E. Norwood, 259–286. Cambridge, UK: Cambridge University Press.

Gilgun, J. F. and Reiser, E. 1992. "The Development of Sexual Identity among Men Sexually Abused as Children. *Families in Society* 71: 515–523.

Gilligan, C. 1982. *In a Different Voice: Psychological Theory and Women's Development.*
    Cambridge, MA: Harvard University Press.
Greenberg, A. 2006 *Grand Soy Vanilla Latte with Cinnamon, No Foam..." Jewish Identity
    and Community in a Time of Unlimited Choices.* New York: Reboot.
Guest, G., Bunce, A., and Johnson, L. 2006. "How Many Interviews are Enough? An
    Experiment With Data Saturation and Variability." *Field Methods* 18 (1): 59–82.
Guidubaldi, J., Cleminshaw, H. K., Perry, J. D., Nastasi, B. K., and Lightel, J. 1986.
    "The Role of Selected Family Environment Factors in Children's Postdivorce
    Adjustment." *Family Relations* 35: 141–151.
Hall, D., ed. 1997. *Lived Religion in America: Toward a History of Practice.* Princeton, NJ:
    Princeton University Press.
Hareven, T. K. 1982. *Family Time and Industrial Time.* Cambridge, UK: Cambridge
    University Press.
Hartman, T. 2007. *Feminism Encounters Traditional Judaism: Resistance and
    Accommodation.* Waltham, MA: Brandeis University Press.
Hayward, R. D., and Krause, N. 2013. "Patterns of Change in Religious Service
    Attendance across the Life Course: Evidence from a 34-year Longitudinal Study."
    Social Science Research 42 (6): 1480–1489.
Heaven, P. C., Ciarrochi, J., and Leeson, P. 2010. "Parental Styles and Religious Values
    Among Teenagers: A 3-year Prospective Analysis." *The Journal of Genetic Psychology*
    171 (1): 93–99.
Henry, C. S., and Lovelace, S. G. 1995. "Family Resources and Adolescent Family Life
    Satisfaction in Remarried Family Households." *Journal of Family Issues* 16 (6):
    765–786.
Hoffman, A. 2011. "Friday Night Light." *Tablet Magazine.* April 29, 2011. Downloaded
    from http://tabletmag.com/jewish-life-and-religion/76226/friday-night-lights.
Hollander, S. 2014. Bat Mitzvah, Brooklyn Style: Laid Back and Do It Yourself. Wall
    Street Journal. July 13, 2004. Available at http://online.wsj.com/articles
    /bat-mitzvah-brooklyn-style-laid-back-and-do-it-yourself-1405304732.
Horowitz, B. 2000. *Connections and Journeys: Assessing Critical Opportunities for Enhancing
    Jewish Identity.* New York: UJA-Federation of Jewish Philanthropies for New York.
Hyman, P. 1989. "The Modern Jewish Family: Image and Reality." In *The Jewish Family:
    Metaphor and Memory*, edited by D. Kraemer. New York: Oxford University Press.
Informing Change. 2015. Finding New Paths for Teen Engagement and Learning: A
    Funder Collaborative Leads the Way. Downloaded from http://jimjosephfoundation
    .org/wp-content/uploads/2015/04/Funder-Collaborative-Case-Study-January
    -2015-FINAL.pdf.
Jensen, J., and Jensen, L. C. 1999. *Families: The Key to a Prosperous and Compassionate
    Society for the 21st Century.* Lewiston, NY: Edward Mellen.
Johnston, M. J. 2012. *Faith Beyond Belief: Stories of Good People Who Left Their Church
    Behind.* Wheaton, IL: Quest Books.
Kadushin, C., Kelner, S., and Saxe, L. 2000. *Being a Jewish Teenager in America: Trying to Make
    it.* Waltham, MA: Cohen Center for Modern Jewish Studies, Brandeis University.

Kahneman, D. 2011. *Thinking, Fast and Slow.* New York: Farrar, Straus, and Giroux.

Kapel, D. E. 1972. "Parental Views of a Jewish Day School." *Journal of Jewish Education* 41 (3): 28–38.

Katriel, T. and Shenhar, A. 1989. "Rituals of Socialization: On Performing Israeli Cultural Identity." *Text and Performance Quarterly* 9 (4): 337–341.

Kelman, S. L. 1979. "Parent Motivations for Enrolling a Child in a Non-Orthodox Jewish Day School." *Journal of Jewish Education* 47 (1): 44–48.

Kelner, S. 2010. *Tours That Bond: Diaspora, Pilgrimage and Israeli Birthright Tourism.* New York: NYU Press.

Keysar, A., and Kosmin, B. A. 2004. *"'Eight Up': The College Years: The Jewish Engagement of Young Adults Raised in Conservative Synagogues, 1995–2003."* Jewish Theological Seminary.

King, A. 1993. "From Sage on the Stage to Guide on the Side." *College Teaching* 41 (1): 30–35.

Kohler Reissman, C. 1993. *Narrative Analysis.* Thousand Oaks, CA: Sage Publications.

Koren, I. 2010. "Talking about the Jewish Wedding Ritual: Issues of Gender, Power, and Social Control." In *Rites of Passage: How Today's Jews Celebrate, Commemorate, and Commiserate,* edited by L. J. Greenspoon, 33–56. West Lafayette, IN: Purdue University Press.

Kosmin, B. A., and Keysar, A. 2000. *"Four Up"—The High School Years, 1995–1999: The Jewish Development of the B'nai Mitzvah Class of 5755.* New York: The Jewish Theological Seminary.

Lam, M. S., and Pollard, A. 2006. "A Conceptual Framework for Understanding Children as Agents in the Transition from Home to Kindergarten." *Early Years* 26 (2): 123–141.

Lareau, A. 2000. *Home Advantage: Social Class and Parental Intervention in Elementary Education.* Lanham, MD: Rowman & Littlefield Publishers.

———. 2011. *Unequal Childhoods: Class, Race and Family Life.* Berkeley, CA: University of California Press.

Lawton, L. and Bures, R. 2001. "Parental Divorce and the 'Switching' of Religious Identity." *Journal for the Scientific Study of Religion* 40 (1): 99–112.

Leach, M. S., and Braithwaite, D. O. 1996. "A Binding Tie: Supportive Communication of Family Kinkeepers." *Journal of Applied Communication Research* 24: 200–216.

Marcus, I. G. 1996. *Rituals of Childhood: Jewish Acculturation in Medieval Europe.* New Haven, CT: Yale University Press.

Markson, S., and Fiese, B. H. 2000. "Family Rituals as a Protective Factor for Children with Asthma." *Journal of Pediatric Psychology,* 25 (7): 471–480.

Maxwell-Stewart, S. 2012. *Roger Ebert Discusses the Up Series with Director Michael Apted.* Retrieved from https://www.youtube.com/watch?v=rGu470P7yfc.

McCullough, M. E., Enders, C. K., Brion, S. L., and Jain, A. R. 2005. "The Varieties of Religious Development in Adulthood: A Longitudinal Investigation of Religion and Rational Choice." *Journal of Personality and Social Psychology* 89 (1): 78.

McGinity, K. 2009. *Still Jewish: A History of Women and Intermarriage in America.* New York: New York University Press.

———. 2014. *Marrying Out: Jewish Men, Intermarriage, and Fatherhood.* Bloomington, IN: Indiana University Press.

McLaren, P. 1999. *Schooling as a Ritual Performance: Toward a Political Economy of Educational Symbols and Gestures,* 3rd ed. Lanham: MD: Rowman & Littlefield.

Measor, L., and Sikes, P. 1992. "Visiting Lives: Ethics and Methodology in Life History." In *Studying Teachers' Lives,* edited by I. Goodson. London: Routledge.

Meiser, R. 2013. Bar Mitzvahs on the Beach. Tablet Magazine. May 17. Downloaded from http://www.tabletmag.com/jewish-life-and-religion/132116/bar-mitzvahs-on-the-beach.

Mendes-Flohr, P., and Reinharz, J. 1995. *The Jews in the Modern World: A Documentary History,* 2nd ed. New York: Oxford University Press.

Munro, P. 2016. *Coming of Age in Jewish America: Bar and Bat Mitzvah Reinterpreted.* New Brunswick, NJ: Rutgers University Press.

Myerhoff, B. 1977. "We Don't Wrap Herring in a Printed Page: Fusion, Fictions and Contingency in Secular Ritual." In *Secular Ritual,* edited by S. Moore and B. Myerhoff, 199–224. Assen/Amsterdam: Van Gorcum.

Ochs, V. L. 2010. *Inventing Jewish Ritual.* Philadelphia, PA: Jewish Publication Society.

Olson, D. H., and Gorall, D. M. 2003. "Circumplex Model of Marital and Family Systems." In *Normal Family Process,* 3rd ed, edited by F. Walsh, 514–547. New York: Guilford.

Olson, D. H., Sprenkle, D. H., and Russell, C. S. 1979. "Circumplex Model of Marital and Family Relations: I. Cohesion and Adaptability Dimensions, Family Types, and Clinical Applications." *Family Process* 18: 3–28.

Oppenheimer, M. 2005. *Thirteen and a Day: The Bar and Bat Mitzvah Across America.* New York: Farrar, Straus and Giroux.

Payne, G. 2006. "Cohort Studies." In *The SAGE Dictionary of Social Research Methods,* edited by V. Jupp, 30–32. Thousand Oaks, CA: Sage Publications.

Pearson, J. 2016. *The Life Project: The Extraordinary Story of 70,000 Lives.* Berkeley, CA: Soft Skull Press.

Peters, J. F. 1985. "Adolescents as Socialization Agents to Parents." *Adolescence,* 20 (80): 921–933.

Pett, M. A., Lang, N., and Gander, A. 1992. "Late-life Divorce: Its Impact on Family Rituals." *Journal of Family Issues* 13 (4): 526–552.

Petts, R. J. 2015. "Parental Religiosity and Youth Religiosity: Variations by Family Structure." *Sociology of Religion* 76 (1): 95–120.

Pew Research Center. 2013. *Portrait of Jewish Americans.* Available at http://www.pewforum.org/2013/10/01/jewish-american-beliefs-attitudes-culture-survey/.

Pickus, A. 2015. *A Closer Look at the Independent B'nai Mitzvah in the Chicagoland Area.* Chicago, IL: Jewish United Fund of Chicago.

Pomerantz, S., Raby, R., and Stefanik, A. 2013. "Girls Run the World? Caught between Sexism and Postfeminism in school." *Gender & Society* 27 (2): 185–207.

Pomson, A. 2004. "Loosening Chronology's Collar: Reframing Teachers' Career Narratives as Stories of Life and Work Without End. *International Journal of Qualitative Studies in Education* 17 (5): 647–661.

———. 2011. "Day Schools in the Liberal Sector: Challenges and Opportunities at the Intersection of Two Traditions of Jewish Schooling." In *International Handbook of Jewish Education,* edited by H. Miller, L. Grant, and A. Pomson, 713–728. Dordecht: Springer.

Pomson, A., and Schnoor, R. F. 2008. *Back to School: Jewish Day School in the Lives of Adult Jews*. Detroit, MI: Wayne State University Press.

Prell, R. E. 1989. *Prayer and Community: The Havurah in American Judaism*. Detroit, MI: Wayne State University Press.

———. 2000. "Developmental Judaism: Challenging the Study of American Jewish Identity in the Social Sciences." *Contemporary Jewry*, 21: 33–54.

Price, S. R. F. 1984. *Ritual and Power: The Roman Imperial Cult in Asia Minor*. Cambridge: Cambridge University Press.

Putnam, R. D. 2000. *Bowling Alone: The Collapse and Revival of American Community*. New York: Simon and Schuster.

Putnam, R. D., and Campbell, D. 2010. *American Grace: How Religion Divides and Unites Us*. New York: Simon & Schuster.

Reimer, J. 2012. "Providing Optimal Jewish Experiences: The Case of Camp Ramah in Wisconsin." *Journal of Jewish Education* 78 (2): 114–134.

Ritual. 2016. In *Merriam-Wesbter.Com*. Retrieved February 12, 2016, from https://www.merriam-webster.com/dictionary/ritual.

Roof, W. C., and McKinney, W. 1987. *American Mainline Religion: Its Changing Shape and Future*. New Brunswick, NJ: Rutgers University Press.

Rosov Consulting. 2015. *"Lifting the Veil": Report on the Retrospective Study of Masa Alumni*. Jerusalem: Masa Israel Journey.

Rossi, A.D., ed. 1985. *Gender and the Life Course*. New York: Transaction Publishers.

Roth, P. 1993. *Goodbye Columbus and Five Other Stories*. New York: Vintage International.

Sales, A., Samuel, N., and Zablotsky, A. 2011. *Engaging Jewish Teens: A Study of New York Teens, Parents and Practitioners*. Waltham, MA: Cohen Center for Modern Jewish Studies, Brandeis University.

Saxe, L. 2014. "The Sky Is Falling! The Sky Is Falling!" *Tablet*. December 3. http://tabletmag.com/jewish-news-and-politics/187165/pew-american-jewry-revisited

Saxe, L., and Chazan, B. 2008. *Ten Days of Birthright Israel*. Waltham, MA: Brandeis University Press.

Saxe, L., Phillips, B., Sasson, T., Hecht, S., Shain, M., Wright, G., and Kadushin, C. 2009. *Generation Birthright Israel: The Impact of an Israel Experience on Jewish Identity and Choices*. Newton, MA: Maurice and Marilyn Cohen Center for Modern Jewish Studies.

Saxe, L., Shain, M., Hecht, S., Wright, G., Rieser, M., and Sasson, T. 2014. *The Impact of Taglit-Birthright Israel: Marriage and Family*. Brandeis University, MA: Cohen Centre for Modern Jewish Studies.

Schachter, L. 2010. "Why Bonnie and Ronnie Can't "Read" (the Siddur)." *Journal of Jewish Education* 76 (1): 74–91.

Schoem, D. L. 1989. *Ethnic Survival in America: An Ethnography of a Jewish Afternoon School* (Brown Studies on Jews and Their Societies). Atlanta, GA: Scholars Press.

Schoenfeld, S. 1987. "Folk Judaism, Elite Judaism, and the Role of Bar Mitzvah in the Development of the Synagogue and Jewish School in America." *Contemporary Jewry* 9 (1): 67–85.

Schnoor, R. F. 2011. "The Contours of Canadian Jewish Life." *Contemporary Jewry* 31 (3): 179–197.

Schuster, D. T. 2003. *Jewish Lives, Jewish Learning: Adult Jewish Learning in Theory and Practice.* New York: UAHC Press.

Sered, S. S. 1992. *Women as Ritual Experts: The Religious Lives of Elderly Jewish Women in Jerusalem.* New York: Oxford University Press.

Sklare, M., and Greenblum, J. 1967. *Jews on the Suburban Frontier.* New York: Basic Books.

Smith, C. 2005. *Soul Searching: The Religious and Spiritual Lives of American Teenagers.* New York: Oxford University Press.

Stake, R. E. 2005. "Qualitative Case Studies." In *The Sage Handbook of Qualitative Research,* 3rd ed, edited by N. Denzin and Y. Lincoln, 443–466. Thousand Oaks, CA: Sage.

Stein, R. 2001. "The Road to Bat Mitzvah in America." In *Women and American Judaism: Historical Perspectives,* edited by P. S. Nadell and J. Sarna, 223–234. Hanover, NH: Brandeis University Press.

Steinglass, P., Bennett, L., Wolin, S., and Reiss, D. 1987. *The Alcoholic Family.* New York: Basic Books.

Stolzenberg, R. M., Blair-Loy, M., and Waite, L. J. 1995. "Religious Participation in Early Adulthood: Age and Family Life Cycle Effects on Church Membership." *American Sociological Review* 60 (1): 84–103.

Tanaka, K. 2009. "The Effect of Divorce Experience on Religious Involvement: Implications for Later Health Lifestyle." *Journal of Divorce and Remarriage* 51 (1): 1–15.

Thompson, J. A. 2013. *Jewish on Their Own Terms: How Intermarried Couples Are Changing American Judaism.* New Brunswick, NJ: Rutgers University Press.

Turner, V. 1975. "Ritual as Communication and Potency." In *Symbols and Society: Essays on Belief Systems in Action,* edited by C. Hill. Athens, GA: University of Georgia Press.

Uhlenberg, P., and Mueller, M. 2004. "Family Context and Individual Well-being: Patterns and Mechanisms in Life Course Perspective." In *Handbook of the Life Course,* edited by J. T. Mortimer and M. J. Shanahan. New York: Kluwer Academic.

Ukeles, J. B., Miller, R., and Beck, B. 2006. *Young Jewish Adults in the United States.* New York: American Jewish Committee.

Warner, R. S. 1993. "Work in Progress toward a New Paradigm for the Sociological Study of Religion in the United States." *American Journal of Sociology* 98 (5): 1044–1093.

Way, N. 1998. *Everyday Courage: The Lives and Stories of Urban Teenagers.* New York: New York University Press.

Weinfeld, M. 2001. *Like Everyone Else—But Different: The Paradoxical Success of Canadian Jews.* Toronto: McClelland & Stewart.

Weiss, A. 2009. "On the Jersey Waterfront, Jews return but Jewish Community Still Struggles." *Forward,* April 24, 2009. Downloaded from http://forward.com/articles/104858/on-the-jersey-waterfront-jews-return-but-jewish-co/.

Wertheim, E. 1975. "The Science and Typology of Family Systems. II. Further Theoretical and Practical Considerations." *Family Process* 14: 285–308.

Wertheimer, J. 2005. "The American Synagogue: Recent Issues and Trends." *The American Jewish Year Book* 3–83.

———. 2010. *Generation of Change: How Leaders in Their Twenties and Thirties Are Reshaping American Jewish Life.* New York: AVI CHAI Foundation.

———. (ed.) 2011. *The New Jewish Leaders: Reshaping the American Jewish Landscape.* Waltham, MA: Brandeis University Press.

Wertheimer, J., and Cohen, S. M. 2014. "The Pew Survey Reanalyzed: More Bad News, but a Glimmer of Hope." *Mosaic Magazine,* November 2. http://mosaicmagazine .com/essay/2014/11/the-pew-survey-reanalyzed/.

Wolin, S. J., and Bennett, L. A. 1984. "Family Rituals." *Family Process* 23 (3): 401–420.

Woocher, M. L. 2014. "Teen Development and Jewish Life: Insights from Research and Practice." Unpublished report: The Jewish Education Project.

Wuthnow, R. 1998. *After Heaven: Spirituality in America Since the 1950s.* Berkeley, CA: University of California Press.

———. 2007. *After the Baby Boomers: How Twenty- and Thirty-Somethings are Shaping the Future of American Religion.* Princeton, NJ: Princeton University Press.

Yerushalmi, Y. H. 1996. *Zakhor: Jewish History and Jewish Memory.* Seattle, WA: University of Washington Press.

Zeldin, M. 1988. *Cultural Dissonance in Jewish Education: The Case of Reform Day Schools.* Los Angeles: Hebrew Union College, Jewish Institute of Religion.

Zerubavel, Y. 1995. *Collective Memory and the Making of Israeli National Tradition.* Chicago, IL: University of Chicago Press.

Zhai, J. E., Ellison, C. G., Glenn, N. D., and Marquardt, E. 2007. "Parental Divorce and Religious Involvement Among Young Adults." *Sociology of Religion* 68 (2):125–144.

INDEX

143–144; on intermarriage, 138–139; Jewish day school and, 1, 2, 129; rituals and, 100–102

Manning family (Sharon and Ed): Bar Mitzvah and, 16–17, 47–49; description of, 162; as interfaith family, 65; Jewish day school and, 47–49; ontogenetic changes and, 44; rituals and, 103–104, 106; role of critical moments and incidents in, 16–17

Marcus, I. G., 93

Masa Israel Journey, 111–112

Maybaum family (Carrie, Ian, and Elijah): Bar Mitzvah and, 11, 17, 49, 62–63; description of, 162–163; educational transitions and, 57; rituals and, 95–96; role of critical moments and incidents in, 17

McGinity, K., 77, 88

McKinney, W., 6

Miller, H., 160n1

morphogenesis, 91–92, 103

morphostasis, 91–92, 103

new voluntarism, 6

Olson, D. H., 79–80, 103

one-child families, 145

ontogenetic change: definition and concept of, 39, 40, 41–46, 147–148; impact on family life of, 87; rituals and, 97, 107

opportunity sampling, 17–18, 25–26, 150–152

Parmer, D., 88

Paul Penna Downtown Jewish Day School (DJDS): impact on family life of, 1–3, 38, 41, 47–48, 52, 53–57, 72–74, 86–87, 144; normalization of Jewish day school education and, 66–68; teenagers on, 126–128

Payne, G., 13

Pears Foundation, 160n1

Pett, M. A., 104

Pew Research Center, 26, 64, 143, 151

PJ Library, 159

Portrait of Jewish Americans (Pew Research Center), 64, 143, 151

power, 20

Prell, R. E., 9–10

purposive sampling, 151

Putnam, R., 8, 26–27, 147

qualitative research sensibility, 155, 156

quantitative studies, 6, 143

reciprocal socialization, 71n1

Reinhart family (Sandra, Donald, and Yael): Bat Mitzvah and, 63, 129; description of, 163; Israel experience and, 58–59; Jewish social and cultural capital and, 29–30; ontogenetic changes and, 44–45; rituals and, 107; Yael as teenager and, 120, 121–122

religious prodigal, 71n1

religious transmission, 144

research participants: Jewish community in Toronto and, 23–26; Jewish social and cultural capital and, 27–35, *31*; as opportunity sample, 17–18, 25–26, 150–152; research process and methodology and, 18–20, 23. *See also specific families*

retrospective narrative inquiry, 13–17, 42

reverse socialization, 71n1

Richards family (Jean, John, and Melanie): as "Apple Orchard Jews," 25; description of, 163; on intermarriage, 135–136; Melanie as teenager and, 119, 122–123, 130–131, 135–136; rituals and, 97–99, 102–103, 107

ritual, 93–94, 109. *See also* home-based family rituals

Roof, W. C., 6

ALEX POMSON (PhD, University of London) is Managing Director of
Rosov Consulting. He is internationally regarded for his research in areas
that include the life course of Jewish families, teachers' lives and work,
and Israel education. He was Koschitzky Family Chair in Jewish Teacher
Education at York University, Toronto, where he coordinated York's Jewish
Teacher Education program. He was a Senior Researcher at the Melton
Centre for Jewish Education at the Hebrew University where he continues
to teach. Among numerous publications, he is coeditor of *The International
Handbook of Jewish Education*, a landmark publication. He was Associate
Editor of *The Journal of Jewish Education* for more than ten years.

RANDAL F. SCHNOOR (PhD, McGill University) is a sociologist,
specializing in the qualitative study of contemporary Canadian Jewish
life. He has been teaching sociology and Jewish Studies for more than
a decade at the Koschitzky Centre for Jewish Studies at York University
and has recently received the John O'Neill Award for teaching excellence.
For nine years he served as the president of the Association for Canadian
Jewish Studies. He has published more than fifteen peer-reviewed academic
articles and book chapters in the field. His recent policy research includes
studies on Jewish day school enrollment patterns, Jewish poverty, and
community approaches to interfaith families.